Church Work In British Columbia: Being A Memoir Of The Episcopate Of Acton Windeyer Silliteo, First Bishop Of New Westminster

Herbert H. Gowen

CHURCH WORK

IN

BRITISH COLUMBIA

BEING A MEMOIR OF THE EPISCOPATE

OF

ACTON WINDEYER SILLITOE, D.D., D.C.L.

FIRST BISHOP OF NEW WESTMINSTER

BY THE

REV. HERBERT H. GOWEN, F.R.G.S.

AUTHOR OF

"THE PARADISE OF THE PACIFIC," ETC. ETC.

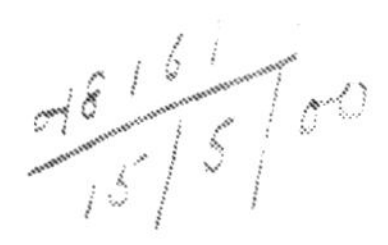

LONGMANS, GREEN, AND CO.

39 PATERNOSTER ROW, LONDON

NEW YORK AND BOMBAY

1899

PRINTED BY
WILLIAM CLOWES AND SONS, LIMITED,
LONDON AND BECCLES.

ACTON WINDEYER SILLITOE.

1840–1894.

Once for the least of children of Manasses
God had a mission and a deed to do,
Wherefore the welcome that all speech surpasses
Called him and hailed him greater than he knew;

Asked him no more, but took him as he found him,
Filled him with valour, slung him with a sword,
Bade him go on until the tribes around him
Mingled his name with naming of the Lord.

F. W. H. MYERS.
(*Saint Paul.*)

PREFACE

OUR only qualification for writing this short preface to Mr. Gowen's excellent work is that we loved, and still warmly love, our old Bishop.

He was to us, for years, not Bishop only, but father, brother, guide, and friend.

Perhaps some apology is needed for our rashness, for we are not men of great reputation or position, either in the Church or the world.

Nor can we lay claim to the possession of what are called "literary" gifts or experience, for we have seldom seen ourselves in print. Love makes us bold.

When others, greater and better men, and in every way more fitted for the task than ourselves, were, for various reasons, unable to take it in hand, it was given to us by those we could not, if we would, refuse. This must be our plea for the kind indulgence of our friends.

For ourselves, and those who were closely bound to Acton Windeyer Sillitoe by ties of kindred and friendship, we gratefully thank Mr. Gowen for giving us this memoir, and for all the valuable time and work he has so generously and lovingly expended upon its production.

It was necessary to curtail and slightly revise it before finally sending the manuscript to press, and with Mr. Gowen's kind permission, one of us (Mr. Edwardes) undertook that somewhat delicate duty. Separated from the author by some six thousand miles, it was impossible to confer together. If faults there are, then they must not be attributed to Mr. Gowen.

To one ever engaged in good work on behalf of the Diocese of New Westminster, we must express our gratitude for the kindest and most patient help in revising the book, and in making arrangements for its publication.

Our thanks are also due to Messrs. Alfred Ellis and Walery, of Baker Street, W.; Messrs. Notman and Son, of Montreal; and Mr. Thompson, of Vancouver, B.C., for their kindly expressed permission to copy photographs taken by them.

This little memoir has been compiled mainly from Bishop Sillitoe's own diaries, from old numbers of the *New Westminster Diocesan Gazette*, and from Mrs. Sillitoe's and the Bishop's letters written to various missionary publications.

The author does not pretend for a moment to give an exhaustive biography of the Bishop's life, nor to do more than give, from the matter placed at his disposal, a graphic summary of the life and work and difficulties of the first Bishop of New Westminster, during the fourteen years he occupied the see.

If a more adequate appreciation of the man,

and his varied gifts and splendid character, especially his spiritual gifts, is looked for, it must be remembered that his letters and diaries did not lay bare his inner self, and that even if they had done so, death does not prohibit reticence. With all his lovable qualities and gifts of sympathy, he was not one who wore his soul outside. There was about him a reserve and dignity in spiritual matters which men understood and respected, as they always do.

He was full of wise, honest, practical common sense, both in the affairs of his Master, and in dealing with the men and women about him.

But his spiritual power and gifts were discovered by all who came in close personal contact with him. If any went to him in spiritual trouble or difficulty, a wonderful depth of sympathy and wisdom, and a rare combination of the knowledge of the Lord Jesus Christ, and human nature, were at once at their service.

And that was exactly the man needed for such a country as British Columbia, and to influence for good the lives of those adventurous spirits who, in rough days, had left the old country to begin life afresh in the far West, under new conditions and with new prospects.

Many a man in British Columbia could testify to faults and vices struggled with, and possibly overcome, through the Bishop's quiet personal influence, appeal, and sympathy.

He did not frighten men with talk too pious

and conventional, but quietly, in familiar intercourse, and with a few kindly, direct, homely words to begin with, the way was opened up to higher and holier things—sometimes to God's grace and pardon and strength. But such things were not talked of, or written about, and for that very reason men trusted him. He understood before many words were said.

It was his constant endeavour, even when harassed by trials and difficulties himself, to cheer and encourage his clergy in their work; to keep their tone high, and their sacred duty to the Church and their flocks ever before them.

He realized the great spiritual dangers to which they were exposed in isolation and loneliness, and the lax moral atmosphere in which they sometimes had to live and work. One by one they were called down to New Westminster for a spell of refreshing, bracing change and intercourse, till they could return to their distant posts with renewed zeal and vigour, both of body and soul.

As often as possible, too, he called the clergy together for a synod, or a short retreat, that, together with their Bishop, they might spend a few days apart with God, for the deepening of their spiritual life and the interchange of mind with mind.

Hospitality was with Bishop Sillitoe a sacred duty. His house was always open, and all kinds of guests were ever welcome, from Her Royal Highness the Princess Louise, and the Marquis of

Lorne, to very humble folk. He allowed nothing to stand in the way of the fulfilment of this part of a Bishop's duty—not even failing health, and the daily struggle to stretch a small income to meet the many demands made upon it.

Every one who received his hospitality found alike a kind, courteous, unselfish, considerate gentleman in their host.

Of his wide influence and his great ability it is unnecessary to speak. It was recognized throughout the broad Dominion of Canada, in the western states of America, and widely at home in England.

Some may think that financial troubles and worries have been treated of at too great length; but it is well that the truth should be told.

Those who knew the Bishop most intimately during the closing years of his life were only too well aware that constant anxiety in these matters hastened his death. The anxiety was never for himself—for he was unselfish to the core—but it was his earnest desire and care to see his diocese well equipped, the Church spreading out her branches and occupying new ground as the population increased, and the clergy receiving to the full, however straitened his own resources, the small stipends due to them, too frequently in heavy arrears.

His English committee, a body of his most trusted and honoured friends, did their very best to supply the needs of the diocese and to lessen his anxiety, but latterly their kind efforts could not well be supported in British Columbia itself. A wave of commercial depression was passing over the country, and one disaster after another left the settlers less and less able adequately to help themselves in providing for the needs of their Church.

Bishop Sillitoe would not approve of all we have written. He would have wished us to say nothing of him, but to say a few prayers for him, that God would grant him peace and refreshment and growth where the faithful departed wait, and eternal joy and rest hereafter.

His memory is still warmly cherished in his old diocese, and in the hearts of those for whom he laboured.

Many loving, gentle hands still carefully tend the grave at Sapperton, where his tired body awaits the resurrection day, though none of his own kindred are there to show their love and reverence in this last way.

In the face of great difficulties the good Bishop spent, and was spent, in the service of his Lord, and laid well the foundations of the Church in his Western diocese.

His name will ever be bound up with the history of the Church in the Dominion of Canada, and is worthy of honourable mention among those who have gone forth in Christ's holy Name, and at His call, and have given themselves a willing sacrifice for their God, His Truth, His Church, and the precious souls of men.

Trusting to the kind and indulgent judgment

of friends, this little book is sent out as a slight contribution to the missionary annals of our Church, and in memory of a true and faithful servant of God and pastor of men.

We would conclude with one word of the country in which he laboured; but it is too beautiful to describe. At this moment its subtle charm and its westerly breezes find their way into the street of the Cornish city whence we write. There is no country on earth to equal it for grandeur of scenery and healthy, vigorous life. There, are mighty, snow-capped, fir-clad mountains, whose summits pierce the clouds; impenetrable forests of kingly trees; great rivers, and turbulent, brawling streams, rushing on their hasty way to the great waters of the blue Pacific; quiet lakes of emerald and opal hue; fertile valleys for the use of man; and over all the fair blue sky.

Who ever lived and worked in British Columbia and did not *love* it? It is a country in which one learns to thank God for His wisdom and His goodness in creation—a country of such exquisite beauty and healthy climate as to make life at once worth living, and God to be thanked for His manifold gifts.

It is easy to predict a great future for such a country, for, added to its beauty, there is untold wealth of gold and other minerals, inexhaustible forests of valuable timber, vast salmon fisheries, abundant and as yet undeveloped coal-fields, and splendid opportunities and attractions for farming, ranching, and fruit culture.

Already, young as the country is, the Great Canadian Pacific Railway, the Imperial highway from east to west, passing as it does through some of the grandest and weirdest scenery in the world, is bearing an ever-increasing flow of population westward. Year by year towns and cities are springing up; places, which a few years ago did not exist, are now numbering their inhabitants by thousands.

Vancouver, the beautifully situated terminus of the Canadian Pacific, can rival even now in prosperity, and the appliances of modern civilization, many an older Western city.

The country, which began its modern history and development half a century ago, on passing from the hands of the Hudson Bay Company to the position of a Crown colony, is now an integral confederated province of the Canadian Dominion. Its people are loyal, zealous, devoted, as is the whole of Canada, to our Queen and Empire. British Columbia is yet in her infancy, but will rise in the future to a proud and prosperous position.

The Indians, the original inhabitants of British Columbia, are gradually dying out before the white man and certain sad consequences of his civilization.

The remnant are a more industrious people than their fathers. Many are at regular work upon the Canadian Pacific Railway, others have their little ranches and fertile farms, while others work the banks of the Fraser and Thompson Rivers for gold.

Bishop Sillitoe loved them well, and spared no efforts for their temporal and spiritual welfare.

Missionary work has been blessed among them, and many an Indian has lived and died in the faith of Christ, and the fear of God.

None can tell of their origin, or speak for certain of their past; but we are told by those who understand such things that, at least three thousand years ago, they were in British Columbia. Many a strange and beautiful legend has been told to the writers of this preface by the Indians, as they have travelled amongst them—legends of the Indian version of the creation of the animal world, and others which seemed to give a glimmering of some dim and ancient knowledge, even of the truth of the Ever Blessed Trinity.

Once simple, happy, healthy, free, it is sad and pathetic to think of them as a fast dying race, the victims of our sins, our vices, and diseases.

Yet it is a comfort to know that, in spite of the white man's poor representation of Christianity, the power and the love of Christ have won their way into hundreds of Indian souls. His Blessed Name is honoured, and His saving Truth held fast.

HENRY EDWARDES,
Member of the Bishop of Truro's Staff, sometime Mission-Priest at Lytton, B.C.

RICHARD SMALL,
Archdeacon of Yale, and the Indian Missions in the Diocese of New Westminster.

TRURO,
June 30, 1899.

CONTENTS

CHAPTER I.

THE FORMATION OF THE SEE.

1879.

CHAPTER II.

EARLY LIFE, AND CALL TO THE EPISCOPATE.

1840-1879.

CHAPTER III.

FIRST GLIMPSES OF THE NEW LIFE.

1880.

CHAPTER VII.

SUMMER CAMP AT YALE.

June–July, 1881.

CHAPTER VIII.

A VISIT TO CARIBOO.

August, 1881.

CHAPTER IX.

THE CHURCH CONFERENCE AT NEW WESTMINSTER.

September, 1881.

CHAPTER X.

TRIP TO THE NICOLA VALLEY, THOMPSON RIVER, AND WORK AT HOME.

October–December, 1881.

CHAPTER XI.

FINANCIAL ANXIETY.

1882.

CHAPTER XII.

REVIEW OF THE YEAR'S WORK.

1882.

CHAPTER XIII.

A TOUR IN THE INTERIOR.

1883.

CHAPTER XIV.

WORK AMONG THE INDIANS.

1883.

CHAPTER XV.

PROGRESS OF DIOCESAN ORGANIZATION.

1883-1884.

CHAPTER XVI.

THE INDIAN GATHERING AT LYTTON.

June, 1884.

CHAPTER XVII.

THE REPORT FOR 1884.

CHAPTER XVIII.

FROM KAMLOOPS TO THE COLUMBIA.

1885.

CHAPTER XIX

GENERAL SURVEY, 1885-1886.

CHAPTER XXIII.

WORK IN THE INDIAN MISSIONS.

1891.

CHAPTER XXIV.

ILLNESS AND STRUGGLE.

1892.

CHAPTER XXV.

TOUR IN EASTERN CANADA, AND GENERAL SYNOD.

1893.

CHAPTER XXVI.

IN HARNESS TO THE LAST.

1894.

CHAPTER XXVII.

AT REST.

LIST OF ILLUSTRATIONS

CHAPTER I.

THE FORMATION OF THE SEE.

1879.

THE wisest, ablest, and most statesmanlike of England's sons are at one in the value they attach to the Colonial dependencies of their wonderful Empire. They realize that the welfare of the children is the welfare of the mother, and that no policy is so futile and inane, even for the mother's sake, as that which fails in sympathy with the career of the children.

And England rightly gives all the honour at her command to the brave pioneers who open up her Colonial estates to her Imperial commerce.

The Church at home is sometimes less wise, and the time has yet to come when the whole Church, from its leaders to its humblest members, shall rightly know the glory of its own Colonial inheritance, and shall take to her bosom with enthusiasm the children given to her beyond the sea.

Yet, as in a national so in a religious sense, the welfare of the children is the welfare of the mother, the strength of the branches the strength of the tree. Interest in and enthusiasm for the Church abroad, so far from weakening the Church's power of maintenance and defence at home, will react in increasing depth and breadth of knowledge, and in enlarged capacity of loving and helping.

And this interest will find both its source and its object in knowledge of the lives of those who have been pioneers, builders, and directors—the Bishops of the Colonial Church.

As contributing to this end, the following memoir is given of one who is truly representative of the noble band of makers of Church history in modern times.

Bishop Sillitoe was one of the last to wish a biography of himself written, and the writer has no intention of attempting any such task. The man must survive on earth in the memory of those who loved him, but the man's work is a legacy to the Church—a legacy not only to the far distant West, where he sowed and planted in faith and hope, but to the whole Church, which values catholicity and believes in the Communion of Saints.

There will be no attempt made to put into strong relief the adventurous or the romantic. The sketches given may seem even monotonous in their record, but if so, the reader will remember that the work was monotonous too, performed often in weariness and painfulness, but in patience and love by one sustained solely by devotion to the Lord Who had called him to labour in His Vineyard.

* * * * *

The diocese of New Westminster, of which Acton Windeyer Sillitoe was the first Bishop, is situated on the Pacific coast of the great Dominion of Canada, and forms part of the Province of British Columbia, which sprang into a colony in 1858, owing to the discovery of gold.

Numbers of people were then attracted to its shores, but previously it was known as a profitable ground for fur traders, who occupied various stations, and did a good business with the various Indian tribes scattered here and there.

The C.M.S. had commenced work in the province in 1856, when Mr. Duncan began his remarkable career among the Indians. A year after the S.P.G. entered the field with two clergy, and in 1859 the venerable Bishop, George Hills, was consecrated first Bishop of Columbia.

It seemed as though the new diocese was destined to great prosperity, but the hopes at first entertained were perhaps over-sanguine, for, owing to commercial crises, a rough population, an unsettled country, and enormous districts to cover, the Bishop had for many years the maximum of hardship with an altogether disproportionate amount of success.

Yet, in spite of all discouragements, the diocese, both on Vancouver Island and on the mainland, was gradually opened up to the Church's ministrations. To mention only work accomplished on the mainland—in Cariboo we are told that the labours of Mr. Reynard were more full of romance than the wildest fiction; the present Indian Missions at Yale and Lytton were begun and carried on successfully by the Rev. J. B. Good; and in the city of New Westminster a handsome stone church and a well-equipped parish testified to the work of the Rev. John Sheepshanks, the present Bishop of Norwich.

But it was early seen that the diocese was too huge for any one man's supervision, and owing to the Bishop's occasional absence in England for the purpose of raising money, large numbers of people remained altogether untouched by the Church's system, and in consequence deserted her for other religious organizations, or else drifted into a state of absolute indifference to religion.

So in 1878 Bishop Hills made the following announcement to his synod :—

"Cariboo, Kamloops, Nicola, Chilliwhack, the Lower Fraser Valley, and Cassiar are needing the ministrations of the Church, but we send them no supply. We seem to neglect them altogether. Yet could faithful ministers of God be sent, the blessing as elsewhere would follow, and great good be done. What is the cause, and is there a remedy?"

It was subsequently moved by Archdeacon Wright and carried—

"That this synod considers the great spiritual destitution of the vast mainland portion of this diocese, as regards clergy, church-buildings, etc., calls for the earnest and immediate attention of the Church, and that a committee be appointed to obtain statistics and all other information that may in any way tend to the relief of such destitution."

At the same synod the real solution of the difficulty was suggested in the following important resolution :—

"That this synod is of opinion that a division of the diocese into three separate dioceses, viz. (1) Vancouver Island, (2) New Westminster, (3) Caledonia, with a view to forming a provincial organization for British Columbia, is very desirable, and that this synod cordially supports the endeavour of the Lord Bishop to carry out the scheme when in England."

From this it will appear that the Bishop had already had the idea of division under consideration. It was his belief that it was clearly impossible to keep in touch with one another different parts of the diocese which were one thousand miles apart, and that subdivision would not only render the ecclesiastical province more easy to work, but would bring increase of clergy and support to each division.

To this end Bishop Hills worked indefatigably during his subsequent visit to England, and the result is shown in the announcement he was able to make to his next synod, as follows:—

> "During my visit to England my time was largely occupied in carrying out the resolution agreed to in the last session of the synod of the undivided diocese with respect to a subdivision into three separate dioceses.
>
> "I laid the resolution before the Archbishop of Canterbury, and received his cordial support; and after many months of hard work in raising endowment funds, I had the happiness of a successful result."

Generous help towards the endowment of the two new sees was given both by private individuals and by the two great missionary societies of the Church, and on July 25, 1879, the first of the two new Bishops, Dr. Ridley, was consecrated to the see of Caledonia.

Shortly afterwards the announcement was made that the Rev. Acton Windeyer Sillitoe, chaplain to the British Legation at Darmstadt and to the Princess Alice, had been selected to fill the see of New Westminster.

CHAPTER II.

EARLY LIFE AND CALL TO THE EPISCOPATE.

1840–1879.

ACTON WINDEYER SILLITOE was born in Sydney, New South Wales, in 1840, and remained in the colony, to which he was ever loyal, till he was fourteen years old.

It is not the purpose of this memoir to do more than allude to the facts of the Bishop's life prior to his episcopate, but one little incident of his almost baby life, told by his own lips to a near friend and relative, illustrates beautifully the tender love which sheltered his early years.

The Bishop's father, who was always spoken of with most reverent affection, had a high degree of sympathy with childish fears very rare in the sterner sex, and this must, one would think, have been combined with some of that quiet sense of humour which was in after years a most helpful constituent in his son's mental character.

Sea-bathing had been recommended to the little boy, and the close vicinity of his parents' house to the Bay of Sydney made the carrying out of this prescription easy of attainment.

But the boy objected to contact with the waves on account of the cold, and therefore as father and son went hand in hand each day to the bay for the bath, the father's free hand carried a small pitcher of hot water, which was emptied into the sea in the sight of the boy. He then no longer feared the cold, and was soon enabled to enjoy his prescription even without the jugful of warmth, which to his childish sense tempered the chill of the great ocean.

He returned to England with his parents in 1854, and proceeded first of all to King's College School, London, and subsequently to Pembroke College, Cambridge. Here he took his degree of B.A. in 1862, and in 1866 proceeded to that of M.A. In later years the degree of D.D. was given him by his University in recognition of his elevation to the episcopate; and a year before his death the University of Toronto awarded him that of D.C.L., in recognition of his services in the consolidation of the Church in Canada.

In 1869 Mr. Sillitoe was ordained deacon, and the following year priest, by the great missionary Bishop, Selwyn of Lichfield. He served his first curacy at Brierley Hill, Staffordshire, where he remained till 1871. For the next two years he laboured as curate in charge of All Saints', Wolverhampton, and then from 1873 to 1876 held the curacy of Ellenbrook, under the Earl of Mulgrave (the present Marquis of Normanby), who became his lifelong friend.

In 1876 he left England and became British chaplain at Geneva, which he left in 1877 for the chaplaincy of the British Legation at Darmstadt. Here—one of the happiest periods of his life—he stayed for two years, combining with his chaplaincy to the Legation the position of chaplain to the late Princess Alice.

The duties of this double post he left at last to

obey the call to the episcopate given him from the far distant West.

Of this episode in the Bishop's life, one high in influence in the Church of England writes—

"I knew nothing of Bishop Sillitoe until he was nominated as chaplain at Geneva, where he had a good many troubles. His work at Darmstadt was signalized by his great influence over the Princess Alice and her children, especially her daughters. . . . He was undoubtedly the means, under God, of bringing the Princess back from Strauss and unbelief to the happiness of the Faith. When the diocese was formed, Bishop Hills asked me if I could suggest a good man, and I at once recommended Mr. Sillitoe. . . . I well recollect his coming to me and saying he wished I had let him alone, that he was by no means the man I took him to be, that he was very human. . . . The result has proved that my estimate of him was truer than his own."

But although the offer of the Bishopric of New Westminster seemed to upset all his plans and to make a radical change in the whole outlook of his life, Mr. Sillitoe felt it would be wrong to refuse so evident a call to harder duty in the distant dependencies of the Empire.

He was consecrated on All Saints' Day, 1879, in the parish church of Croydon, by Archbishop Tait of Canterbury, assisted by Bishop Jackson of London, Bishop Thorold of Rochester, Bishop Hills of Columbia, Bishop Jackson of Antigua, and Bishop Tufnell.

The sermon was preached by the Bishop's old friend and former rector, the Earl of Mulgrave, who continued to be his commissary till the close of his arduous episcopate.

That the service was never forgotten by him will have been evident to all who have been privileged to share in the beautiful services the Bishop always arranged for All Saints' Day, as that festival and anniversary came round in the course of the Church's year. Stronger and more solemn to the end seemed to grow the impression of the responsibility of his office, and it certainly could not have been fresher or truer on All Saints' Day, 1879, than it was on All Saints' Day, 1893.

The Bishop then addressed his first letter to the diocese through its representative, Archdeacon Woods. Writing on November 13, 1879, he says—

"My dear Archdeacon,

"Yours of the 12th reached me yesterday. I heard also from Mr. Good, and am very thankful that you have been remembering me at the Throne of Grace. God has blessed me with a very real faith in the efficacy of intercessory prayer, and has so often allowed me to see it abundantly answered, that I feel a happy assurance that we shall not have asked in vain in this instance. My consecration was full of blessing to me personally, and especially in the full satisfaction of those who have known me best and longest, and I enter on my holy office in the full conviction that He Who hath called me will be with me to further my weak endeavours, and to supply all my defects. May one of the first benefits be to fill all of us whom He has appointed to be His fellow-labourers in His field with the spirit of godly union and concord in and through His Son Jesus Christ. Please convey a loving greeting to Mr. Ditcham and Mr. Baskett, and publicly to the congregations of Holy Trinity and S. Mary's, Sapperton. . . .

"I have had a letter from Archdeacon Wright, and a copy of a report on the spiritual destitution of the mainland. The letter is a gloomy one, but it has not made me gloomy. I am prepared for trials and for disappointments, but I don't believe we shall overcome them any the easier by magnifying them or dwelling too much upon them. The bitter has pretty well mingled with the sweet in my life already, but nevertheless I find I get on very fairly by remembering the sweet and forgetting the bitter as much as I can.

"Let us take courage and go forward. God bless you and your house.

"Faithfully yours in our Lord Jesus Christ,

"A. W. NEW WESTMINSTER."

To a correspondent he wrote at this time what proved to be indeed the guiding principle of all his dealings with his clergy to the end of his life.

"I hope to be in a most real sense a 'father' to my clergy, and though they may differ as widely as the wide comprehensiveness of our Church permits, I shall never *as Bishop* lean more to one way of thinking than another. I shall claim the right to hold my own views and to express them, and to place them in the most favourable light I can, but I shall never regard a fellow-worker with less affection because he fails to see things from my standpoint; and my clergy will, I hope, honour my fairness in this respect by equal confidence in one another."

With this wise resolution in his heart, he took his farewell of old friends in England on Thursday, April 29, 1880, at a celebration of Holy Communion in the church of S. Margaret's, Anfield. The rector here, the Rev. John Sheepshanks (now Bishop of Norwich), was bound by ties of long and devoted work to the Diocese of New Westminster, having held for many years the position of Rector of Holy Trinity Church, New Westminster.

For this church the Bishop carried out with him a present from the Abbey Church of Old Westminster, an altar cross presented by Dean Stanley, and the altar pedestals, which will be referred to later on.

Then in the blessed consciousness of that Communion of Saints which annihilates the barriers of time and space and binds together the whole family of God in earth and heaven, the new Bishop and his wife said adieu to the shores of England, to carry with them the gospel of glad tidings to a people in spiritual darkness and destitution.

The old Church at home will never suffer as long as she thus gives of her light to those who are far off in a land of darkness. God forbid that the time should ever come when her thoughts are only for herself. As England's empire extends year by year over the continents and across the seas, the appeal comes to her with ever-increasing force—

"Oh, let the thought within thee stir
  Of thy lost children, Island Mother!
They hear no more, when Sundays come,
  The old bells ring in village towers,
A message from the angels' home
  To this poor work-day world of ours.
For them no calm, chance words are said
  By pastoral lips in love and meekness,
Like breathings from a violet-bed,
  That touch the common air with sweetness.
Therefore lift up thine arm this day,
  Bid the Church meet them, Island Mother,
Lest they forget her as they stray,
  And falsely deem they find another."

CHAPTER III.

FIRST GLIMPSES OF THE NEW LIFE.

1880.

At 2 p.m. on Thursday, April 29, 1880, the *Sarmatian* put out from Liverpool with the Bishop's party on board. The voyage across the Atlantic was not devoid of peril from the quantity of ice encountered, "hundreds of acres of it, ten and fifteen feet thick," and "icebergs—some little ones with smooth round tops, like hillocks; others, enormous ones with straight-up, cliff-like sides. One was fully two miles long, and at least two hundred feet high. Struggling and crashing and frequently obliged to lie to, in company with four other big steamers and a perfect fleet of sailing-boats, the good ship ploughed her way through a hundred and forty miles of ice, nearly half of it fully twenty feet thick."

The Bishop conducted several services on board during the voyage, both for the emigrants and for the saloon passengers, and gained some little experience of the various classes of people on their way to settle down in the great Dominion.

The landing was made at Quebec on May, the 12th, and thence the Bishop journeyed by short stages to Montreal and Toronto, keeping Whit

Sunday at the former place, and Trinity Sunday at the latter. Then, as there was no C.P.R. in those days, the journey had to be made to San Francisco, which was reached on June 8th. Thence by boat the Bishop journeyed to Victoria, arriving on June 14th; and, leaving Victoria on the 18th, he reached New Westminster, the first point in his own diocese, on the same day.

The first impression of New Westminster is thus given—

"This is really a very lovely place, though of course we have the advantage of the first fresh brilliancy of summer to heighten its natural beauty, but the whole situation is well chosen and picturesque. The ground rises suddenly from the river on both banks, so that in the town the houses stand one above another; every one has a view, and indeed a view more or less panoramic, since abundance of space has given nearly every house a garden. The opposite bank of the stream is covered with pine forest, rising suddenly to about a hundred feet above the stream, and over this ridge, from the higher parts of the town, is seen the snowy summit of Mount Baker, nearly seventy miles away to the south-east. Down the river, to our right, about a mile distant, two fir-clad islands divide the stream into three great arms, and form a basin just above them fully two miles wide, across which we look over to the mountains of Vancouver Island; while upstream, to our left, the view is bounded by the mountains of the Cascade Range, thirty miles off, and still, at midsummer, largely covered with snow."

But lovelier even than the scenery it was to enter into the sanctuary which was henceforth to be in a very real sense a home. A special service was held in Holy Trinity Church, the cathedral designate, at which Litany was said and the *Te Deum* sung.

The next morning (Saturday) there was a celebration of Holy Communion at eight, and the following day the Bishop preached morning and evening to large congregations of his new flock. In a very short time he had fallen in love with his see-town and its churches. Upon the architectural demerits of the cathedral he was indeed (and not unjustly) severe, but with the work going on there he was much pleased.

Sapperton, a village a mile and a half from New Westminster, now included in the city limits, he selected for his residence, as there was the old Archdeaconry House ready to hand and a beautiful little church. The latter he thus describes—

"S. Mary's Church stands in the grounds of the Archdeaconry House, and is a model of what all wooden churches might be and ought to be. It was designed and built by the sappers, who came out on the original survey expedition under Colonel Moody. It was the 'fashionable church' of those days. Government House stood near; officials and their staff had their residences round about; an English tone pervaded the little society; and they took pride in the church they had built for themselves, and in its services."

Getting down to business without delay, Bishop Sillitoe at once began to find out for himself the work before him. After a day or two spent in New Westminster organizing an S.P.G. committee and other work, he went down the river with Mr. Baskett to visit Ladner's Landing. Here he made his first acquaintance with the salmon canneries, then as now the life of the riverside districts. Here, after the good folks had astonished him with the processes of can-making and the farming, with land producing twenty-four tons of onions per acre, and cabbages twenty-four pounds in

S. MARY'S, SAPPERTON.

Photo: Thompson.]

NEW WESTMINSTER.

weight, the Bishop in his turn brought forth the good things he had come to bring.

There was a large congregation at the service held, and the Bishop writes—

"It was very cheering and a little pathetic to see the people turning up as the hour approached by all manner of conveyances, some by boat on the river, some in waggons, some on horseback, and of course many on foot. . . . After the service we had a meeting. . . . I told them I thought they could raise £80 if they tried, and that if they did, I would undertake to provide an equal sum and find them a clergyman. I have since heard that that £80 has been promised and that probably more will be forthcoming; and that they are also prepared to undertake by degrees the erection of church and parsonage, for which they offer sites."

Back in New Westminster, and preaching at Sapperton and elsewhere during the week, the Bishop held his first Confirmation on the Sunday following at Holy Trinity Church, when thirty-five candidates were presented by Archdeacon Woods. During the week thus inaugurated a great Congregational Meeting was held in the Drill Shed, at which the Bishop established a formal acquaintance with the citizens of New Westminster, and the next day went down by steamer to the North Arm to make the acquaintance of some of the logging camps.

"We called first," the Bishop writes, "at a logging camp, where we were hospitably entertained. About thirty men, all whites, are employed. The work consists in felling timber up in the forest, which, being stripped of its bark, and sawn into lengths of about twenty-five feet, is dragged by mules or oxen down a specially constructed road to the river, where a number of logs are roped together in the form of a raft, technically called a *boom*, and towed away to a saw-mill. The road consists of logs laid crossways about three paces apart, called *skids*, with smaller ones between to form what is termed *bridging*. In the centre of the skids a hollow is scooped out, in which the log is dragged along, a boy preceding the train with a can of oil to keep the way greased. This oil presents irresistible attractions to bears, who watch the passage of a team, and then regale themselves on what the friction has left of the savoury delicacy. The oil is extracted from a fish called the *oolachan*, which abounds in these waters, and is of such an oleaginous character as to burn like a candle after being dried in the sun."

A service was held in the camp, at which about fifty were present, although a small proportion consisted of Church people. The Bishop was from this day forth quite at home in the logging camps, where all men admired his frank and manly spirit.

The same week found the Bishop on his way by stage to Burrard Inlet and Moodyville to visit the large saw-mills and logging camps there. Granville, as the settlement was then called, impressed the Bishop as likely to become an important place, and his impression was justified, for the Granville of 1880 is the Vancouver of to-day, the busy terminus of Canada's transcontinental highway.

It would be wearisome to give an account of all the work done by the Bishop during these first few days, so we set down here only a few instances of its wonderful variety, leaving the reader to imagine the days not spoken of as not idle, but filled with a multiplicity of engagements such as speedily rob bishops of any hope of leisure time.

A new scene was reached on July 7th, when a visit was paid to Yale, the centre of the Rev. J. B. Good's earnest and successful work among the

Indians. At this time, however, the railway works had brought a large increase of population. It had now risen to the number of two thousand, including the Chinese labourers. As a consequence, the town gained an unenviable notoriety for rowdiness and license, and the work among the Indians was terribly hampered by the intercourse of the aborigines with vicious and unprincipled white men.

Several days were spent at Yale, during which the Bishop inspected Mr. Good's work, appointed Silas Nalee as catechist, worked hard with his usual devotion in training the choir, married an Indian girl to a Chinaman, and had his first experience of British Columbia rain. As a consequence of exposure to the latter, he spent the Sunday in bed.

We have here the report of a correspondent to a Canadian paper, describing the railway works, to help us in our glimpses of the Bishop's work at Yale.

"A few days ago," he says, "we drove to the engineer's camp about five miles from here. The drive was beyond description beautiful—huge mountains on all sides, and the river foaming below. The waggon-road runs high above the river. One is thankful to have a steady horse and a careful driver; for a shy or a swerve on the part of the horse, and we should be sent hundreds of feet down into the river, running in places at the rate of twenty miles an hour. The water is now fifty feet above what it is sometimes, and in the cañons it rises one hundred feet during the freshets. The windings of the road are such that at times there seems to be no outlet, but mountains in front and around, and in some places the mountain quite overhangs the road. The air was heavy with the scent of meadowsweet and syringa, and the ferns were quite beyond description. . . . At the engineer's camp, at the special request of the *employés*, the Bishop of New Westminster held a service, at which every one was present. . . . I attended an Indian service this afternoon at which representatives of two different tribes were present. It was a curious sight; some of the women were in fashionable dresses, and others almost in rags. The first prayer was sung beautifully—it was like monks chanting a Latin psalm; but the hymns were pitched too high, and were dreadful. The Bishop preached, and one gentleman interpreted to the Yale Indians, while another translated for the edification of the Spuzzum Indians. . . . It was very amusing to see the Bishop gesticulating and pointing, and then to hear one interpreter in a deep voice repeating the sentence in the Yale tongue, dropping his voice at the end of each sentence; while the other, in highly pitched tones and elevating his voice as he proceeded, gave it in the Spuzzum tongue."

After this, the journey was renewed by canoe to Hope, fifteen miles being made by the two Indian paddlers in an hour and a half. Then Yale was once again reached, and the Bishop shared in the excitement of a big fire. The church and mission house had a very narrow escape, taking fire twice, and being under a rain of cinders; but strenuous efforts succeeded in saving the property. Others were not so fortunate, and, worse than all, two men were so severely burned that they died the next day. The Bishop buried them, and on the same day that he laid them to rest received five members into the Church by baptism.

Agassiz and Chilliwhack are the next places to appear in the Bishop's itinerary, and once more Yale was revisited, and an arduous day was spent by the Bishop in examining and preparing the adult Indian candidates for baptism. An open-air service was held in the evening, and on the Thursday the baptisms were held, also five marriages. These latter convinced the Bishop that, in the case of Indian weddings, a rehearsal was absolutely necessary, unless the officiant had unlimited time at his disposal.

The Bishop returned to New Westminster on August 6th, having fairly tasted of the work before him, at least, in the lower country.

CHAPTER IV.

A TRIP INTO THE OSOYOOS COUNTRY.

SEPTEMBER–OCTOBER, 1880.

THE month that followed the visitation of the Yale country was spent at home in necessary but prosaic duties, and in establishing some sort of diocesan organization — one day a committee meeting to discuss the condition of the beautiful peal of bells presented by the Baroness Burdett-Coutts for the cathedral; another day arranging for and conducting a service at the Provincial Penitentiary, writing reports for S.P.G., arranging for school-building, rowing up and down the river to take services at the logging camps—at some of which, by-the-by, no one turned up—and so on, *ad libitum*.

Work of this kind filled up the time till the beginning of September, when a very interesting visitation was made of the Osoyoos country, which may well be described in detail.

The Bishop left New Westminster on September 8th by steamer, accompanied by Mrs. Sillitoe, George the Indian, and "Punch" of the genus *Equus*.

At Hope a landing was made, and an agreement with the Indians for Antoine and five horses at $4.50 a day, and Susap and one horse at $1.50

a day. In spite of rain the stay at Hope was busily occupied in buying stores, paying visits, administering baptism, and recovering strayed horses.

On Friday the cavalcade started at 7.45 a.m., the Bishop, Mrs. Sillitoe, George, Antoine, and Susap riding, and accompanying them three pack-horses carrying luggage. Twenty-four miles were accomplished during the day—a good distance considering the rain and soft roads. Then came camping out. The night was cold and frosty, and the beds hard to those inexperienced in their use. They are made of twigs of fir or cedar, in the spreading of which the Indians are adepts. If skilfully laid, they form a very easy, springy bed, but woe betide the unfortunate traveller who tries to sleep on a brush bed when not scientifically spread.

Next day, Saturday, Mrs. Sillitoe describes the journey thus—

"Our way was a narrow trail round the mountain side, and there were some frightful places to cross. 'Punch' jumped beautifully with me over a tree lying across the road fully three feet in diameter. It was amusing to see the pack-horses get over. They managed by jumping to get their forelegs over, and were then quite at fault; finally, with their hind legs they scrambled over like cats."

Groves of young fir trees, through which rippled beautiful trout streams, tracts of burnt timber, forests full of grouse, and, moreover, infested with myriads of caterpillars—then the open country at 2 p.m. After this came the descent through a bleached forest full of grasshoppers, and at last the halt at Powder Camp, where the night's camp was made.

On Sunday, after a hunt for the horses and a bath in the creek, service was held in camp, and the day's rest was a welcome preparation for the toil yet to come.

Next day for several hours a very rough country was experienced, but the labour received its recompense when the party entered upon a beautiful open and undulating country like an English park, with this difference, that white pines took the place of the ancestral oaks. In the middle a great herd of cattle was encountered.

Similkameen came in sight during the afternoon from a high bluff overlooking the river, and, after one hour's descent, the river was reached, only to find the bridge broken. Camp was made on the level plateau at 5 p.m.

On Tuesday twenty-six miles were traversed by Five Mile Creek, through the cañon, past Indian ranches, over the fork of the stream to a camping-place 2200 feet above the sea. Wednesday's experience was a similar one, ending in a breezy night, during which the would-be sleepers could only watch the straining cords of the tent and wait for the day. On Thursday two *divides* were crossed, and the first sight was obtained of Osoyoos Lake (790 feet above the sea). Here a welcome rest awaited the travellers, and a hearty reception. On the following Sunday everybody in Osoyoos attended the services.

The Bishop observes that the soil here was apparently barren, but with sufficient irrigation it seemed capable of producing anything. Potatoes were seen weighing three and four pounds each, and garden turnips twenty-seven inches round, while melons and tomatoes ripened freely in the open air.

On Wednesday, September 22nd, Osoyoos was

left behind for Penticton, along a good trail across the mountains, with copses in the hollows of the hills, and small lakes full of wild fowl. Rain fell all day, and after twenty-two miles' travelling, even a bad camp, wet, hard, and without brush as it was, proved very welcome.

The Bishop reached Penticton on Thursday, September 23rd, a promising settlement on low land separating Okanagan Lake from Dog Lake. The approach was through a marsh, where the horses sank to their knees in mud. Once arrived, however, troubles were for a while at an end, and the Indian train was dismissed and sent back to Hope.

Leaving Penticton on horses borrowed for the occasion, twenty miles more were accomplished, and a point of the lake reached opposite Mission. No soul was then living within many miles of the house in which the Bishop was staying, and the four younger children of the household had only twice before seen white people other than members of their own family. The Bishop baptized the children, and then proceeded with his journey. The first attempt to cross the lake was unsuccessful owing to the coming on of the darkness, but a second attempt was made soon after, and the Lequines' house reached after some wanderings.

On Saturday a further stage brought the Bishop to Mr. Forbes Vernon's farm in the Mission Valley, where services were held on Sunday in the barn. About twenty men were present, and everything went well with one exception, described by Mrs. Sillitoe—

"A small *contretemps* occurred during afternoon service in the shape of a hen who, having laid an egg, flew upon some hay to announce the fact, and so persistently and loudly that the Bishop could not proceed with his sermon till she had been turned out. Among other unbidden visitors at the same time were the little chipmunks running lightly and gracefully along the rafters—little animals in size between a rat and a mouse, but in appearance more like squirrels, having long bushy tails."

Mr. Vernon's was left behind on Monday, and Lake Head was reached after a journey of twenty-three miles. The Bishop describes the scenery as being very beautiful, especially near Otter Lake, in which there was a wonderful reflection of the surrounding mountains. Calls were made all along the road as usual.

On Tuesday the Bishop rowed down to the landing, and took passage on the *Lady Dufferin* down the river to Eagle Pass, and up another long arm to "Cape Horn" through the narrows. All day long the only people seen were one Indian family in a canoe. The Bishop's party had, like the Apostles of old, "forgotten to take bread," and as the boat was scantily provisioned, they suffered some inconvenience, but managed to appease their hunger by sharing some bread and beef with the crew.

Next day at 8 a.m. they entered a small lake, and thence passed into the Thompson River, where they came across an Indian fishing-camp, and witnessed the spearing of hundreds of salmon, although the fish were at this time out of season. One baptism was administered *en route*.

At 5 p.m. Kamloops, one of the largest towns in the upper country, was reached, and, with a eeling of being once again within the borders of civilization, the party put up at Spelman's Hotel.

Kamloops boasted an hotel, a store, a flour-mill, and a saw-mill; but the Bishop did not stay at this time, taking a drive of forty miles on the Friday to Grand Prairie.

On Saturday the return journey was made to Kamloops, and here on Sunday there was a full day's round of services. The Court House was used as a church, and this in the evening was filled to overflowing. Next day was occupied in visiting, and the Bishop began to give practical attention to the calls he had heard everywhere for a Church school. Large families, he found, were growing up without education for the want of some centrally placed boarding-school conducted on Church lines. A Roman convent school had just been started in Kamloops, but parents naturally objected to send their children there. The Bishop went over this, and he also tried to find some suitable premises which might be converted into a school—with what amount of success we shall see by-and-by.

On Tuesday the journey was resumed by steamer as far as Savona's Ferry, where the Bishop stayed for service, and also looked up candidates for confirmation.

The next point was Ashcroft—a very English settlement, for two of the farmers were found keeping a pack of foxhounds with which to hunt the coyotes.

An incident occurred during the stay here which we give in Mrs. Sillitoe's own words—

"Whilst we were sitting in the drawing-room one evening during our stay at Ashcroft, an extraordinary noise was heard. Some supposed it to be an earthquake, but we finally came to the conclusion that it was nothing more than the moving of some chairs or tables overhead. The next morning, however, we heard that the sound had been caused by a tremendous landslip three miles distant from where we were, and which had dammed up the river until it should have forced its way through this immense dam. However, in company with our hosts, we drove to the river to judge for ourselves. We found that the dam was half a mile long and eighty feet high. The river above had already risen forty feet over its usual level, and was almost dry below. As it had still forty feet to rise before it could break through, and as it would then almost certainly carry away the only bridge by which we could cross, we decided on continuing our journey to Cook's Ferry, where we were able to cross safely. It was painful to see the salmon—some floundering in shallow pools, others lying dead in the dry bed of the river."

From Cook's Ferry the journey was resumed to Nicomen, where there were many Indians mining in the river-bed rocks, and from thence to Lytton, the well-known Indian Mission Station, like Yale, under the charge of the Rev. J. B. Good.

Returning, New Westminster was reached on October 25th, after an almost continuous journey of six weeks, and covering nearly eight hundred miles.

The next day the Bishop wrote to England—

"We returned yesterday from our journey through the interior of the diocese; we travelled a distance of over seven hundred miles, through a country very rarely travelled by ladies, and into a portion of which no Church of England clergyman has ever before penetrated. I don't say this to exalt our performance, for in truth the 'hardships' we underwent were rather of a pleasant and exciting character than otherwise; but I want you in England to feel that we do not call upon you for earnestness we do not ourselves endeavour to feel in practice. We do not intend to 'sit at home at ease,' and send you lively reports of wants derived second-hand from the complaints of others, but to go and see for ourselves, and force no demands on your faith and charity beyond what we can make ourselves personally responsible for."

The visitation must have brought cheer to many a lonely settler. Everywhere the Bishop found himself able to supply touch with home. Here he would come across a schoolmaster acquainted with friends in England; here a postman who was an old Woolwich cadet; here a University man, now the solitary inhabitant of a log hut, whose only other occupants were a cat and some chickens; here a blacksmith from a familiar parish in England; and here a Yorkshireman with mutual friends and acquaintances—all ready to give and receive a friendly greeting.

It was a journey, too, which helped to make the Bishop familiar with no inconsiderable portion of his huge and bewildering diocese.

CHAPTER V.

A WINTER JOURNEY.

OCTOBER, 1880–FEBRUARY, 1881.

WHEN one kind of work was impossible it was the Bishop's happy faculty to turn straightway to that which was possible; and so, when the end of summer made it impossible to do much in the way of up-country travelling, the time had fortunately arrived when it was possible to do most in the cities on the coast.

So, although for the two or three months which closed the year 1880, the Bishop did not go far from New Westminster, yet he had anything but an idle time.

It was a time, too, which was marked by much deepening of the spiritual life in and around him. He knew too well that the only result of activity sometimes is to be "busy, but not for God," and he feared "the barrenness of a busy life" as much as idleness itself. To escape this, it was his constant practice year by year to have a short retreat for himself and his clergy in which they could gather up their spiritual force and gain closer touch with the Source of all power.

This year the retreat was held at Sapperton, commencing on October 30th, and so including the first anniversary of the Bishop's consecration. It was a time deeply appreciated by the wearied workers—one of those times when the human tenderness of our Master is felt, as He says, "Come ye apart and rest awhile."

The Sunday following the Bishop held his first ordination.

It is needless to dwell much on the work of this time, but we may mention that it included the opening of a girls' school, in accordance with the Bishop's earnest desire to establish an educational institution on Church lines, and the taking of the first steps towards the publication of a diocesan magazine.

Beyond this he was hard at work, preaching, organizing, and working everywhere in the neighbourhood, sometimes riding over to Granville, a journey so slippery that many hours were consumed where now we glide over in electric cars in less than one. The snow came on November 30th, but still by stage, canoe, sleigh, or on foot the Bishop accomplished his work.

* * * * *

With the winter well advanced and the engagements in the neighbourhood of the cathedral city fulfilled, the Bishop's desire grew to undertake a winter visit to some of the remoter parishes, and at the beginning of February he started out.

With regard to this trip a local newspaper made the following significant comment:—

"A Live Missionary.—The Bishop of New Westminster, accompanied by his wife, paid Yale a missionary visit last week, and held services in S. John's Church. Even hardy pioneers shrank from making the trip at such a season."

But as the reader may like to have some fuller

account of this adventurous journey, we cannot do better than quote Mrs. Sillitoe's own description.

"The Bishop had been since Christmas wishing to go to Yale, as Mr. Good was in Victoria with his family, and the place, therefore, was left without a priest, Mr. Blanchard being only in deacon's orders. But the river being frozen, no steamboats were running. Now, to travel the whole distance by road is costly, and occupies a good deal of time. He determined, therefore, to wait till the river should be open, at least as far as Chilliwhack, whence we might get on overland. At last a thaw having set in, with almost incessant rain lasting for nearly a week, the *Gem*, one of the smallest of the steamers, arrived from above, where she had been for some time frozen in. George, our Indian, was sent into New Westminster, and late in the evening brought us word that the *Gem* would start next morning for Chilliwhack. It was not till after night-school—which lasts from 7.30 to 9—that we thus learned for certain that we should be able to go. We had consequently not much time to make arrangements for our absence, or to pack up; but packing up is a simple process when one does not take more baggage than is absolutely necessary.

"The *Gem* did not get off as early as was expected, and it was nearly nine o'clock on Wednesday, February 9th, before she called for us at the Sapperton wharf. Our three dogs very much wished to accompany us. The day was fine but the wind cold. The *Gem* is not a passenger boat, and has, therefore, no proper accommodation for passengers, but two chairs were provided for us near the boiler, and the officers did all in their power to make us comfortable, whilst they were profuse in their apologies that the accommodation was no better. We had not long started before the tiller-rope broke, and the boat swung in, and threatened to go ashore. The accident was soon remedied, and we steamed on again. Towards one o'clock, feeling very hungry, we began to speculate on the probability of getting dinner, and as we could discover no place resembling either kitchen or dining-room, we considered our chances small. However, at one o'clock dinner was announced, and we followed our guide over bales and boxes of goods, till we reached a small place partitioned off from the engine-room. It could not have exceeded six feet in width, and of this two feet at least was taken up by two bunks, in one of which a man slumbered peacefully. A long narrow slab against the partition was our dining table, and between that and the bunks there was scarcely room to slip in. The Bishop sat on a flour-barrel at the end of the table, and as the machinery was working close behind him, he had to be careful lest his coat-tails should be caught.

"We thoroughly enjoyed our dinner, and soon left to make room for other hungry people, as only five could sit down at once, and there were several other passengers as well as the crew. As our chairs had been taken for the dining-room, I had to ensconce myself on a big case with a bale at my back, and so managed to make myself very comfortable, amused also listening to our very loquacious fireman talking to the Bishop. He was an American, and spoke with great scorn of British Columbia farmers, saying they would stop the boat to send off eleven eggs, and ask if the boat would wait whilst the hen laid another to make up the dozen! I give this only as a good story, not that I would have anything so libellous believed of our farmers. From all accounts they are doing very well now, and if there has been formerly lack of energy, it was for want of a market. We arrived at Chilliwhack at 6 p.m., and found Mr. Baskett on the landing-place awaiting us. A sleigh was soon got ready to take us to Chilliwhack proper, about a mile from where we landed. The mail sleigh left for Yale at eleven the same night, but we had arranged to remain the whole of the next day at Chilliwhack. We spent most of the day on Thursday trudging about in the snow, and visiting whites and Indians. The

Chilliwhack Indians want a little 'Church house' of their own, and there was a great deal of talk as to where it should be built and about the cost. The Bishop promised on his next visit to look at the site they propose.

"Our driver wished to start at seven the next morning (Friday), but we objected so strongly that he consented to make it eight o'clock if we would be punctual. He it was, however, who kept us waiting, and it was 8.30 before we made a start. Our conveyance was a very primitive one, a long shallow box on runners, a plank laid across as a seat, and, for my comfort, some hay behind to lean against. The day was very fine, not very cold, and the sun shining brightly. The road not being used except for a short time in winter, when the river is closed by ice, is not kept in repair, and a nice shaking we had, scrunching over stones, through the rocky beds of streams, and over other almost impossible places. There are dips in the road as deep as a ditch, and into these the sleigh goes, standing up on the front end, and then on the back. We had to keep in as best we could, since there was nothing to hold on by. At one place one runner was on the rock, and the other on the ground; the Bishop was on the lower side, and out he was thrown with one foot only left in the sleigh. I followed helplessly, and then came the hay. Happily, we were going slowly, and the driver noticed us, and pulled up. A yard further and we must have been deposited in the bed of a stream, which, although not deep, would have given us an unpleasant wetting.

"Our driver told us there was one 'bad' place, where the road goes round the face of 'Murderer's Bar Bluff.' A few nights before he was driving some of the mail passengers, and seeing they were quietly asleep, intended to drive round without waking them. One man, however, started up just as they were coming to the place, and seeing the character of the road, without a moment's hesitation rolled out at the back of the sleigh. It so happens that just at this part of the road there is no snow, but a smooth sheet of ice, with nothing to prevent the sleigh slipping off the road down into the river below. The sleigh got round safely, but the efforts of the passenger to get around on foot seemed hopeless. So slippery was the ice that he could not even stand, and at last had to take off his boots and follow barefooted till he succeeded in reaching the sleigh. Our autumn trip had made us callous to such places, and we were driven safely round. At three o'clock we reached the Indian village of Oham'l, and there stopped about an hour to rest the horses and get dinner, which was prepared for us by an Indian woman. There were not many people on the road, but we met one picturesque-looking Indian, with gun slung at his back, moccasins on his feet, snowshoes in his hand, and surrounded by five dogs. About 6.30 we reached Hope, the last part of our drive being in bright moonlight. We were tired, stiff, and very cold, but had thoroughly enjoyed our drive. Dock and Boundary, our two steeds, were as pleased as we were to have reached the end of their day's journey.

"The Bishop had arranged that a team should meet us on the other side of the river on the following morning, Saturday, to take us on to Yale, and at half-past ten Captain Bristol, the mail-guard, came to say that a canoe was waiting to take us across. We started on foot over the hard snow, down the steep bank of the river, and then paddled across, landing on the ice on the other side about half a mile higher up. The ice was so slippery and the wind so strong, that had I been left to myself, I should have been reduced to take the same measures as the gentleman going round the Bluff. Happily, there was no necessity for this, as Captain Bristol had provided a small hand-sleigh, on which the Bishop and I seated ourselves, and we were drawn, or rather, the wind blew us, across the ice to the shore. The sleigh which awaited us was of the same description as that we had had the day before, only now it was nearly filled with goods, and we had nothing against which to rest our backs. Twice we had to get out when the sleigh went through streams, the bridges over which had been burned. It was thought more than probable that if we remained in the sleigh we should be overturned into the water. The snow on this side of the river was much deeper than on the other, and for about eight miles we could hardly advance beyond a walking pace. Nearer Yale there had been more traffic, and we progressed more rapidly. We found Mr. Whiteway and Mr. Blanchard at the door of the Mission House to welcome us on our arrival, and very soon we felt ourselves quite at home again. Many Indians came to the Mission House in the course of the afternoon and evening to see the Bishop.

"The following day, Sunday, Holy Communion was celebrated, and other services held for both whites and Indians.

"On Monday the Bishop was occupied the whole day arranging business matters and seeing people. On Tuesday morning we started homewards, the morning being fine and bright, though the East wind was very cold. During the night the thermometer had been as low as 10° Fahr. Thanks partly to the numerous wraps with which our sleigh was provided at Yale, we were warm enough, and the road being in better condition than it had been on Saturday, we managed our fifteen-mile drive comfortably. Soon after leaving Yale, two deer crossed the road a few yards in front of us. At the river, after being again drawn over the ice in a hand-sleigh to the open water, we found the canoe awaiting us, and were paddled across by two Indians. It was no easy matter to climb the steep, slippery path on the other side; but that accomplished, we soon reached the inn, where as usual we received a hearty welcome.

"On Wednesday morning at 7.30 we took our places in the sleigh, this time seated on the bottom, and without any hay for our backs. The bare boards seemed very hard, and every jolt shook us severely. The cold was intense, and we watched the sun rise, first over one mountain and then over another, longing for it to reach and warm us too a little. We had intended to get out and trust to our own legs going round the Bluff, thinking it safer, as one of our horses had lost a shoe. Our driver, however, never stopped, thinking that he could take us safely round. My heart seemed to stop beating as I felt the sleigh sliding, sliding, till one corner where I sat was off the road overhanging the river. The chain which forms a drag round one of the runners turned the hinder part of the sleigh outwards. Happily, the horses kept a firm hold of the ice, and we were soon on safer ground. The road round the Bluff is not more than fifteen feet above the level of the river, but it is directly below, and runs, as at all the bars, very swiftly. The road certainly was worse than when we came up, but on the whole we felt little disposed to quarrel with our jolting.

"We reached Chilliwhack about four o'clock, and found the place in great excitement over a 'Social' that was to take place that night, and at which I had promised to sing. I was very tired, and it was kindly arranged that both my songs should be in the second part, so that we might remain quietly in the hotel during the first half.

"Much to our relief, the *Gem* arrived that very evening. Ice had formed on the river during the last few cold nights to such an extent that there had been grave doubts whether she would be able to get up. We embarked about nine on Thursday morning, and were soon on our way down the river. There was much floating ice, and, for the protection of the boat, rough planks had been nailed on to the bows. The ice, however, made short work of these. Then they tried lashing two trees at a sharp angle before the bows, but the ice soon cut the lashings through. At Langley there is a small loop of the river, into which the captain tried to go to land the mails, but it was so blocked with ice that this was found to be impossible, and it was a difficult matter to get out again. It took a whole hour to get out where we had been but a few minutes getting in.

"The *Gem* is not a boat in which one can feel much security. The ice here was but a few inches thick, while that we passed through last year in the Gulf of S. Lawrence was some feet, yet we were in more danger in the *Gem* than we had been in the *Sarmatian*. After getting out of our difficulty, and proceeding a short distance down the river, we encountered a fresh obstacle. The ice was closely packed across its entire width. The captain determined to try to get through, but soon found he must back out, and quickly, too, if the *Gem* was not to be fast shut in, as large masses of ice were coming down from above. When, after hard work, we were clear, it was decided to make fast to the shore and wait till the ice broke up. The ice had done some damage, which the crew set to work to repair. We were in sight of Maple Ridge, a settlement where we should have been hospitably received, and should have found comfortable quarters. We made for it, but, alas! there were no means of crossing the slough which lay between us and the wished-for goal, so we had to return to the steamboat, and spend the night on board. The weather had been warm all day, and rain seemed imminent. The captain and the engineer gave up to our use a small cabin on deck, their own sleeping quarters, and into this five persons were crowded. Sleep was out of the question, and at midnight (it was snowing hard), when looking out, I heard a curious roaring sound down the river. The captain came soon after, and explained that it was the tide coming up, lifting and breaking the ice, which by morning would be floated out to sea. He proved to be right, and at 6.30 on Friday morning we made a fresh start.

"The engineer told us that during the night, finding that the boat was making more water than he could account for, he took a light and went round to examine, and found that one of the main planks had been started by the ice, and that but for a coating of ice she would have filled still faster.

"By 9 a.m. we were landed at Sapperton, heartily glad to be at home again, after a trip which, in spite of its roughness, had been on the whole thoroughly enjoyed."

CHAPTER VI.

SPRING WORK IN 1881.

IT is not to be expected that a Bishop's work, any more than any other man's, can be always interesting. There are those who fancy that the life of a missionary in foreign parts, and particularly that of a missionary Bishop, must be one long series of exciting and thrilling adventures. Unless these are forthcoming, the idea gains ground that there is not much in his work after all. It is difficult to see why more should be expected of the daily life of a colonial missionary than of a clergyman at home, except in so far as he may move among new and unexplored surroundings. Drudgery comes alike to all, and no novelty of environment, no romantic scenery, no peril of travel, can save a biography from being for the most part a record of duties performed over and over again, till every charm is gone from them, except that which belongs inherently to duty done for duty's sake.

So the spring of 1881 passed quickly with Bishop Sillitoe, in routine work of that uninteresting but necessary kind by which, more than by any brilliant exploits, the foundations of dioceses are well and truly laid. There was abundant parochial work, both at Sapperton among his own special flock, and at New Westminster, where he was an ever-welcome assistant to the Archdeacon. The arrangement of Lenten work afforded employment dear to the Bishop's heart, for in that which concerned the deepening and strengthening of spiritual life in the hearts of earnest and sincere believers, he ever found a peculiar joy. Mission work was dear to him too, but he did not allow it to blind him to the needs of the growing Christian, nor did he ever permit his public work to distract his attention from that which must be done more or less in private in dealing with individual souls.

A night school at Sapperton, at which there was an average attendance of about twenty, occupied the Bishop and Mrs. Sillitoe several evenings a week, and then there was the rowing here and there, up or down or across the river, to visit lonely settlers, hold services wherever such could be arranged, and consult with fellow-workers as to the extension of the work.

On Sunday, March 13th, the second ordination was held at New Westminster, when Mr. Bell was ordained deacon, and the Rev. G. Ditcham raised to the priesthood. During the preceding Ember week, the whole clerical staff of the diocese, supplemented by Mr. Bell and Mr. Whiteway, assembled at S. Mary's Mount. The early days of the week were spent in the examination, conducted by the Archdeacon of Columbia; Thursday was devoted to the reading and discussion of the Epistle to the Philippians; and Friday was observed as a day of retreat and devotion, addresses being given at intervals by the Archdeacon and the Bishop.

The two newly ordained clergy went out at once to their work, and the Bishop, after making arrangements for a conference of Church people to be held in the autumn, quickly followed on a round of spring visitations. The following extracts from letters of Mrs. Sillitoe's will give some idea of the general character of these visits. The picture of the Bishop in the kitchen blacking boots, as given in the first extract, and that of his helping to put out a fire in the third, will afford to the uninitiated some valuable glimpses into the daily life of a colonial diocesan.

However, we will let the letters tell their own story.

"*April 23rd.*—We left Sapperton last Saturday, and the steamer landed us at Chilliwhack the same afternoon. Mr. Baskett was at the landing, and we were driven to the parsonage by the chief farmer of the settlement. You may like to picture us in our morning's occupation at the parsonage. The Bishop is in the kitchen blacking boots; Mr. Baskett also there washing up the breakfast things; I am sweeping out the dining-room and doing our bedroom. We were driven on Tuesday to a farm to inspect a cow we were thinking of purchasing, but she proved too expensive. As we were returning, a lynx or panther ran across the road in front of us, and then doubled back again behind the waggon and into the woods. We unfortunately had no gun with us. In the evening, whilst we were taking part in an entertainment held at the school towards providing funds for completing the parsonage, there was an alarm that the parsonage itself was on fire. Off we rushed, splashing through the deep puddles in the school-yard, through a hole in the fence, only to find it was a false alarm. On Wednesday we left in a canoe for Maple Ridge. The Bishop's throat was still so bad that we should have postponed our visit there, only that he had been obliged to disappoint them on a former occasion, and was determined not to do so again. Captain Jem, an old Indian, and his wife Susan were the paddlers. Their two small children had to accompany us, as they could not be left at home alone. There was a third paddle, which the Bishop and I took by turns, and we became quite skilful in handling it. We left Chilliwhack at 9 a.m., and did not reach Maple Ridge till 6 p.m., very tired and cramped and cold. The cost of the canoe was six dollars, so you see how expensive travelling is out here. We ran against a snag (a log, one end of which is fast in the river bottom, the other end slanting up out of the river), but our Indian woman was equal to the occasion. With bare feet she climbed on to the snag, pushed the canoe off, and then jumped or rather crept back again. We had service on Thursday morning at Maple Ridge, and in the afternoon went about four miles up the river, landing on the other side at Derby to see a church and parsonage built there about twenty-one years ago, when that place was selected for the capital. I cannot say much for the architectural beauty of the church, but it is in good repair. The boat we went in was of the very crankiest description, dug out of a log, and it leaked so much that the Bishop and I had to bale the whole time. I am not given to be nervous, but I own to having felt very thankful to be on dry land again. Immersion in the Fraser means almost certain death, even for the best swimmers, the water is so intensely cold, and the undercurrent very strong."

On May 6th the following programme is outlined :—

"We are off to-morrow for Trenant, staying there till Tuesday; the following Sunday we shall be at Burrard Inlet for the dedication of the new church. The third Sunday in May we shall be at home, and on the last Sunday go down the North Arm. After that we go up the river, and shall be at Chilliwhack for a Sunday, and then go on to Hope, where we intend to camp out under canvas for some time; thence on to Yale, where we shall be for the two last Sundays in June."

The visit to Trenant, or Ladner's Landing, as it

is generally called, is referred to in a letter under date of May 16th.

"On Saturday, May 7th, we left by the steamer, taking our horse Punch with us, and in almost an hour reached Trenant. In the afternoon I rode Punch and the Bishop Mr. Bell's horse to make a few visits. The corduroy roads are bad enough, but where not so made are still worse. It is not till May that people can ride at all without getting 'mired.' The Bishop's horse in one place refused to jump a ditch, and walked deliberately into the mud, into which he disappeared all but head and shoulders, the Bishop having only just time to roll off first. We got back at 8.30, tired with our long day, including a rough ride of fifteen miles. Next morning, Sunday, after eleven o'clock service at the school, the Bishop and Mr. Bell rode to Mud Bay, fifteen miles distant, for afternoon service. I could not go for lack of a third horse to ride. This was a very tiring day for the Bishop, not so much from the length of the ride (thirty miles), as from the nature of the roads making the riding very slow. The following day, Monday, I was able to borrow a horse, and we all three rode out to a small hill, which it is wished to obtain as a cemetery, and then on to a cannery further down the river, returning to Trenant by water. On Tuesday afternoon we were to return home, and there being no particular business cut out for that day, we congratulated ourselves on the prospect of a quiet time till two o'clock, when the steamer would call. The Bishop had just sat down with his book, and I with my work, when the lady in whose house we were staying rushed in to say the next house was on fire. Off we flew, and found that Mr. Bell had just arrived before us. All three then set to work to extinguish the fire. There was only one man on the premises, working in the garden; the owner of the house was absent at his cannery, and his wife, who was at home with a three-year-old child, was naturally very much alarmed. Mr. Bell got through a trap-door between ceiling and roof, and the Bishop on a ladder outside. There was a difficulty in getting water, as the tide was out, and I had to cross a shore of soft mud. We managed to extinguish the fire before aid came from the cannery, though but for our being on the spot the house must have been burnt down."

On Sunday, May 15th, S. James' Church, Granville, was dedicated, and proved the commencement of a great work, one of the most important in the diocese. The Bishop, accompanied by the Rev. G. Ditcham, was met at the church doors by the members of the church committee, and the service of dedication then took place. Immediately after Holy Communion was celebrated, the Bishop being both celebrant and preacher. The church was much admired, and was declared to be a credit both to the architect and to the diocese. It is worthy of note that the Communion vessels used, a handsome double set, including alms dishes, were presented to the diocese by the Rector of S. James', Wednesbury, England. They were afterwards burnt in the Vancouver fire in 1886.

The visit to the North Arm of the Fraser River is thus described by Mrs. Sillitoe—

"*May* 28, 1881.—We started from here yesterday morning at nine o'clock in a little steamer, the *Princess Louise*, which carries cargo. The crew consisted of the captain (a German) and his two sons, one of ten years old, who was steersman, the other of twelve, who was engineer. As rain was falling heavily, we had to take shelter in the pilot house; but before long the weather cleared, and the sun broke out. After various stoppages to deliver cargo, we arrived at 12.30 at the house of an English family, with whom we were to stay that night. The Bishop had promised when next he went up the North Arm to visit the Indian chief at his ranche. So after dinner we again started in the steamer. Though the distance in a direct line to the chief's residence is very short, yet, there being no road, and the ground very soft, we had to go a distance of eight miles by water before reaching his ranche. A shrill whistle from the steamer brought down Pete, who piloted us through a very soppy meadow to the chief's house. Similano, the chief, and his wife Sh'alee, came out to meet us, and after shaking hands, we went into the house. We were ushered into a large room, with a kind of bunk running all round. Bunk and walls alike were covered with matting, which the Indians make. The matting was so clean that I seated myself without hesitation, while the Bishop (through an interpreter) talked with Similano, Sh'alee in the mean time squatting on the not too clean floor. She had her hair hanging down in two plaits, the parting dyed a deep brown. After a while I expressed a wish to see the blankets they make from the hair of the mountain goat, and Sh'alee fetched two bright-coloured mats—curious, but not very pretty. All round the room were bundles of reed mats. George, the engineer, told me that they are kept for a *potlatch*, the Chinook word for a gift. (*Cultus potlatch* is the expression for a gift, no return for which is expected.)

"A *potlatch* is a large party to which the giver invites all his *tillicums* (friends), and gives away his presents. Sometimes it is a flour potlatch, when numbers of bags of flour are given away, sometimes blankets or mats. At one potlatch I heard of lately, two hundred pairs of blankets were given away by a chief. The giver is no loser, as he seems always to get an equivalent at other potlatches.

"Our visit ended, we shook hands all round and left. Noticing outside a strong platform on high poles, we found on inquiry that at a potlatch the blankets are thrown from this platform, and scrambled for by the guests. We examined curiously some canoes in process of manufacture, being dug out of the trunk of a tree, and our remarks afforded Similano great amusement, making him go off into fits of laughter. We did not get back from our expedition till seven o'clock.

"The following morning, Sunday, we started at half-past nine for the church, picking up on the way, as we did again in the afternoon, various boat-loads who would form the congregation.

"In the evening we again embarked, and steamed up the river homewards, arriving about eight o'clock."

CHAPTER VII.

SUMMER CAMP AT YALE.

JUNE–JULY, 1881.

THE summer of 1881 was spent by the Bishop chiefly under canvas at Yale, with the special purpose in view of ministering to the spiritual needs of the navvies working on the railway in course of construction at that place.

Yale bore at this time a most unenviable reputation. Pay day was signalized by the most fearful riots, with which the all too slender police force was powerless to contend. Drunkenness and disorder filled the place day and night. Fires kindled by lights held in hands unsteady with drink were of almost daily occurrence, the jail was overflowing, and the justices weary. Tattered, dirt-bespattered drunkards rolled about the streets, wallowing in the mud, cursing and fighting, and driving all respectable people into the recesses of their homes, while saloon after saloon was added to the number, already terribly in excess of the needs of the community.

It was in such a society that the Bishop and Mrs. Sillitoe decided to spend their summer; and as the whole visit has been graphically described by Mrs. Sillitoe, we cannot do better than quote from her account.

"We left home on the first day of June. It was a real June day too, bright and sunshiny. Our first day's journey was not a very long one; it extended only to Maple Ridge, a settlement fifteen miles up the Fraser. The steamer landed us there about 10 a.m., and the captain promised to call for us again on his next 'up trip.' We passed three very pleasant days in this place. The steamer, according to promise, called for us on Saturday morning, and landed us late in the afternoon at Chilliwhack, where we had promised to spend Whitsuntide. Mr. Baskett is in charge of Chilliwhack and the surrounding districts, and we stayed with him at the parsonage."

Here let us interrupt Mrs. Sillitoe's narrative a moment to mention another incident in the Bishop's Sunday work, which illustrates both his manner of dealing with individuals and also the influences against which the Church had continually to be fighting.

An old Indian chief, named Whalem, had been inveigled into joining the Church of Rome, and had been rebaptized. He was also given to understand that his change of religion would result in a speedy recovery from a sickness under which he was suffering. This consummation, however, fortunately or unfortunately, was not realized, and Whalem now desired to be readmitted into the English Church. The Bishop had a long "palaver" with him, and told him that if he returned his recantation must be made publicly, and he must also give substantial proof of his sincerity. Whalem said he was weak and insensible at the time he was perverted, and promised to remain faithful for the future.

This proselytizing by priests of the Church of Rome was often a sore annoyance. Not all the Indians were as staunch as the young chief belonging to Mr. Good's mission, who replied to the priest's assurance that Protestantism would surely end in hell, that if Mr. Good was leading him thitherward, he would go along and take his chance.

But we must return to Mrs. Sillitoe's guidance.

"A picnic had been arranged for Whit Monday, and up to the very time of starting the weather, which for the last few days had been very wet, made us doubt if it would be wise to venture further. We did, however, make a start at 10 a.m., and were rewarded by soon seeing a clear sky. Our destination was Cultus Lake, some eight miles further on. A very slow and jolting ride over some rough ground brought us to the Chilliwhack river—a rushing, foaming mountain torrent. It was decided to have lunch here, and I was considerably surprised to hear that we were to proceed by canoe *up* the river. This seemed hardly possible. Soon two canoes appeared, each manned by two Indians, who had long poles for punting the canoes along. The canoes were the smallest and crankiest I have been in. Very gingerly we got in, and I was much amused by one of our Indians remarking, '*Hyas cumtax*' ('She very much understands'), which referred to the manner in which I got in. The way to get into a canoe is to step in, and without another movement collapse at the bottom. It was very exciting work this making our way up the river. The poles with which the Indians punted bent till one thought they must snap in two. We had to land about a mile before the lake was reached, as the canoe could proceed no further. Following a narrow trail, across which many fallen trees were lying, we were not long in finding Cultus Lake. It is very beautiful, surrounded by mountains, but we had seen finer ones on our last autumn trip in the interior. 'The canoe ride,' as it is termed in this country, was the principal feature on our return journey. We seemed almost to fly through the water, and the skill with which the Indians turned and guided the canoe was simply wonderful.

"We left Chilliwhack on Wednesday afternoon, and were landed at Hope between three and four o'clock next morning. It had been a moonlight night; we had made capital time from Chilliwhack, as we had raced the greater part of the way with a rival steamboat, and we should have reached Hope that night, only that, when two miles short of our destination, some driftwood got foul of our rudder, and for some ten minutes we were at the mercy of the Fraser in full flood, with difficulty avoiding either bank. Then the captain 'guessed we had better tie up,' and proceeded forthwith to do so, much to our chagrin.

"It was useless to undress, as we might at any moment be clear and proceed, so we settled ourselves on a sofa and armchair. The cabin being very near the screw, we required no waking when the vessel began to move on, and, not having any delay occasioned by dressing, we were ready to land at once. We had sent on our tents a week before, and we found them pitched ready for us in a field adjoining the church. They were already occupied by our Chinaman, Sing, who bestirred himself on our arrival, under the impression that it must be quite time to get up. We, however, begged him not to disturb himself or us for the next four hours at least, and then turned in to our couch of fir twigs, fragrant as the proverbial 'roses.' When we had refreshed ourselves with sleep and breakfast, and got all straight, we proceeded to call on all our friends in the village. Our camp consisted of four tents—two of our own and two which had been borrowed. Ours were used as bedroom and drawing-room, the others as dining-room and for Sing to sleep in. All cooking was done in the open air.

"The first night in camp is rarely a success, and ours was no exception to the rule. First of all, it rained, and we were not sure that the rain would not find an entrance. In the second place, it blew, and we were not quite sure that the tent would not be blown away, and leave us *sub frigido Jove*. In the third place, Punch was very restless, and spent the night galloping about, and now and then catching his feet in the tent ropes, and arousing the ire of Sam and Bran, the dogs who shared our calico quarters. Mr. Sheldon arrived next morning, and was not over pleased to find that an Ashantee hammock, in a rather ragged tent, was all the accommodation we could offer him. It still continued to rain very heavily, and, fires having become necessary, the Bishop and Mr. Sheldon had to go into the forest to bring in logs for fuel. But, though fires made our circumstances a little less cheerless, they could not dry a two-acre field, or keep off the rain as we went from tent to tent, so we were always more or less wet. Sing was greatly amused at the hammock having to serve as a bed, and sententiously remarked, '*Him very good catch fish; him no good bed.*'

"The weather partially clearing on Saturday afternoon, we took a walk to dry and air our clothes, visiting some falls about three miles distant along the Hope trail, the only exciting incident of our walk being the crossing of a stream on a log which served as a bridge. Just as we had turned in for the night there arrived by steamer from New Westminster a greatly welcomed joint of beef.

"There was every appearance of Sunday being a fine day, despite the fall of the barometer. The services were Matins, Sermon, and Holy Communion at 11 a.m., and Evensong and Sermon at 6 p.m. Before evening the barometer vindicated its character, for the rain fell heavier than before, and our evening congregation was in consequence a small one. So as not to have any cooking on Sunday, we had kept our joint for Monday's dinner, but when Monday came bitterly did we regret this. The first news with which Sing greeted us in the morning was that the joint had disappeared. We wondered whether Punch had been carnivorously inclined, but as our Chinaman said he had noticed a strange dog prowling about, Punch was given the benefit of the doubt. The dog must have been very agile, for the meat was hung at least eight feet from the ground, and Sing's slumbers must have been somewhat heavy, as the dog must have sprung at his prey within a foot of the Chinaman's pig-tail. On Monday afternoon we took another walk, and on our return were told that the dog had again paid us a visit, and this time taken a fancy to our bacon. We thereupon instituted a search to find some traces of the culprit, and had not far to look, for just outside the fence lay the remnants of a bag of oatmeal, which our nimble visitor must, with no little difficulty, have dragged there and contemptuously abandoned, not fancying its contents. The following day, whilst we were out, he again got into the tent, and, finding nothing better to his taste, carried off our bread.

"On Thursday, June 14th, we left Hope by steamer, and in three hours reached Yale.

"Arrived at Yale, our tents were pitched behind the church, and it was not very long before we were straight and snug again."

After describing work in Yale and a temporary return to New Westminster to fulfil various engagements, Mrs. Sillitoe proceeded to describe the departure from Yale in order to be within easier reach of the railway camps.

"These cannot well be worked from Yale, so we found a very good camping ground about seventeen miles off, and by the side of a running stream. On our drive up the heat was intense, and I have never seen anything to equal the clouds of dust we met with. The road the whole way follows the course of the river, which above Yale is a rushing torrent quite unnavigable. The road at the best of times is a very dangerous one, there being nothing, in case the horses swerve or shy, to prevent them rolling down into the river below. Just now it is worse than ever, having been cut up by the railway works and plentifully strewed with large stones from the blasting operations which they necessitate. It is, moreover, so

Photo: Thompson.]

IN THE JAWS OF DEATH: THOMPSON CANYON.

Photo: Notman.]

SAILOR-BAR BLUFF, BELOW SPUZZUM.

narrow that one holds one's breath while passing another team. One conveyance stands still on the road's very edge, while the other creeps past on the inside an inch at a time, and with one wheel up the bank. There are places where one may pass more easily, and at these the drivers wait when they see another team coming; but some of the worst places occur where one cannot see ahead, and it is here that there is the difficulty and danger. Another source of danger is to be found in the fact that the blasting is perpetually going on, a loud report and a shower of stones being sometimes the first and only notice you receive of the discharge. I was told the other day by a gentleman in Yale that nobody who can avoid it now drives over the first thirteen miles of the road. 'If you are riding,' he said, 'you can dodge the rocks flying about, but if you are driving you are powerless.'

"The Fraser runs through the Black Cañon, about two hundred feet below our camp, and the 'Line' on the other side passes along the face of the mountain, and where even that is impossible, through tunnels. The men are working on small sections, which can only be reached from above by means of ladders in some instances, and in others by ropes. The work consists entirely in blasting. It is a great amusement, as soon as we notice the men beginning to run, to watch the blasts go off. The rocks fly in all directions, and roll down into the torrent below. The day after our arrival we determined to make the tour of the camps. We started about 10 a.m., and had a very hot, dusty walk down to the bridge, a distance of four miles. Here, however, the hard work only began. We called in at 'Camp 8' at the bridge, but the men were just going in to dinner, so we did not stay. At 'Camp 10' there is quite a number of houses. The men there are at work in the big tunnel, sixteen hundred feet long, and several of the officers have their wives living in camp.

"We called on all the wives, had some lunch, and the Bishop arranged for a service on the following Monday. We then proceeded up the mountain, over a fearfully rough trail, with the sun blazing down upon us. A sharp descent brought us to 'Camp 11.' Here I was too tired even to enter, but sat outside in the shade of a tent while the Bishop interviewed the authorities. It was about three o'clock when we trudged on again, climbing up the steep rocky path. The heat of the sun on the one side and of the rocks on the other was fearful, and we were *cheered* by meeting two men riding, who told us that the *worst* had yet to come. And so indeed we found it, for the trail continued to ascend almost to the top of the mountains. Here we found the camp of one of the Government engineers, and near it a stream of the coldest and most delicious water I ever tasted. From this point we could look down upon our own camp on the other side of the river, still in a blaze of sunshine, whereas for us the sun had now set. A steep zigzag descent brought us to a fork in the trail, and we had to go about half a mile down the river again to get to 'Camp 12.' Then followed another hard climb, for about three quarters of a mile, and a still steeper zigzag descent brought us to 'Camp 13,' with the most exquisite waterfall I have ever seen. Here we had supper, and promised to pay a visit on the following Tuesday, that the Bishop might hold a service first, and later on in the evening assist in giving the men an entertainment. The boat was soon manned to take us across, a very large one—the *A. Onderdonk*, named after the contractor for the section, and manned by six men besides the captain. The river is a fearful one to cross, and this is the last of the boats remaining, the rest from other camps having broken away and been carried down. The course taken in crossing is a somewhat erratic one. The crew row for quite a long distance in an eddy up the shore, or rather under the rocks. As soon as they turn to cross, the stream catches the boat, and carries her down at a tremendous rate, the men meanwhile rowing with all their might, the captain steering with an oar. They strike an eddy on the other side, and have to row some distance up to the landing. A walk of about half a mile brought us to our camp, very tired, and very glad to be back again. I am the only woman who has ever walked over that trail, and not many men have done it either.

"We were obliged next day to return to Yale for the Sunday services. We left again at three o'clock on Monday afternoon, and arrived at the big tunnel at six. They had promised to have everything ready for service at seven, to allow our getting to our camp by daylight, but it was eight o'clock before they had the supper cleared away, and the room ready. We employed the interval in seeing the tunnel, going in on a lorry drawn by a mule. They had penetrated to a distance of four hundred feet at either end. The noise inside was deafening, the drills being worked by machinery, and shouting our loudest we could hardly hear one another speak. The men work in two shifts of twelve hours each—the day-shift lasting from 7 a.m. to 7 p.m., with only twenty minutes for lunch, and the night-shift from 7 p.m. to 7 a.m. There was a good congregation, which surprised me, as I should have thought that after twelve hours' work in the close atmosphere of the tunnel and the deafening noise of the engine, the men would have been too tired for anything but their beds. We did not get away till 9 p.m., and it was already dark. I cannot say I should wish to repeat that six-mile drive home, for in broad daylight it is bad enough. Twice the horses got frightened and started off, but a good driver and a good brake soon stopped them. In about the worst part of the road two men were lying drunk, and we had to go on the very outside to pass them. Had the horses swerved in the least we must have gone over into the river fifty feet below. We had not much difficulty in finding our tents, and were very glad to turn in.

"Tuesday was a bright day, and we sat under the trees, the tents being unbearably hot, and wrote letters and worked. Shortly before seven we started off for 'Camp 13.' The boat's crew was on the watch for us, and as soon as they saw us began to get the boat ready. She had got below a small 'riffle' in the river, and they set to work hauling her up with a rope, two men in the boat keeping her off the rocks with the oars. Suddenly the rope broke, and off she went with the two men in her at a fearful rate down the river. There did not seem to be a chance for the boat to escape capsizing in such a torrent. We commenced running along the road to watch. The men seemed to keep cool, and guided the boat cleverly past the rocks which stand up in the middle of the stream. Several times the boat got into an eddy, and it seemed as though they might get her to shore, but again the stream caught her, and whirled her along. The excitement of watching was intense. Twice they got into a whirlpool, and the boat spun round like a top. We watched them right through the Black Cañon, and then a bend in the river hid them from view, but we continued to run on, remembering a part opposite 'Camp 11,' where the river broadens a little, there is a good eddy, and where Indians can cross in canoes. At one time we saw a log in the stream looking just like a capsized boat; but on we went, hoping almost past hope that as they had got safely through the Black Cañon, they might escape, and just opposite 'Camp 11' we saw the boat tied up, looking as quiet and serene as if it were her proper place, and she had not made such a mad rush down the river. The men had landed and started across the trail home. The boat will have to stay down where she is till she can be brought across, and will then have to be carried up the road, which, I imagine, from her size, will be no easy matter. This mishap to the ferry effectually prevented our service, and in fact has cut us off from all communication with the camps."

It is no wonder that, with all the work open to him in Yale and its neighbourhood, the Bishop felt almost overpoweringly the need of more men to take advantage of such grand and pressing opportunities. Before starting he had written—

"Oh, the opportunities Yale just now affords! Hundreds of men are now going up every week, and what can one man do, and he only a deacon? I purpose being there all June and July, but we want *ten* men, and then we might do something. There is not a fitter illustration in the whole mission-field of the Lord's lament, 'The harvest truly is plenteous, but the labourers are few.'"

And now that he returned he felt the need weighing on him with a thousand-fold its former force. In writing home an urgent appeal for help, he expresses in striking language his personal sense of the awful burden God had given him to bear in taking the oversight of such a work.

"I have acted," he writes, "and purpose always to act, God helping me, on the principle that the work is not ours, but His; that it is His will the work should be done, that He Himself is the real doer of the work. Only He moves some to come out to the field of labour, while He moves others who stay at home to provide those temporal means which enable the work to be prosecuted. Their obligation is as great as ours, and I doubt not they feel it as deeply. All, therefore, I need do, as God's husbandman, is to mark out the ground, to describe to those at home its character and capacity, and to explain how it may be most profitably tilled. I cannot doubt but that He will direct me in this, and for His work's sake enable me to carry it out. I am not so foolish as to suppose that my judgment will always be right, or my plans always allowed to succeed. We are all apt to lean on the arm of flesh; and so often as this is the case must come failure and disappointment. But guided by the judgment of the All-wise, and relying on the arm of the Almighty, with His glory only in our mind, then the work will be allowed to prosper in our hands, and the dew of the Divine Blessing will rest on it and on us."

CHAPTER VIII.

A VISIT TO CARIBOO.

AUGUST, 1881.

OF the first part of this journey the Bishop gives his own account as follows:—

"We should never have started had we listened to the gloomy vaticinations of anxious friends. They painted the perils of the road in most ghostly colours, and ransacked the pages of history (an unwritten history at present, and existing only in the memories of the 'oldest inhabitants') for illustrations of the dire results of *amateur* coaching on the waggon-road. All kindly meant, no doubt, but scarcely helpful or to the point. For the point was to get to Cariboo, or rather, Cariboo was the point to get to, and, unless we could drive ourselves, the point was unattainable.

"In the first place, the public stage travels day and night and makes but few stoppages, and would give us no opportunities of making the acquaintance of people on the road, which was an important part of our purpose; and in the second place, the stage charges would be £15 a piece each way, and this was altogether beyond our means. So, having already one horse and what is here called a *buckboard*, we decided to buy a second horse and drive ourselves, rather than give up the journey.

"It does not take long to buy a horse in this country, and, having had an eye on a particular one for some

Photo: Notman.]

TRUTCH SUSPENSION BRIDGE ON OLD CARIBOO ROAD.

time, an exchange of proprietorship and £12 made our team complete. On August 12th all was ready for a start from Yale, and with many words of caution, and a farewell almost as sorrowful as an Ephesian elder's, we set out on our drive of four hundred miles.

"There are few things more dull than a diary, and I will therefore spare you the infliction of days and hours further than clearness makes necessary, and aim rather at a connected narrative broken chiefly by Sundays, and otherwise only as interest shall seem to warrant.

"The first fifty-seven miles of our journey lay through the Fraser Cañon, a narrow gorge in the Cascade Mountains, through which the river has at some time forced a passage by some power which it seems a weak expression to call supernatural. Here is a river five hundred and fifty miles from its source, without reckoning its windings, contracted between sheer rocky walls that approach each other in some places within fifty yards. Its depth is unknown, for so impetuous is the current that the heaviest plummet is carried furiously away before it can reach the bottom. And this at the lowest stage of water; while in June and July, when the winter snows are melting, there is in some parts of this cañon a vertical increase of water to the extent of ninety feet. It is scarcely conceivable that salmon can make head against this torrent dashing along at the rate of eighteen or twenty miles an hour, with long stretches where the straight walls offer no opportunity for an eddying resting-place. And yet in every little eddy they were to be seen in such marvellous numbers that I am almost afraid to speak of them lest I should be accused of romancing. There was positively not room enough for them; they jostled one another out of the stream; in fact, there was more fish than water. Supposing a tub were filled with salmon, and then as much water poured in as there was room for—this would give you an idea of the appearance of the eddies as we saw them during the whole course of our first day's drive. Perhaps even a more striking illustration of the abundance of the fish is afforded by the fact that the Indians were selling them to the canneries for *one halfpenny* each. We get them even cheaper than that, for there is a cannery within a hundred yards of our house at Sapperton, from the proprietor of which we have *carte blanche* to send for a salmon when we want one. Unfortunately, we are away from home during the best of the season, and although, up-country, at roadside houses there is the same cheapness, and you get salmon at breakfast, dinner, and supper—*toujours saumon*, in fact—yet the culinary arrangements have the Chinese stamp too rudely impressed upon them, and one never sees a boiled fish.

". . . If the character of the river is extraordinary, equally so is that of the road, and, to people with nerves, equally terrible. There are places here and there where the river is lost sight of, and the road passes safely enough through woods which form a perfectly secure barrier on either side, but for the most part the cañon is so narrow and the cliffs so precipitous that the road had to be cut out of the rock, and in some places the rock is not only beneath one's feet and on one side, but overhead as well; while, on the other hand, the Fraser is sometimes so near that in high water it overflows the road.

"Here and there bluffs formed by spurs of the mountains have proved impassable by excavation, and then the road is built out from the face of the cliff and supported by struts. There are two such places between Yale and Lytton—China Bluff and Jackass Mountain—and after driving four times over them last year, I don't mind acknowledging that nothing could induce me to do it again but the call of duty. The risk is too great to run except of necessity. Not that these particular places are the most dangerous, for one may just as well fall five hundred feet as fifty. But the danger is more obvious. It is pressed rather too forcibly upon one's attention, and suspended conversation, a moment's introspection, a quick glance over horses and harness and wheels, and a 'taking fresh hold,' generally of things inward and outward, teach one with a force often wanting in sermons that 'there is but a step' between life and death. The width of the road is eighteen feet, ample enough—it might be supposed—to drive upon, and perfectly secure if it were across a plain, just as a plank is wide enough to walk upon when it lies upon the ground. But elevate the plank twenty feet above the ground and flank it with a wall, and it takes a Blondin to traverse it successfully.

"And so this eighteen-feet road, with a precipice on one side and an abyss on the other, seems to dwindle to a ribbon under the most favourable aspect, and it becomes something very little short of appalling when one comes face to face with ten yoke of oxen and a pair of freight waggons. By the rule of the road the heaviest team always takes the inside, and the oxen therefore invariably go to the wall. The light team looks anxiously for a lucky spot where nature or accident may have added a few inches to the width, and there, pulling up, awaits the *rencontre*. The dangers of the road teach men consideration, and in all our travelling up and down, we could name but one instance of anything but the most uniform courtesy and goodwill.

"An amusing circumstance which occurred on one of the first days of our drive illustrates the primitive character of the administration of justice in the country districts of the province. We had passed without stopping at a farmhouse where a number of people were assembled, and had driven on perhaps half a mile, when a shout behind us drew our attention to an Indian furiously galloping in our wake. We pulled up and allowed him to overtake us, and he handed me a scrap of paper on which was written, 'Have you got a Bible with you?' My acquaintance with Chinook is still in its infancy, and, though not a complicated language, its intelligibility was not increased by the gasping utterance of a man out of breath with hard riding, and I utterly failed to elicit from the messenger any explanation of the purpose of his mission. However, the fact that a Bible was in requisition was sufficient reason for turning back, and fortunately we had been overtaken at a portion of the road where turning back was not an impossibility. Arrived at the farmhouse, we found a court sitting, and a magistrate hearing a complaint of assault. The magistrate was a teamster. He had come along that morning in the course of one of his journeys, not expecting to be called upon to exercise his judicial functions, and was unprovided with the legal instrument for administering oaths. The farmhouse being equally unproductive, the course of justice seemed likely to be arrested, when lo! a *deus ex machinâ!* A bishop surely must have a Bible with him! But since the *machine* was whirling away the *deus* at the rate of eight miles an hour, it was necessary to send post-haste after him, and there was no time for more than the brief message we received. We soon had our 'pack' unstrapped, and produced the book, and when the witnesses had been sworn, left the court sitting, and went our way.

"Magistrates are not always so particular as this as to the character of the volume used on such occasions. There is a tradition that the book long used in one of the courts of this province was a copy of 'Gulliver's Travels,' and that the mistake was only discovered by a Jew, who, a little fastidious about kissing the New Testament, opened the volume that he might get at the right end, and naturally objected to swear on it at all.

"The second day out from Yale we reached Lytton, the dreariest, dullest, and driest place in the country. A great scarcity of water prevails, and there is consequently but little cultivation. Five days out of six a strong wind prevails, and the sand gets into one's eyes, and into one's throat, and down one's neck, and plays havoc with one's temper, and since the hotels are the worst managed houses on the road, one has comfort neither indoors nor out. Nevertheless, we were obliged to spend a Sunday there on the Indians' account. We had Matins and a Celebration in the court house for the white people at nine o'clock, and service in the Indian church at eleven. The native catechist said prayers in the Indian tongue, and then I celebrated Holy Communion, administering to twenty men and eight women—as devout a body of communicants as I ever ministered to. I could not preach, however, for want of an interpreter, the catechist not being yet competent for the office.

"We drove on in the afternoon seventeen miles to where there is a cluster of houses occupied by the C.P.R. engineers and their families. Here we had evensong, and I preached.

"We had now left the valley of the Fraser, and were following the Thompson. The Thompson River is chiefly interesting in a missionary point of view from the fact that it is the central field of our Indian Church work. From a few miles above Yale to Lytton, and then branching off in two directions up the Fraser and Thompson Rivers to Lillooet and Kamloops respectively, one language prevails, called commonly 'Thompson,' but more correctly, 'Neklakapamuk.' Into this language the greater part of the Prayer-book has been translated and printed through the instrumentality of the S.P.C.K. During fifteen years these people have been under instruction, so far as one missionary could cover so large a district. Churches exist in many of the villages, and a kind of service is held regularly by the chiefs and head men of the tribes, although they can do no more than repeat *memoriter* what they have learned at the mouth of the missionary, no opportunities of secular instruction having been afforded them as yet by Church or State. That they are capable of such is evidenced by the fact that there are individuals who by their own endeavours have learned both to read and write. A remarkable instance of this natural ability is furnished by a young man of whom I have frequently written. John Teetleneetsah lives on the Thompson, a few miles above Spence's Bridge. There he has built himself a house more comfortable than many in which white men live. He frequently writes me letters on the subject of his farm and about Church matters in his neighbourhood. This mission has been carried on by the Rev. J. B. Good, who has just resigned. I earnestly hope an endeavour will be made to establish a new departure, and provide these Indians with the one thing they require to lift them above their present civilization, namely, simple but efficient secular education.

"This is all, however, by the way. We are on the road to Cariboo, and must get forward.

"Two days' journey from the Thompson River brings us to Clinton, a busy little town almost in the centre of the province. It has two hotels, a large store, a school, and a court-house. Alas! no church. It is very prettily situated in a broad valley at an elevation of three thousand feet above the sea, and has a climate so bracing and dry that the inhabitants enjoy a perfect immunity from all those varieties of domestic insect life which sometimes seriously embitter existence on a lower level.

". . . They have never had a resident clergyman or minister of any kind in Clinton, but depend for religious services upon the stray visits of missionaries located in districts around. If I am successful in establishing a mission station at Kamloops, Clinton can occasionally be served from there.

"Immediately on leaving Clinton, the road enters what goes by the name of 'Green Timber,' a high table-land about fifty feet across, covered chiefly with low brushwood, and abounding in lakes. At present wholly unutilized and too elevated for grain produce, this district might, at small expense, be made available for the pasture of unlimited herds of cattle in the days, not far hence, when bunch-grass shall have become extinct.

"I must not omit to notice in the interest of lovers of nature a most remarkable natural feature about fourteen miles from Clinton, called by the people 'The Chasm.' It consists of a deep fissure of rock about fifteen hundred feet wide at the top and about nine hundred feet deep. The road passes round the point of its commencement, and from thence one looks along the length of it a distance of about a mile, though it is said to extend much further. The sides of the chasm are perpendicular cliffs of rock for about halfway down, below which sand blown over the edge on either side has accumulated in sloping banks, on which is a growth of fir trees. The cliffs are clean cut, but here and there on the face of them are patches of a smooth and rounded character, evidently acquired under the action of fire. The cliffs themselves are of sandstone, with veins (apparently) of iron running through them at various heights. Along the margin the ground seems full of human bones in larger and smaller fragments, with specimens here and there of pointed flints. I hazard no conjecture on the origin of this wonderful freak of nature or its ghastly accompaniments. I am not afraid to be silent when more scientific heads than mine have been puzzled.

"On emerging from Green Timber we come upon a beautiful open country of rolling hills, of which Lake La Hache forms a kind of centre. Here agriculture and dairy farming are in full force, and nothing is wanted but a market to multiply a hundred-fold the present produce of the district. Cariboo is at present the farmer's only market, the cost of freight being too high to enable them to compete in the lower country, and unfortunately the Cariboo market is failing, for the reason that mining itself is failing, chiefly from want of encouragement by the Government. This was our second day from Clinton, and we had driven since morning forty-six miles, when we arrived at a comfortable farmhouse by the roadside, occupied by a large family of Church people. This was a log house, most substantially built, consisting of one great room in front, which served for dining-room by day, while round it were ranged, head to foot, clean, inviting looking beds to be occupied by the men of the family by night, and a wide open fireplace at one end, in front of which an ox could have been roasted whole; behind this room were three or four smaller rooms and a kitchen. Just the kind of place to reach late at night, tired and hungry, where one can feel the horses will be well looked after, and can sit down by the fire while the good wife prepares a supper of 'bunch-grass' beef of their own rearing, with wholesome home-made bread and rich butter and cream, all made pleasanter by the welcome, not only expressed, but made evident in the kind faces and manner of host and hostess, and the interest manifested by them all in one's self and journey.

"On the next day, by the margin of the lake (wherein are to be caught trout of from fifteen to thirty pounds in weight !), we passed through the same open rolling prairie country, with a farmhouse every six or seven miles, and great fields of grass and oats ready to gather for the harvest. Then across another 'divide,' and down once more into the valley of the Fraser at Soda Creek, about two hundred miles higher up its course than where we left it at Lytton.

"It was Sunday again, and we gathered a congregation in the large room of the hotel, our numbers being augmented by the arrival during the day of the mail from Cariboo. A scarcity of Prayer-books prevailing, the service partook of a somewhat old-fashioned 'parson and clerk' character, the latter *rôle* being courageously and indefatigably sustained by Mrs. Sillitoe.

"For the next two days our road lay along the river —sometimes on the very brink, sometimes high up the benches or terraces, which are a peculiarity of this river and its tributaries. . . . They are of sand and gravel, and full of gold, for which they are being worked profitably by Chinamen in many places, but the proportion of dirt to gold is so great that a large supply of water is absolutely necessary, and until means are devised for cheaply pumping the Fraser water to the level of the benches, mining operations will not be extensively pursued.

"Fifty-four miles separate Quesnelle Mouth from Soda Creek, and along the road are some of the largest and most prolific farms in the province. Oats are the chief production, but wheat, too, will ripen in most seasons, though early frosts sometimes surprise it. The fields are of prodigious extent, and though not so large as many in California, are to be found not infrequently of a hundred, a hundred and fifty, or even two hundred acres. Quesnelle Mouth is the junction with the Fraser of another large river which drains the western slope of the district of Cariboo. It is the chief forwarding station for the supplies of the Hudson Bay Company's stations in the north, and though still a town of some consequence, its fortunes have waned through the establishment of depôts on the coast, and the advantages of quicker and cheaper communication by sea. Its enormous distance from the more settled parts of British Columbia completely shuts it out from any share in general trade. It is nearly two thousand feet above the level of the sea, and before us was an ascent of two thousand two hundred feet more in the sixty miles that still separated us from Cariboo.

"We had not appreciated the elevation much before, but now every mile seemed to make a difference. We had lovely weather, and the road was mostly smooth and hard, and driving in the dry, bracing air was very exhilarating. Moreover, a drive of four hundred miles is not an everyday occurrence, and now it was drawing to a close our hearts were naturally lifted up with thankfulness for the abundant prosperity and gracious protection accorded to us, and occupied besides with bright anticipations of the place and people we had come so far to see."

Here the Bishop's description stops. A drive of twenty-six miles on Wednesday brought him to Boyd's, and the next day, starting off at 8 a.m. and visiting various farmhouses by the way, he succeeded in getting over the remaining thirty-four miles, and reached the residence of Judge McCreight at Richfield by evening.

The description of the journey is thus completed by Mrs. Sillitoe—

"We had just one week to stay in Cariboo, and we began our visit very lazily, for our first evening was spent sitting over a fire and talking with our host. Although it was August, there were sharp frosts every night, and there seemed little prospect for the strawberry crop in the garden outside, for the plants were only just coming into blossom, while the first radishes of the season had that day been pulled for us. A night's rest, however, in such a climate, over four thousand feet above the sea level, made us as brisk as possible again.

"Our first visit was to S. Saviour's Church, which stands in the middle of the street at one extremity of the queer-looking town of Barkerville, which in the irregularity of its houses resembles in many respects an old German village. The church and the houses are all on stilts (so to speak) of various heights, for the reason that the process of hydraulic mining above the town is gradually washing the mountain into the creek below, and every year when the freshet comes down, it brings with it and leaves behind a large deposit of *débris*, locally called 'tailings,' which during the last twelve years has raised the bed of the creek twenty feet above its original level. The town, built in the first instance on the margin of the creek, has had to be raised correspondingly, but the houses being of wood, this is not a difficult matter. One store building that could not be so treated is now buried up to the roof. The side-walk is from six to ten feet above the level of the street, and varies with the height of the houses, so that walking along one is constantly ascending or descending a few steps, and it is necessary to keep a careful look out. Besides which, in many places the side-walk comes to a sudden end, without any warning or any barrier to prevent one tumbling over into the road below. How they manage in high water, when the street becomes a rushing stream, I don't know, but I heard of two children falling off and being nearly drowned before they were seen and rescued.

"The church was built eight years ago, and it was

only used during one winter, and has since been shut up. In spite of this it looks as new as though it had just come out of the builder's hands.

"The services during our stay were remarkably hearty, and seemed to express the thankfulness of the people for again being able to take part in the services of their church. It made us regret that our stay was to be so short. On Sunday evening there was a general request for another service on the following Wednesday, with which the Bishop of course complied. The altar was covered with a dilapidated red cloth, and the alms dish was an old tin plate. A concert had been arranged to take place the evening of our last day in Barkerville, towards raising funds for putting down a second floor to the church, and repairs to the adjoining rooms. Mr. Blanchard, the clergyman in charge of Yale, had shortly before been up to Barkerville, and as the result of his visit, a petition had come to the Bishop for a resident priest, and a list of subscriptions towards stipend amounting to over $800. . . . The Bishop promised that as soon as the Yale Mission station could be filled, Mr. Blanchard should be at liberty to proceed to Cariboo. . . .

"But to return to our doings. Early in the week we visited a mine about six miles distant. We had dinner in a miner's cabin, and though we were unexpected, the dinner that was very soon ready seemed almost the work of a conjuror. Chicken, beef, strawberries, and peaches were among the delicacies set before us (all canned, of course), and tea, without which no meal is complete in this country. After dinner we went down the 'Brothers' mine on Jack o' Clubs Creek. It is one hundred and eighty feet deep. We saw the process of getting out the earth and sending it to the surface to be washed. Some of it was 'panned' out, as it is termed, for me, and, much to the annoyance of the miners, who are most generous, the pan showed but few 'colours.' Still I carried away with me some specimens of gold dust. The 'Brothers' mine connects with the 'Sisters,' and we crawled through the low passage between the two, and came up to the surface by another shaft. Next day we went to see the wash-up of an hydraulic claim, and the same day went down another shaft, popularly known as 'slum tunnel' from the amount of slime and mud in it. I brought away two very pretty specimens of gold.

"On Wednesday night the church was crowded for service, and so on Thursday night was the 'Theatre Royal,' a large building put up years ago for theatricals and concerts, not only all Barkerville, but numbers from the surrounding creeks, some six or eight miles distant, being present, besides a large number of Indians. The dogs had all accompanied their masters to the concert, and loudly joined in the applause. All efforts to quiet them or turn them out only made matters worse.

"We left Richfield on Friday, and a large party assembled to see us off. Just before starting a note was brought me, which, upon opening, I found to be from the principal residents asking me to accept a beautiful gold nugget, the largest found in the 'Brothers' during our stay in Cariboo. This nugget I have now in the shape of a bracelet, made as a broad gold band, with 'Cariboo' in raised letters on it, and I shall always greatly value it in remembrance of our first visit. We stayed for a few hours in Stanley, and spent the night at Beaver Pass, a few miles further on. Next morning, before starting, the Bishop married a couple. Sunday we spent at Quesnelle Mouth, holding services in the schoolroom, and the congregation was so large that many had to leave, not finding room. Our journey down was not so enjoyable as that on our way up.

"From Quesnelle Mouth to Clinton we had rain every day, and the roads were so fearfully muddy that we were obliged to walk the horses nearly all the way. The drivers of ox-teams told us they could only make four or five miles a day, having constantly to take the oxen out of the one waggon to hitch them on to the other team.

"We spent Sunday at Clinton, where the Bishop had

Celebration and Morning and Evening Prayer. We reached Boston Bar on Wednesday night, and here made arrangements to leave our horses, as we were to return in a week for our journey through the Nicola Valley. The stage was quite empty, so we ascended to the very elevated seat beside the driver. Our friends need not have been so urgent on us to go by the stage and so avoid the great danger of driving ourselves, for we encountered more dangers in the twenty-five miles in this conveyance than on all the journey beside. Twice we were very near having an accident—the first time from a blast going off below us without any warning, so close as to blow the dust right in our faces, and of course frightening the horses; and a little later, while quietly driving along, a nut came off the whiffletree and fell on the heels of one of the leaders, and then the more he kicked the more the whiffletree flapped about, frightening both him and his three companions, till they galloped off, and it was some time before the driver could get them in hand again. Fortunately, the stages are very heavy and have powerful brakes, otherwise we should have been over the bank before the horses could have been stopped.

"We arrived in Yale late that afternoon, and the steamer landed us in New Westminster next evening. We were very glad to have a few days at home again."

CHAPTER IX.

THE CHURCH CONFERENCE AT NEW WESTMINSTER.

SEPTEMBER, 1881.

"HOTEL SILLITOE" was the name often applied to the residence of the Bishop of New Westminster, and no *sobriquet* was ever more appropriate. It was seldom, indeed, that the house was not full of visitors, and the sick, convalescent, and homeless clergy and laity, were always sure of the heartiest welcome from the Bishop and his wife.

The Bishop reached home on September 16th, and the first meeting of a conference called by him was on Monday, the 19th.

One sentence in the Bishop's address was prophetic.

"I venture to look forward," the Bishop said, "to the day when besides the great confederation which joins together politically the various provinces of the Dominion, there will be a confederation, too, of the Church of England in Canada, joined together in the unity of the spirit and by the bond of peace, and strengthened in her work by the happy realization of the fundamental truth that we are 'all of us members one of another,' living stones of one temple built upon 'the faith once delivered to the saints.'"

It was the Bishop's joy in the last year of his

life to see this prediction fulfilled—nay, more, to help materially by his personal influence to secure its fulfilment.

Among other subjects dealt with in the address were the means of securing clergy and their stipends for various parts of the diocese—a perennial question this—the supply of churches and parsonage houses, insurance and repair of Church property, registration of births, marriages, and burials, the Christian education of the young, the formation of a Diocesan Endowment Fund, and the establishment of a Diocesan Synod.

The subject of religious education was ever in the Bishop's mind.

> "I may say," he said, "that this is a subject never absent from my thoughts. I feel its incalculable importance as much as any of you; and months before I ever set foot in the country, I occupied myself in laying plans for the education of both boys and girls."

He described the result of his efforts. Columbia College for girls had been only moderately successful, the support of Church people not being commensurate with that which had been expected. In a new country, where free education prevails, where few people are at all wealthy, and where a good secular education is provided in the public schools, it is difficult to convince people of the fatal defect in a non-religious system of teaching; and perhaps, after all, the real remedy will come in time rather from the clergy finding opportunity to teach Church children for an hour a day in the public schools than in the maintenance of separate schools. With regard to a school for boys, the Bishop had plans, not, however, sufficiently matured to be laid before the conference.

It is greatly to be regretted that the Bishop's recommendation with regard to diocesan endowment was not carried out. Parochical endowments are unadvisable in a land where parishes are continually changing shape, size, and character, but the suggestion that "there should be immediately started a Diocesan Endowment Fund, on ever so small a scale, which should be allowed to accumulate and be invested in the names of a missionary board, who should have the management of it, and apply the interest only in augmentation of insufficient incomes, or in starting new parishes," is exactly what is wanted to secure to every colonial diocese in time freedom from pressing insufficiency of funds, independence of the grants of our great missionary societies, and a proper regard for the future as well as for the needs of the present.*

The formation of a synod was a step requiring careful consideration, so, much as the Bishop desired to hasten the provision of this means of constitutional Church government, he deemed it best for the present, to appoint a committee to study the whole question and report on the difficulties to be encountered and the way to overcome them.

Of the general work of the diocese the Bishop spoke as follows:—

"To pass in general and brief review the work of the diocese, I would say that we had very much reason to 'thank God and take courage.' There is no district that is not showing signs of growth, if all are not growing alike. Everywhere I have found earnest hearts and willing hands, and, best of all, a sense of the necessity for sacrifice if any good work is to be done. Personally, I have no language to acknowledge

* A Diocesan Fund was eventually established.

the kindly warmth of the greeting which has awaited me in every corner of the diocese; it makes me sometimes afraid lest I should be unable to make the return of spiritual help which so much heartiness deserves. And indeed, 'I can, of mine own self, do nothing,' but I try to humble myself by the recollection that it is only the grace of God in me that can make me acceptable to any of you, and I know that that grace in me God can make sufficient for all His Church's needs."

No sooner was the conference over than another special and no less important task was taken in hand in preparation for the ensuing ordination. We cannot do better than give the following account written at the time by one present:—

"The whole staff of the diocese was present. The Bishop, realizing most acutely the dangers that beset the clergy in their lives of comparative isolation in this extensive diocese, knowing how much the spirituality of the work depends upon the maintenace of a high tone of piety and devotion in all to whom the care of souls is committed, and deeply alive to the importance of fostering a spirit of brotherly kindness between himself and his spiritual sons, 'yea, rather, brethren beloved,' is aided by his zealous and honoured wife at no little cost and trouble in the preparation he makes for affording a retreat whilst the examination of candidates proceeds.

"At 6 a.m. the calling bell arouses all from slumber, and by seven the chapel is occupied by silent worshippers preparing for the Eucharist, celebrated by the Bishop himself every morning at 7.30.

"It is needless to any one acquainted with the Bishop's regard for order and reverence, to add that the administration of Holy Communion is invested with the solemnity and impressiveness that befit the Divine Mysteries.

"At eight breakfast is partaken of in silence, whilst each in turn reads from some book of an edifying character. This season we read Milman's 'Love of the Atonement.'

. . . At ten the examination of the candidates is conducted by the Archdeacon. . . . Dinner at 1 p.m. with reading in turn, as also at tea, which is at six. . . . It is with almost a feeling of reluctance that one returns to the custom of making such occasions periods of social relaxation and common talk. Friday is passed in a still more marked manner, though it is generally termed 'a quiet day.' Absolute silence is enjoined on all by the Bishop, himself not excluded, from the rising of the sun till the breakfast on the day following. On the walls are posted the proceedings in which all are expected to take part; . . . subjects for meditation suitable to the ministerial life, and earnest addresses by the Bishop and others are given in the chapel, concluding with a special service at 7.30, to which the parishioners generally are invited. So the day of separation from the world, of self-communing, and personal exhortation passes away, —but not so, we trust, the deeper insight into ourselves, the high resolve, the kindled desire and the chastened spirit. . . .

"The ordination on Sunday last was an event to be remembered. Three were to be admitted to the diaconate, and one to the priesthood,—in itself a circumstance of no light moment in the present condition of the diocese.

"A large congregation was gathered at 11 a.m., Mattins and Holy Communion having taken place at 8 a.m. The Bishop and clergy entered while the processional hymn, 'When God of old came down from heaven,' was being sung, after which the Bishop ascended the pulpit and announced his text, Matt. i. 23: 'God with us.' The burning words which fell from his lips, weighted and tremulous as they evidently were from the anxious sense of responsibility resting upon him as chief pastor admitting so many as co-workers with himself in his arduous field of labour, will not pass away with the occasion that called them forth; they all live in the recollection of many who will not forget the impression that fell on all as he turned to address the candidates, or that eloquent, 'not I, but the grace of God within me,' that brought his discourse to a sudden close, amidst a scarcely suppressed sob from many overpowered by the force and power of his words."

It is not hard, even after the lapse of fourteen years, to imagine the impression made by the direct appeal of the following exhortation :—

"Oh, dear young brethren, who are to take upon you this day the yoke of Christ, . . . remember that wherever your Lord sends you He goes with you. He does not bid you go in your own strength, but in His. Your weakness in Him is omnipotent power; your foolishness in Him omniscient wisdom. 'You can of your own selves do nothing, but you can do all things through Christ strengthening you.' You can 'bind up the broken-hearted' by His love working in you; you can 'preach deliverance to the captives' by His Spirit operating through you; by the light of His word you shall recover sight to the blind, and by the authority of His commission you shall heal those whom sin hath bruised. 'God was in Christ reconciling the world unto Himself,' and Christ in you will carry on the work. But you must have *faith*. Yes, faith is the connecting link that joins you to Christ. 'According to your faith will it be unto you.' 'If you have faith as a grain of mustard seed,' you shall be able to remove mountains of prejudice and corruption, and cast out devils of unbelief, hard-heartedness, and pride. Believe in your commission, believe in your sacred calling, believe in the reality of that glorious heritage of grace which by the love of Christ has been mercifully preserved from age to age, and then Christ Himself will 'add to your faith virtue, and knowledge, and temperance, and patience, and godliness, and brotherly kindness, and charity,' and if these things be in you and abound, they make you to be not idle nor unfruitful unto the knowledge of our Lord Jesus Christ."

The candidates at this ordination were the Rev.

C. Blanchard, ordained priest, and Messrs. A. H. Sheldon, R. C. Whiteway, and T. H. Gilbert, admitted deacons. The last named was an accession to the Church from the ranks of the Methodists.

The new clergy were distributed as follows : Mr. Blanchard to Cariboo, where the people had enthusiastically risen to the occasion in the matter of providing a stipend ; Mr. Sheldon to the curacy of Holy Trinity Church, New Westminster ; Mr. Whiteway to the Indian Mission at Yale ; and Mr. Gilbert to the charge of Maple Ridge and Langley.

Several of the newly licensed clergy had a narrow escape on proceeding to their destinations, for the steamer in which they travelled was burned to the water's edge, and although able to save their lives, they had to endure the loss of most of their effects.

Unfortunately, being "burned out" is not a rare experience for colonial settlers.

CHAPTER X.

TRIP TO THE NICOLA VALLEY, THOMPSON RIVER, AND WORK AT HOME.

OCTOBER–DECEMBER, 1881.

THE Bishop only escaped participation in the accident referred to at the close of the last chapter through having been obliged to defer his up-country trip for two or three days, but on October 5th he left home to pay his first visit to the Nicola Valley and Kamloops. A short abstract of this journey is given as follows:—

"After visiting the settlement at Nicola in severe weather, Kamloops was reached on the 18th, and next day a Confirmation was held in the Court House, the Rev. J. B. Good having gone on previously to prepare the candidates. A meeting of Churchmen and others was held on the 20th, at which the Bishop announced that a lady was coming out from England to undertake school work in the district. . . . From Kamloops the Bishop and party travelled to Cache Creek.

"On his way down from Kamloops the Bishop paid a visit to an Indian farm on the south side of the Thompson, nine miles above Cook's Ferry. The farm is in the occupation of a young man named Teetle-neetsah (referred to in Chapter VIII.), who, although not the chief of this tribe, ought to be, if intellectual and industrial superiority were among the qualifications for the office. . . . A boat had been provided to convey the Bishop and Mrs. Sillitoe across the river, and a salute of an uncertain number of guns greeted them on landing. Teetleneetsah and his wife conducted them with much ceremony to the house, and chairs of state, covered with bear-skins, were provided for them at one end of a large room, Teetleneetsah occupying a place by the Bishop's side, and his wife by Mrs. Sillitoe, while the opposite extremity of the room was occupied by about forty Indians of the neighbourhood, with their chief prominently in front. The room was gaily decked with evergreens, and on the walls were some pictures of no mean order—one a life-size portrait of Mary, Queen of Scots, and another a representation of Balmoral Castle; besides which were one or two sketches by the hand of Teetleneetsah himself. After the usual compliments, the chief informed the Bishop that the next building to be erected was a 'Church house,' which they hoped to have ready for use this winter, and they would be glad of a flag and a bell. The Bishop promised to supply these, and then gave a short address, complimenting the Indians generally and Teetleneetsah in particular, on their progress and industry, which, if persevered in, would, he said, enable them in the future to take a position second to none in every useful and profitable pursuit. A short service concluded the proceedings."

Flag and bell were duly sent, and an interesting letter of thanks was received in acknowledgment of the welcome gifts, together with a present of fur for Mrs. Sillitoe.

"89 Mile Ranch, Thompson River,
"January 18, 1882.

"*To Bishop and Mrs. Sillitoe, New Westminster.*

"We received some time ago the flag and the bell sent us, for which please accept our sincere thanks. Mr. Campbell, of 89 Mile Stables, read us also the piece you put in the *Gazette* regarding our tribe. We cannot thank you enough for the praises we received, and we will always try to do right towards the white people, and will be most happy to receive another visit from yourself and Mrs. Sillitoe when you will come again on your tour to the mainland. We just commenced to put up the 'Church house,' and we are sawing lumber ourselves—two of us sawing timber and two more putting it up. We had a big meeting on Christmas Eve in Teetleneetsah's house, praying to Jesus Christ, and Teetleneetsah reading to us all he could. We do not forget Sundays; we are holding service every Sunday. We do not forget either the good advice we received from you.

"Simichulta wishes to be remembered regarding what you sent him, and says every time he sees it he remembers you. Also Mrs. Teetleneetsah thanks Mrs. Sillitoe for the work-basket sent her. We would write to you long time ago but we were trying to get hold of something in the shape of fur—a foxskin, silver grey,—but after many hunts all we could get of any account at all was what we send you along with this letter. It is sent by Simichulta, the chief, and Teetleneetsah, second chief, and they will count themselves happy if you will accept it as a small gift, and we are sorry we could not get anything better; and we will be expecting your answer to this short note as soon as convenient, and also your advice.

"The chief Simichulta's youngest daughter is very sick, and two other young lads of our tribe are not keeping well at all for some time back. We are having good winter up here—the mildest for years as yet; our stock is doing very well out on the mountains. We remain

"Your obedient servants.

"× Simichulta's mark,

" JOHN TEETLENEETSAH. (*Signed.*)

"× Dick Blimdouse's mark."

Arrived in New Westminster once again, the Bishop found himself confronted by work amply sufficient to keep him busily employed during the winter.

The synod committee kept up meetings as frequently as was necessary, and got through an immense amount of work. There were many different questions needing solution, such as—

1. The expediency of applying for State recognition.

2. The position of the diocese relatively to the mother Church.

The misunderstandings, rife at the time, in connection with the Church in South Africa, made it all the more necessary to proceed very warily. Scylla and Charybdis threatened equally; for, if it were necessary to pay due heed to the special legislative power of the province of British Columbia, it was equally advisable to remember the source whence all the Church's gifts and endowments were derived. The Bishop of Tasmania was at the time declaring that "the 'Church of England' is, outside of England, a misnomer," and was strongly advocating the formation of independent Churches in communion with the mother Church. On the other hand, the Chief Justice of Cape Colony, in alluding to the Grahamstown case, expresses himself thus:—

"I feel bound to express my individual opinion as to the necessity of legislation, whether Imperial or Colonial, to regulate the relative rights of the Church in S. Africa and the Church in England in respect to their endowments under private deeds of trust, and to legalize the transfer, to the Church of S. Africa, of property secured by the law for the uses of the Church of England."

It will thus be seen that the synod committee had thorny work before it, and wise and strong counsels were necessary to prevent the idea of a diocesan synod coming to shipwreck altogether.

It was not till the end of February, 1882, that the draft constitution of the proposed synod was ready for printing and distribution, and the wise step was then taken of calling together a general conference of Churchmen to consider it again.

Of this conference we shall speak in due course, but, in sending out the copies of the draft constitution, the Bishop wrote—

> "It is of the highest importance that the constitution of the synod should be adopted by as full a meeting of Churchmen as possible, and it is hoped, therefore, that no one will fail to be present except for the most urgent reasons. It is suggested that Churchmen unable to come should give written authority to sign the constitution on their behalf to some friend who expects to be present."

No more democratic form of government could be imagined than that of a diocese under a constitution drawn up and sanctioned in such a manner.

In other ways, the Bishop was at this time devoting himself to the social and moral development of the laity of New Westminster. Two instances may be mentioned out of many.

First, he flung himself heart and soul into the movement for reducing the number of liquor saloons, by which New Westminster was being demoralized. Fifteen saloons to a population of 2500 seemed a sufficiently large allowance for a not very thirsty community! and so large a provision could only result in bringing many, hitherto strong, within the reach of almost irresistible temptation.

But if in this way the Bishop exemplified his

desire to save men from the false pleasure which lured them to perdition, on the other hand he was strenuous in endeavouring to secure for men the true pleasure which would lift up their lives into a region far removed from sordidness and vice. We shall have reason often to mention the passionate love of Bishop Sillitoe for music, and his great gifts in this respect were used in the highest of all ways—the raising of the standard of the Church's service to the highest level attainable with the material at his disposal. There was no recreation so delightful to the Bishop to the end of his days, even when worn with illness and wearied out with a long journey, as to take the conductor's bâton, and infuse into the choir of Holy Trinity Church something of his own estimate of the quality of the praise we are bound to offer to Almighty God. And it may also be said with truth that to no one so much as to Bishop Sillitoe is the city of New Westminster indebted for the creation and maintenance of a high musical standard, and a sincere appreciation of the most beautiful among the arts.

It was at the close of this year that a very interesting presentation was made by the Bishop to Holy Trinity Church, New Westminster, a presentation serving to link the church in that old Westminster by the Thames with its smaller namesake on the Fraser, and also connecting the diocese with the illustrious name of Dean Stanley.

During the rectorship of the Rev. John Sheepshanks (now Bishop of Norwich), the church of Holy Trinity had received the gift of a beautiful altar cross from the Mayor of Coventry, in which city Mr. Sheepshanks was preaching for his colonial work. The benefaction, valued as it was by many, was not by any means unanimously approved, and the report of the churchwardens in 1875 announces with sorrow that some sacrilegious fanatic had stolen the cross from the church. According to rumour, it was thrown by the thief into the Fraser, and was of course never recovered. Its place was filled by the best substitute which could be obtained, and no further objections were raised.

In the mean time, however, the see of New Westminster was created, and Dr. Sillitoe appointed and consecrated. In November, 1881, we have the following letter written to the churchwardens :—

"DEAR SIRS,

"During the term of office of your predecessors, I made them an offer of an altar cross and four pedestals, presented to me by the late Dean of Westminster, England, as a mark of sympathy and union between the old and new cities. The altar cross is made of wood which had formed part of the Abbey of Westminster from the time of King Henry V. The pedestals were those which had for many years supported the altar slab in King Henry VII.'s Chapel. These were valuable gifts, and their value is now increased by the recent death of the donor. It seemed to me that the most suitable place in which we could treasure these mementoes of the old church of England, was the parish church of the chief city of the diocese, and hence my offer. . . . I now hereby renew it to you, and I do so without further conditions than that, with respect to the cross, due precautions shall be taken for its safe custody, and with respect to the pedestals, that I shall be consulted as to the use to which they are put.

"A. W. NEW WESTMINSTER."

The gift was unhesitatingly and gratefully accepted by the churchwardens, and Dean Stanley's cross was placed above the altar, where it stands to-day. It bears the following inscription :—

"Presented to the first Bishop of New Westminster by Arthur Penrhyn Stanley, Dean of Westminster, being a portion of a rafter of Westminster Abbey of the date of King Henry the Fifth."

It will ever remain a token of the famous Dean's breadth of sympathy, and of his intolerance of sectarian prejudice of every kind.

The history of the pedestals referred to is as follows: Up to about thirty years ago there was no altar in Henry VII.'s chapel. The marble slab existed, but the pedestals were missing. Drawings of them, however, were in possession of the Dean, and in accordance with these he had new pedestals modelled and the altar erected. About fifteen or sixteen years ago, in overhauling the contents of a lumber room in the roof of the Abbey, the original pedestals were discovered, and were at once substituted for the new ones, which were given by the Dean to the newly-consecrated Bishop of New Westminster. A further interest attaches to them, inasmuch as it was at this altar (before the substitution of the original pedestals) that the Revisers of the Old and New Testaments assembled for a celebration of the Holy Communion, previously to commencing their labours on June 22, 1870.

Unfortunately no place has yet been found for them in the Cathedral, although it was the Bishop's desire that a new altar should be constructed in which the pedestals should form the supports. It is to be hoped that this wish may in time be carried out.

So the year 1881 passed away, bearing with it its burden of many cares and anxieties, but leaving much good work accomplished, and foundations laid for work yet to come.

CHAPTER XI.

FINANCIAL ANXIETY.

1882.

THE year 1882 is marked by the absence of journeys on the Bishop's part into the more distant portions of his diocese. Two causes contributed to this.

First of all, the Bishop was engrossed at home with an overwhelming amount of parochial and diocesan business. The preparations for the formation of a synod demanded increasing attention and care; the negotiations for the transfer of property from the old diocese of Columbia to the new diocese of New Westminster dragged their slow length along in the most unpromising way, and the absence of Archdeacon Woods in England threw upon the Bishop much extra work of a parochial kind.

But, in the second place, the Bishop had begun to realize what to the lay mind is often an inscrutable mystery, that a Bishop's income is not a purse of Fortunatus, from which he may draw to an unlimited extent for the needs of himself and everybody about him.

It must be remembered that a Colonial diocese is destitute of much that the Church at home has received as her inheritance from bygone ages. It has no endowments for its clergy, few churches to supply the needs of a population coming in like the tide, no parsonages and schoolrooms to serve all the various purposes of a parish, and the parishioners are for the most part poor and struggling, and unable to contribute much in support of religious ministrations.

Thus the Bishop has added to his pioneer work of building up new churches and parishes the grinding anxiety of providing for the maintenance of the existing work and of keeping up the scanty stipends of the clergy. In such circumstances he soon finds an income, which looks large enough on paper, shrink to very modest dimensions indeed.

Bishop Sillitoe had now had time to discover this fact, that an income of less than $3000 required careful guarding to make it hold out to the year's end, and that it was absolutely requisite to resist the encroachments of the diocesan work upon his own private funds.

At a meeting of the synod committee in March, 1882, the Bishop was obliged to make an important statement with regard to the manner in which he had been obliged to draw upon his own resources, and subsequently he published the following explanation, which it is believed will be of interest at the present day to many Churchmen in the diocese, as well as to those all over the world who have the interest of the Colonial Church at heart:—

"The statement made by the Bishop at the last meeting of the synod committee demands the careful attention of Churchmen. It points to a state of things, unavoidable perhaps in the peculiar circumstances of a new diocese, but nevertheless involving such a measure of personal hardship and injustice as to require the immediate application of some remedial measures, if only of a partial character.

"The foundation of the Bishop's statement was a letter from the manager of the Bank of British Columbia, calling his attention to the fact that his private account exhibited a debtor balance of $3234, and suggesting the necessity of a speedy reduction of the overdraft. The Bishop took advantage of the meeting of the general synod committee to lay before them the circumstances that had placed him in this unenviable position. He produced a statement showing that since his arrival in the diocese he had spent no less a sum than $4253 on Church account out of private funds. Two-thirds of this was swallowed up by necessary repairs to the property at Sapperton, and though this might at first sight appear to come naturally within the limits of individual expenses, two simple considerations may be set against such a consideration.

"In the first place, the Bishop is not a settler establishing himself in the country voluntarily in search of material prosperity. To such an one his home is his own concern and no other man's. He comes of his own accord, and his coming is a matter only of the most indirect interest to others. Whether or no the time was ripe for a division of the old diocese and the erection of a new bishopric is doubtless a question which comes into consideration, but certainly not into that of the new Bishop. He supposes, naturally enough, that this question has been affirmatively decided before the invitation reached him to take the oversight of the diocese; and he has a right to expect that the diocese which asks him to devote to it his services will make proper provision for the fulfilment of his duties without unnecessary and undue personal sacrifice. And when it is remembered that the endowment of the see ($2880 per annum) was raised independent of any contribution whatever from the persons most deeply interested, *i.e.* the Churchmen of the diocese themselves, the expenditure by the Bishop of a considerable sum for a suitable residence, out of an already inadequate income, was not an encouraging inauguration of his episcopate.

"But there is another consideration in the same connection. When a man lays out money on a property which is his own, he has the satisfaction of the security that his heirs will enjoy the benefit, if not himself. But this property is not the Bishop's. He has not even a life tenure of it, for if his health were to fail, and he obliged to resign, the property immediately falls to his successor in office without compensation to himself or family. Repairs following on the occupation of a residence by a clergyman are undoubtedly his affair, so far as tenants' obligations go, but it is not a usual thing to charge a new incumbent with all the dilapidations of his predecessor. Moreover, there is a further obligation on this property in the shape of a mortgage of $2000, of which the Bishop has had to assume the obligation, and on account of which there is an item of $430 for repayment of mortgage and interest.

"Travelling expenses have consumed more than $600 over and above the offertories collected on the road. The expenses of the last conference, rent of the *Gazette* office, and other items, make up the total. But in addition to all these the Bishop has had to render himself personally liable for all the legal expenses which have been incurred since his incumbency of the see, amounting to between $600 and $700.

"Again, we say these circumstances were perhaps unavoidable in a new diocese in a poor country, but they are not the less unsatisfactory or intolerable on that account, and no one can be surprised or complain at the decision arrived at by the Bishop in regard to them.

"Considering rightly that all retrenchment should begin at home, the Bishop has largely reduced his own domestic establishment. He has determined to relinquish for the present all visitations except at the expense of the parish requiring his services, and has given notice to his legal adviser that he will incur no further liability on account of diocesan business. The visitation of the diocese has been already so complete (Kootenay alone remaining unvisited) that this part of the Bishop's decision will entail but little inconvenience. It was in contemplation to hold an Indian Industrial Exhibition in the autumn, and the abandonment of this, or, at any rate, its postponement for a year, will probably occasion some disappointment. Work, so far as present means allow, is fairly organized in every district. Confirmations were held last year at Chilliwhack, Yale, and Kamloops; and most of such other business as can arise can be dealt with by correspondence.

"By far the most important matter involved is the delay in the completion of the transfer of property from the old diocese to the new. But even here it is difficult to see how the Bishop could have acted otherwise than he has. To go on incurring expense would be to go on inflicting personal injustice for the public benefit, and it would be none the less injustice because it was self-inflicted. The synod will probably meet in the autumn, and the property of the diocese will be the most appropriate business it can first take up."

It will be seen later that the Bishop was able to undertake more work abroad than he had at first anticipated, but still the anxiety of carrying on the Church's work with very insufficient means pressed very heavily upon him all through the third year of his episcopate.

CHAPTER XII.

REVIEW OF THE YEAR'S WORK.

1882.

THE inability of the Bishop, through the financial situation, to pay his usual up-country visitations, was to a large extent atoned for by the splendid volunteer mission to the railway camps carried on during the year by Father Hall and Father Shepherd of the Society of S. John the Evangelist, which, to our regret, we are unable to describe here.

The diary for this year shows every day fully taken up by labours of more or less importance. Here an ordination by which another missionary district obtains the services of a resident priest; here and there a confirmation, sometimes attended with no little difficulty, as, for instance, that at Trenant in July, after which there was a row home which occupied no less than seven hours against the Fraser at its fullest and strongest. Temperance work in New Westminster also occupied a good deal of time with very happy results, while the two successful concerts given by the Choral Union afforded testimony to the reality of the association's first year's work. The diocesan conference, the clerical synod, the clergy retreat, and the first meeting of the diocesan synod were, each in its respective way, evidence of a very real growth in the organization of diocesan work; while that the extremities were not allowed to suffer from lack of attention is shown by visits paid to various places up and down the river. A fortnight's camp at English Bay enabled the Bishop to minister to the spiritual needs of Granville and hold confirmations there. Chilliwhack was visited September 10th, and Yale had its turn in November.

Maple Ridge, too, was visited a few days before Christmas on the occasion of the opening of the new church of S. John the Divine.

Besides these visits paid within the diocese, the Bishop was also enabled to take a short trip to Victoria to confer with his brother Bishop of Columbia, and also to make a long-promised excursion into the sister Church of the United States for the purpose of assisting Bishop Paddock in his convocation. Arriving in Seattle on June 21st, Bishop Sillitoe spent a very busy week literally overflowing with engagements, not only bringing encouragement and friendly greeting to his fellow-Churchmen "across the line," but also learning much himself, and imparting valuable information respecting the needs of his own diocese. The Bishop came back deeply impressed with the reality and power of the work going on in the sister diocese, while not failing to note the points—few in number, it is true—in which our American cousins seemed to lay themselves open to criticism. One thing comes in for lavish and unstinted praise, viz. the energy and business-like zeal with which the "Women's Auxiliary" was engaged in furthering the work of the American Church.

It was the Bishop's privilege this year to entertain the Governor-General of Canada (the Marquis of Lorne) and the Princess Louise, and the fact of his having once been chaplain to Her

Royal Highness' sister, the lamented Princess Alice, made the visit one of great interest and pleasure on both sides. This royal visit extended from September 29th to October 1st, and the Bishop omitted to show their excellencies few of the beauties of the royal city.

We come now to the Bishop's first annual report, in which there is proof that he has obtained a real grasp of the work with him and before him, in spite of the almost killing worry consequent on slender resources. The growth of Church principles is evidenced on every hand, and the clerical staff during the year contained one clergyman whom the Bishop had received from the ranks of the Methodist ministry and another whom he had received from the fold of Rome.

The report opens as follows with a reference to the synod :—

"I congratulate you most heartily upon the accomplishment of this important work of organization, and I am most thankful for the relief it affords me from the burden of much of my responsibility. Hitherto I have been obliged by circumstances to fulfil the duties of a multitude of offices entirely foreign to the spiritual oversight of the diocese, which is my proper function, and to which I would gladly devote all my time and energy. Now, I may hope, and increasingly more and more, to transfer the care of financial and other secular matters to the hands of trusty laymen, willing and more competent than myself to deal with them. The distance which separates us prevented a full representation of the laity of all our parishes at the first meeting of the synod, but it was a source of much satisfaction to me that all our clergy were able to be present."

Of the clergy he had to say that as the losses just balanced the gains, the staff remained just as in the preceding year; but he confessed an incalculable obligation to Father Benson for sending the two mission clergy, "who, besides their special mission work among the railroad hands, gave us much brotherly help in many of our parishes, as well as at the meeting of synod, and also conducted a retreat for clergy, which, in its results, was perhaps the most far-reaching of all their work."

Of *finances* the Bishop wrote at length, giving a full account of all the difficulties mentioned in a previous chapter, but at the same time cordially recognizing the great assistance given to the diocese both by private friends at home and by the great Church societies, the S.P.G. and the S.P.C.K.

In *educational* matters he gave an encouraging account of Columbia College for girls, which although not yet self-supporting had gained ground during the year, while advance was marked in the opening of the new Mission School of All Saints', Nicola, into which Mr. John Clapperton and other laymen threw great energy and heartiness of support.

The negotiations for the opening of a boys' school in New Westminster failed at the last moment, and the Bishop had to consider the subject *de novo.*

In Granville, whether due to the bracing sea air or not, there was a life and vigour prophetic of the future position of the Church in Vancouver (as Granville was subsequently called), and S. James' Church, Granville, began to be known as an example to the diocese for taste and orderliness.

In Yale, where the irreligion and public depravity had been a byword throughout the province for many years, the Church, under Mr. Horlock's supervision, had become influential and powerful;

and the opening of a reading-room and club in connection with the Church supplied a very urgent want, and kept many from yielding to temptation.

In Barkerville, where Mr. Blanchard had been called to minister, there was an earnest congregation, about whom the incumbent could write in a tone of cheery optimism, and who certainly did their part well in raising money for the support of the Church's ministration.

In the Chilliwhack district, Mr. Gilbert kept both S. Thomas', Chilliwhack, and the new church at Cheam supplied. At Trenant the debt on the church was paid off, and Mr. Bell's work found abundant encouragement; while the dedication of the church at Maple Ridge has already been recorded.

At the same time, the Bishop, after speaking of the work already accomplished, was careful to point out the new work ready for the "labourers" who had yet to be found. He says—

"I have used all my influence with the S.P.G. the last three years to induce them to help us at Kamloops, but so far in vain, and I am disposed to wait no longer, but to send forth a labourer at once in faith that the Lord of the harvest will provide him his hire. It is an enormous field that would tax the energy of two men, but if we cannot provide two, we must find one who will do the work of two, and I hope he will be forthcoming."

Of the need for a special Chinese Mission the Bishop says—

"Our responsibilites towards these heathen sojourners are in no wise diminished. There are about seven or eight thousand of them in our midst, and no endeavour whatever is made to evangelize them. I have again applied to S.P.G. on their behalf, but even without this aid I feel that something must be done. A native Chinese missionary, at present working in San Francisco, has offered himself to me, but an engagement with him will involve the responsibility of $930 or $1000 a year. I am still considering whether or not to incur this obligation."

The Indian work had been a subject of deep anxiety to the Bishop, especially since the loss to the diocese of the Rev. J. B. Good, but the visit of the Fathers had already suggested to him a plan for the future if only the men and the means were forthcoming.

He was able to state that through the generosity of a lady in England he hoped shortly to appoint a priest to take charge of the Fraser River Indian Mission.

"Of the Lytton Mission I can only say that work is necessarily suspended during the vacancy in the post, excepting such ministrations as Mr. Whiteway is able to afford in the town of Lytton itself. Every effort is being made to find a thoroughly efficient man for the mission; in fact, I hope two men may be appointed, the society having consented to a division of their grant for this purpose.

"In association with this work there is a good prospect of a branch of the sisterhood of All Hallows', Ditchingham, being established in the diocese, with the object of supplying an industrial education for Indian girls. With this and a similar institution for boys, we shall take the first step towards dealing in a practical way with the problem of Indian improvement. . . ."

The report, which, all things considered, is most encouraging and hopeful, concludes with a humble acknowledgment of the abundant grace and mercy of Almighty God, and also of the generous support and co-operation of clergy and laity within the diocese, and hosts of friends outside. The Bishop had so far got acquainted with his work that he knew not only the fields of labour, but the characteristic difficulties of each, and he cheerfully braced himself with the Christians' impregnable armour to face and conquer them.

CHAPTER XIII.

A TOUR IN THE INTERIOR.

1883.

THE year 1883 was one of very great activity and considerable progress, marked by a very extensive journey into the interior, and by a new start in the important Indian missions at Yale and Lytton. Many other incidents of the year are deserving of notice, but we must pass them by with only the briefest mention. The Bishop was able this year to carry out the project (long entertained) of opening a boys' school at New Westminster, and, on All Saints' Day, Lorne College was inaugurated with good (though, unfortunately, delusive) prospects of success. Confirmations were held as usual in various parts of the diocese, and two ordinations at New Westminster, at which three clergy were added to the working staff of the diocese. The annual meeting of synod was held in October, when a very important charge was delivered by the Bishop, dealing with the financial position of the diocese, the appointment of attorneys for S.P.G. for the diocese, the marriage laws, and other pressing questions. On the vexed question of his financial responsibility, the Bishop spoke very strongly, as was only too necessary. Yet, after ten years, this question was still the canker eating away at the Bishop's heart, and it is not too much to say that the worry consequent on financial difficulties did more than physical disease to shorten the Bishop's life.

The return of Archdeacon Woods from a busy tour of deputation work in England, towards the beginning of June, opened the way for the Bishop to make his long-contemplated visit into the remote interior of the diocese.

A start was made, even before the Archdeacon's return, early on the morning of May 16th, when the Bishop and his indefatigable wife left the wharf at Sapperton for Chilliwhack, Yale, and the interior.

Nicola was reached on the 26th, in time for a full day's services on the Sunday. The following days were occupied with an examination of the pupils of the Mission School, and in visiting the settlers in the valley. The school was shown to have thoroughly justified its establishment, and seemed to be highly valued by the settlers.

On the return journey to Spence's Bridge a call was made upon Naweeseskan, an old Indian chief. He was lying at home alone and very sick. Except himself all the men were in the mountains herding horses and cattle. Naweeseskan has perhaps done more for the improvement of his people than any other chief in the district. He is opposed to the ruinous custom of *potlatches*, and is able, therefore, to spend money on substantial buildings and home comforts. The whole village presented a striking contrast to the miserable shanties that constitute the houses of Indians generally. The houses are all first-class log buildings with shingle roofs, and the church would be a credit to any prosperous white settlement. It is to this tribe belongs the so-called "Prophetess Mary," a victim of catalepsy, who claims to have received a revelation from heaven while in a trance.

Spence's Bridge was reached on June 2nd, and arrangements were made for next day's services. On Sunday, June 3rd, there was a large gathering of Indians in their little rough chapel at 8 a.m. Between sixty and seventy were present, some having come up from Nicomen, and a few from Pakeist. Prayers were said in Indian by one of the watchmen, and then the Bishop celebrated the Holy Communion, and gave an address through the interpreter.

On June 6th a departure was made for Ashcroft, where service was held for the household, and two sermons preached in the Indian church. We have here an interesting glimpse of the Bishop's method of work among the Indian population. One of the watchmen had died, and at the next Indian service his cap and badge were formally returned to the Bishop, who thereupon had to make selection of a successor and duly invest the chosen one with the insignia of his office. The choice fell on Harry Nitaskut, a native of Lytton, but long a resident of Ashcroft, were he acted as whipper-in of Mr. Cornwall's pack of hounds. Four Indian children were also baptized, and a marriage solemnized between two young people of the tribe. A preliminary examination of the bride and bridegroom was held to elicit their ideas of the sanctity of the marriage tie, and they were warned that the union, ratified in the Church, was indissoluble, except for just cause, by the Church herself. The young lady seems to have been very shy, and it was only after much persuasion that she could be induced to make a public profession of her love. This, however, being at length accomplished—the suggested postponement of the ceremony possibly had something to do with it—the prescribed vows were exchanged, and the pair were pronounced man and wife.

Other services were held here during the week, and on Thursday an early start was made for a drive of fifty-three miles, which had to be accomplished before evening. There were several fresh arrivals in the Green Timber to be called on, and a long halt had to be made in the middle of the day for the horses' sakes. The road, however, was in splendid order, and no difficulty was experienced in reaching the Hundred-Mile House by half-past six, eleven hours from Clinton, including three hours and a half rest on the way. Here was found a candidate for Confirmation, who was examined and her Confirmation appointed for the following Sunday at a house sixteen miles up the road, where service was to be held. A short drive of sixteen miles, and two or three calls along the road, occupied Saturday afternoon, and about six o'clock Mr. McKinley's house on Lac la Hache was reached. Mr. Blanchard—the clergyman in charge of Cariboo—arrived from the opposite direction about half an hour previously.

The drive along the margin of William's Lake was inexpressibly beautiful. The road follows the course of the valley past one or two comfortable Indian settlements till the lake is reached, and then mounts up by a steep incline to a picturesque bluff some three hundred feet above the lake, past which a prettily wooded flat is traversed for two or three miles, until, around the foot of the lake, the valley expands into a seemingly limitless garden of meadowland and cornfield. At this farm the travellers received an hospitable welcome; and after supper—though the visit was unexpected—a congregation of some five and twenty men was soon gathered together, and a short mission service held, the hymns being well taken up.

The Bishop was much struck by the beauty and

productiveness of the Lac la Hache Valley, but the next day the journey was resumed, and the Hundred-and-Fifty-Mile House reached.

A meeting held the following day to consider the building of a church affords an illustration of the vague ideas entertained respecting the Church, and of the weakness induced everywhere by sectarian differences. The meeting was not restricted to Churchmen, and while all wanted a church, the general opinion leaned to the idea of a public church for the use of all denominations. The Bishop explained that he could not use the Diocesan Fund for such a building, but that of course he would rather see a church of any kind, if used for public worship only, than no church at all. So the committee was appointed to consider cost and obtain contributions.

Barkerville was reached on the 25th, and it was a great refreshment once more to be within a *real* church, and enjoy the privilege of daily services. It was more than five weeks since Yale had been left behind, six hundred miles had been travelled, and this was the first Church of England building the travellers had seen, except here and there the humble temples of the Indians.

The Bishop was much pleased to note the success of the work which he had inaugurated in the previous year. Adjoining the church was the Rectory, from which Mr. Blanchard could watch the movements of the greater number of his parishioners, and although the building only contained three rooms, it was commodious enough for a bachelor, and warm enough to keep him comfortable in the by no means unknown temperature of 40° below zero. This severity of climate is due, not to latitude, but to elevation, since Barkerville is in the neighbourhood of four thousand feet above the sea level, while the only approach to it is over a *divide* five hundred feet higher still. There was considerable snow on this *divide* when the Bishop crossed, the last week in July.

The Bishop was still more gratified at the evidence of spiritual progress on the Sunday. Ten years of spiritual famine had been a sore trial for many, and there could have been but little wonder if some had been altogether exhausted by it, or permanently enfeebled. But lost ground seemed to have been quickly recovered and new ground occupied. Large congregations attended all the services, and the Confirmation in the evening was very impressive. Four of the male candidates were adults.

On July 16th the Bishop pursued his journey southward as far as Hundred-and-Fifty-Mile House, and here, for the first time, found the road impeded by fire. The stage, however, had gone through ahead of them, so they drove on without much anxiety. Service was held at Hundred-and-Fifty-Mile House in the evening. A drive of forty-six miles next day necessitated an early start. A halt was made at the Blue Tent for a baptism, and other calls made during the day. At the farmhouse where the last halt was made, the evening was spent in preparing a woman for Confirmation, and next day the sacred rite was administered, and Holy Communion celebrated for the family and neighbours. The following evening saw the journey to Seventy-Mile House completed, and here a burial awaited the Bishop. The travellers arrived for the Sunday at Clinton.

Almost immediately after leaving Clinton a shroud of smoke was entered, with which the party was enveloped for many days. Almost every object was obscured; the sun seemed obliterated, breathing became a difficulty, and the loveliest landscape in the world seemed converted into a dismal wilderness.

Ashcroft was reached on July 27th. Various services and classes were held during the next few days. Of the Confirmation the Bishop writes—

"I do not like the work of preparation of Indian candidates, for I am not accustomed to it, and don't understand it; but these poor souls have been waiting so long that I could not for shame wait longer. When, when am I going to have a man from England for the Indian work? I cannot keep it going myself. If it languishes, it will not be through my fault, though I shall have to accept all the responsibility and blame."

Next day the Bishop passed on from Ashcroft to Cache Creek, making several calls by the way, and after a night's rest at Savona's, Kamloops came in sight the following afternoon.

Of this latter part of the journey the Bishop gives us the following account:—

"It was fearfully hot at Ashcroft. There is no water in the neighbourhood and the earth gets so hot that the air passing over it becomes heated. Moreover, the whole country was on fire. We drove into the smoke about twelve miles out from Clinton, and we have never been out of it till to-day, and now only comparatively. . . .

"It may not seem to some people that driving ordinarily not more than twenty or thirty miles a day in a fairly comfortable trap need exhaust an ordinarily healthy man, and yet, whatever any one may think, a day's journey under such conditions as ours is quite enough work for twenty-four hours. After breakfast comes a visit to the stables, and in most instances such a job as cleaning the collars—a matter otherwise unlikely to be attended to. Then the axles require oiling, and if you don't see it done, or do it yourself, the men will put on axle-grease instead of oil, and give you a rare job the next day cleaning your axles; or (as has happened three times this trip) they will put on harness oil, for no other reason than that they see a can of it in your box, and they can't conceive that you should take the trouble to clean your harness, so conclude that this is for the axles. Then the 'pack,' or luggage, has to be strapped on, and this I never suffer any man to do for me. If your pack is not on tight, or you are not sure that it is so, you have to keep one eye behind all the time. We have only once lost anything this year, and I have never been able to understand how it happened. Well, then you 'hitch up.' You may as well do it yourself, because you must look over everything when done, or they will send you away with twisted traces, or the martingales strapped on to the collars, or some such mistake. Then your day's journey begins. The roads are fairly good, but nevertheless there is seldom a hundred yards when you can venture to take off your attention. It's either going up hill, and you have to see that both horses are doing their share of the work, or it's going down hill, and then you have to watch everything; or, if you get a bit of level and straight road, you have to look out for rocks, over which you may spring an axle or dent your wheel. Then you come to a creek, and you pull up and unstrap your bucket, and water your horses; and then you drive on till you come to your midday halt, and there is unhitching to do, stabling and feeding. Then there comes a second half-day just like the first, except for the matter of oiling axles. When you reach your journey's end, you don't feel any *cacoëthes scribendi*, not a bit. . . .

"I try hard not to think of money, but the thought will creep in sometimes. The responsibility of seeing people paid is very heavy. Men are continually coming into this colony, and a very good class of men, I am glad to say. Another district—the Kootenay District—is being opened out; a number of miners and farmers, the latter comprising English gentlemen, are going in. This means more work for me and longer journeys. All this points to our living some day in a more central part than New Westminster."

The Bishop attended to the spiritual needs of Kamloops, and proceeded on his journey. Travelling by way of Grand Prairie and Salmon River Valley, the whole of which was literally on fire, and the road so encumbered with fallen, burning trees as to render progress very tedious and somewhat dangerous, Spallumcheen was reached on the 10th, and a kind welcome found at the house of Mr. Fortune. This stage completed the one thousand miles. As the community here was a very scattered one, the Sunday service was held at 2 p.m., when a large congregation assembled, and the Bishop preached a harvest thanksgiving sermon.

Of the remainder of the journey we have Mrs. Sillitoe's account—

"There could, I think, be scarcely imagined a more dismal picture than was presented by the tract of country situated around the head of Okanagan Lake. The smoke here was denser than anywhere else, and the country, naturally bare and destitute of trees, and parched with the long drought, derived increased dreariness from the overhanging shroud of smoke that effectually concealed everything beyond a distance of a quarter of a mile, and completely blotted out the sun.

"The following day, however, a change occurred. A storm was evidently gathering throughout the day, and in the evening it burst with all the fury of a cyclone, the roar of which we could hear a full quarter of an hour before it fell upon us, tearing huge branches off the stronger trees, and levelling the weaker ones with the ground, and raising a cloud of dust that darkened the air even worse than before. In about half an hour the wind ceased, and for a few minutes there was a dead calm, succeeded shortly by a second outburst as heavy as before, but from the opposite quarter. Very little rain fell, but the atmospheric disturbance had worked a wonderful change in the appearance of things. The smoke had been rolled away, and in place of a dismal waste there was a fair prospect of harvest fields and craggy hills and grassy vales. . . . For us the storm came most opportunely, for our next day's journey from Mr. Vernon's to the Mission is one of the most beautiful drives in the country, and to have been deprived of its enjoyment would have been a very great disappointment. Even apart from the lovely scenery, it rejoiced one's heart once more to see the sun shining in the clear blue sky. . . .

"At the Mission we had to part company with our buckboard, for the waggon-road goes no further; a trail—and unquestionably the worst in British Columbia—is the only means of reaching the country to the south of this. Along this trail we started next morning, under the guidance of a good-natured friend, who, much to his own hindrance in time and convenience, volunteered to pilot us and drive our pack-horse as far as Penticton.

"There are some curious roads in British Columbia. Even the waggon-road (*par excellence*) itself, much vaunted as it is, is pretty full of places where its purposes would have been more effectually attained by a little less engineering and a little more common sense, not to say anything about defects of management, which seems to aim at the largest possible expenditure for the most meagre of results. But the trails! The trails give one the idea of having been constructed for the purpose of being abandoned. They are very good here and there, where Nature alone is responsible for them; otherwise they give one the impression that human ingenuity had been exercised in rendering them as tortuous and difficult as possible.

"But of all the trails the roughest and steepest and worst is that we were now on. It speaks volumes for the enterprise of men that they ever go on them at all, and volumes more for the surefootedness of animals that men ever go over safely. And yet this is the trail over which the mail is taken once a month, and one would suppose that there was implied in that a sufficient argument for its being kept in efficient repair at the public expense.

". . . Here Mr. Wade kindly welcomed us in the absence of Mr. and Mrs. Ellis, who only reached home the following Sunday. On Sunday, August 19th, we had celebration of Holy Communion at 7.30, Mattins, Litany, and Sermon at ten, and a mission service in the evening. On Tuesday, with an Indian guide, we set off on the last stage of our journey southwards, and reached Osoyoos, thirty-five miles distant, in ten hours and a half. Osoyoos, on the Canadian side of the line, consists of but two families, and it was arranged therefore that service should be held on the United States side of the line, where a considerable number of people reside, and where was also the encampment of the troop of United States cavalry that had formed the escort of General Sherman. About ten o'clock we started in a row-boat for the foot of the lake, and proceeding to the camp, found arrangements made for the accommodation of quite a large congregation.

"The service was held *al fresco* under a leafy awning in front of the officers' quarters. Sacks of oats formed the seats, and an erection of camp chests the pulpit. The sacrament of baptism was first administered to four children, and then, in the absence of sufficient Prayer-books, a mission service was held, with hymns, and the Bishop preached.

"After being hospitably entertained by the American Collector of Customs, the Canadian visitors returned across the line on horseback. We took four days to return to the Mission, having only to make Okanagan by next Sunday. . . .

"The next day we were again bowling along in the buckboard, and after four days' trail-riding, nor heat, nor dust, nor smoke could have wrung a complaint from us. We were not tried, however, for the road to the head of the lake is in splendid order; there was no dust or smoke, and the day was pleasantly warm. The magnificent scenery displayed itself to advantage, and, in addition to all, there was the joy of feeling that our faces were really turned towards home at last.

"We reached Coldstream in the evening. On Sunday, September 2nd, Mr. Vernon's men were engaged with the hay harvest twelve miles up the valley, consequently our gathering was but a small one."

After recording visits to Grand Prairie, Kamloops, Nicola, and Indian settlements, and work done at each place, Mrs. Sillitoe continues—

"*Sunday, September 16th.*—The Bishop celebrated Holy Communion in S. John's Church, Yale, at 8 a.m., and preached morning and evening, preaching also in the Indian church in the afternoon, and addressing the Sunday school children. At Evensong there was also a Confirmation.

"On Monday morning the Bishop and Mr. Sillitoe left Yale by the *William Irving*, and landed at New Westminster at midnight."

The whole journey lasted exactly four months, and extended over a distance of 1682 miles. The Bishop preached forty-eight times, and celebrated Holy Communion thirty-one times, baptized fifteen persons, and confirmed twenty-nine. The whole sum raised by offertories and donations amounted to $403.50, and the expenses to $230.

The expenses would have amounted to far more but for the generous hospitality extended to the travellers in almost every district, both by Churchmen and others, and by innkeepers as well as by private individuals. And in this acknowledgment must be included the worthy blacksmith at Spallumcheen, who would accept no remuneration for a long half-day's work. These many acts of kindness formed a refreshing compensation for the weariness, hardships, and dangers of the road, and that it needed some compensation will be vouched for by any one who, whether for pleasure or profit, has travelled in the interior of British Columbia during the summer of 1883.

One result of this extended tour was to convince Bishop Sillitoe of the need of organizing three new missionary districts, and of appointing a resident clergyman to each, with as little delay as possible. How this desire was brought to a happy fulfilment we shall see in future chapters.

CHAPTER XIV.

WORK AMONG THE INDIANS.

1883.

THE Indian work of the diocese had a large share of the Bishop's thoughts in 1883. The resignation of the Rev. J. B. Good had necessarily drawn the Bishop into closer personal relationship with the Indians and their spiritual needs, and during the journey just described he had seen a great deal of the work that might have been going on provided the men and the means had been at hand.

In the early part of the year the Rev. G. Ditcham went, at the Bishop's request, on a tour of inspection through the whole of the district comprised in the Lytton Mission. Commencing at Chapman's Bar, he travelled, on foot all the way, to Lytton, and from there to Nicola, Ashcroft, and Lillooet. Visiting each village, he questioned the chiefs and watchmen on the moral and religious condition of their people, inspected the churches, and made a careful enumeration of the members of the Church baptized and confirmed. His report was on the whole very satisfactory, but all along the line of railway construction the Indians were found suffering grievously from the increased temptations to drink, which the increase of licensed houses had naturally brought about.

The same fact is elicited by the evidence of others at the time.

In most of the Indian villages many material improvements were observable. Churches had been finished, and some attempts at any orderly arrangement and adornment of the houses had been carried out. The pleasure of the people at having a clergyman to visit them was shown by the most open and cheerful welcome, and the enthusiasm in the prayers and close attention in the address was very cheering. Every now and then was heard the "Oh! oh! oh!" of some one in the congregation, and occasionally several voices would exclaim together, "Good, good!" "Good is the word!" "The talk is good!" When taught by such a story as that of the Roman sentry standing at his post till death, they would show all the eagerness and attention of children. An account in the *Gazette* goes on—

"Oh, but what weak Christians many of them were! The Church needs to train them by her ancient discipline, at the same time remembering that they are only *children* in Christ, bearing patiently with them. The Indian missionary should be that alone, doing nothing else, and should be on his beat continually. He will have many enemies, but at the same time will find not a few friends."

The following further extract from the *Gazette* speaks of the sad condition of the Indians at the time—

"So many are the crooked ways by which bad intoxicating liquors find their way into the hands of Indians that in this province at least a change in the law is required at once. Something should be done, and that quickly, to stop a traffic which is a heavy expense to the exchequer, and causes untold misery to the Indians who wish to live quiet and orderly. From one end of the country to the other, from Cariboo to the sea, in every town and settlement, is heard the one complaint. Whisky finds its way in abundance to every *rancherie*. In New Westminster men well known to be in the business go at large. At Burrard Inlet the mad cries and demon shrieks of drunken Siwashes sound over the water; at Yale there is no trouble in obtaining the 'chain lightning;' while tales are told such as this of the hell it causes in the villages higher up the river.

"A drunken son had his father down on his back and beat his head on the floor; three men tried to hang themselves; the whole *rancherie* was drunk, and this in one day. The chiefs say they are powerless to stop it, and so great is the evil that it has outgrown the ability of the whole country to put an end to it under the present laws."

During the year a great deal of good work was accomplished by the Rev. D. H. W. Horlock, acting under a commission from the Bishop. He visited the Spuzzum Indians at the beginning of July, and was warmly welcomed.

The Bishop's efforts to provide supervision for some part of this immense field of work were rewarded at last by the offer of two English clergy to come out as missionaries to the Thompson River Indians. One was the Rev. Richard Small, then chaplain to the House of Mercy, Ditchingham, the present head of the Lytton Mission; the other was the Rev. H. G. Fiennes-Clinton, late Principal of Bishop's College, Calcutta, and Vice-Principal of the Missionary College of S. Boniface, Warminster, now Rector of S. James' Church, Vancouver. This accession to the ranks of the Bishop's *aides-de-camp* greatly cheered and brightened his heart, and gave him fresh stimulus in the further development of the diocesan work.

We append Mr. Horlock's interesting report, and a copy of the statement signed by all the male householders of the tribe in the presence of the magistrate of Boston Bar.

"Left Yale February 28th by handcar borrowed from the C.P.R. Co., and worked by Mr. Wright, the two Indian interpreters, and myself. We arrived at the crossing of the Fraser about three o'clock, and with some difficulty procured a boat to cross. Arrived at Boston Bar, I called on Mr. Pearson, J.P., to whom I had written by the previous mail, asking him to give notice to the Indians at Yankee Flat of my coming. He assured me that the whole tribe would be in waiting for me on the following morning, and kindly consented to accompany me on the visit. Mr. Pearson also called my attention to the affairs of a tribe living three-fourths of a mile from Boston Bar, and asked me to visit them. I did so immediately, and found that they had half built a church, being obliged to relinquish it for want of funds to purchase the necessary materials. I found there a young man apparently dying of pleuro-pneumonia. Here, as everywhere else, the Indians are without medical attendance. The chief being absent at work, I left word for him to call on me in the morning. He did so, and complained bitterly of the spiritual destitution in which he and his tribe were placed. I hear on all hands that he is a really good man, and has been making the most strenuous efforts to keep his tribe from the usual effects of approximation to the white man—drunkenness and fornication. At his urgent request, I consented to visit the tribe the following day and give them a service and address.

"Crossed the river 8 a.m. on Friday and worked the handcar to the settlement. There we found the whole tribe assembled—numbering about forty adults and twenty children—in the chief's house. The Indian service was very creditably performed, after which I addressed the tribe concerning the proposed school, and found a perfect unanimity as to the expediency of establishing it. I also expressed a hope that a church would also be built ere long, which they seemed exceedingly anxious to effect. After I had finished, the chief, who is a splendid fellow, asked permission to speak. He said neither himself nor his people could think what 'the Church' was doing to leave him thus entirely alone and neglected; certainly it was not acting according to our Blessed Lord's commands. All he said was in sorrow, not in anger. I replied with the oft-repeated excuse of 'no men'—God only knows how my soul revolts against it. I promised to do all I could for them—of course, it is but little. In common with all other tribes I have visited, almost none were baptized. I shall have to visit the place again in a fortnight to baptize the infants. How can one see a great field of work like this and not try to do it? And how *can* I do it? The whole tribe are excessively anxious to have a school established, and a church, and I believe would do all in their power to help.

"Business ended, I baptized a dying old man, and then left for Boston Bar. About six of the chief men of the tribe accompanied me in their canoe, to attend the other service. The Indian service was sung very sweetly, the most musical I have ever heard, the chief who conducted it showing really great untaught musical ability. I promised this tribe I would endeavour to get them the necessary lumber for completing their church as soon as possible. . . . I had to listen to the same bitter complaints repeated, and to reply in the same strain, of course. . . . I left Boston Bar at 2.30 and arrived at Yale at 5.15—a fine run of twenty-five miles. I must *try* to visit these tribes once a month, till something is managed permanently. . . . One cannot help feeling that the Church will have to answer for many souls lost during these past years of trouble and grievous temptation to the Indian tribes."

The statement referred to above is as follows:—

"We, the undersigned Indians of Yankee Flat, desire a certain sum of money due to us from Mr. Onderdonk to be paid over to the Lord Bishop of New Westminster, for the purpose of building and establishing a day-school for our children in the neighbourhood of our village."

It was signed by twenty-three householders of the tribes and by the witnesses to the act, and so forwarded to the Indian Superintendent.

We append a description, by the Bishop, of the Indian Mission and its needs and possibilities.

"The Indian Mission at Lytton—S. Paul's Mission, as it is called—includes all Indians speaking the 'Thompson River' tongue, and extends from about eight miles above Yale to the foot of Nicola Lake, a hundred and twenty-three miles along the main waggon road, with an offshoot from Lytton in the direction of Lillooet, and another from Spence's Bridge as far as Ashcroft.

"The number of the people is variously estimated at from two thousand to two thousand five hundred, of whom about one-fourth have received baptism, and about one-tenth have been confirmed. These are the results of the sixteen years' work of the Rev. J. B. Good, who resigned the Mission last year. . . . This year we hope to invoke God's blessing on a faithful endeavour to bring the widest influence of Christianity to bear upon this people, not only to build them up in spiritual things, but to minister also to their mental and physical improvement and elevation. The Mission staff in this wide and important field has consisted hitherto of but two persons, for whose support the S.P.G. has made annual grants of £300 and £50 respectively. The catechist resided at Lytton, where his labours were limited to saying prayers in the absence of the missionary. He was a catechist only in name, because he was never able to acquire sufficient knowledge of English to study for himself, and was not, therefore, more perfectly instructed than the congregation. Mr. Good resided for a while at Lytton, but for the last six years of his incumbency he occupied the Mission House at Yale, visiting the Lytton district from time to time as other duties allowed. Under these circumstances, the wonder is that the Church retained any hold at all upon the people, and it is the most eloquent testimony to their steadfastness that they accepted thankfully such desultory and deficient ministrations as were afforded them, and are to this day true and loyal to their first instructors in the faith.

"Now for the due administration of such a mission it is equally imperative that the missionary should occupy some central headquarters, and that he should at frequent intervals visit the distant villages; and so the first conclusion arrived at was, that at least two men must be associated together in the work. I obtained the consent of S.P.G. to a division of their grant of £300, to which I propose adding £100 more from private sources, and I have found (D.G.) two devoted men who, for the reduced stipend, have given themselves to the work. . . . Not hastily or unadvisedly, but after long and prayerful consideration, have these appointments been made, and I earnestly plead, on behalf of these new fellow-labourers, for a share in the intercessions of the Church that their devotion and labours be not in vain.

"For a priest's house at Lytton I am indebted to the generosity of the Rev. R. C. Whiteway, who has placed his cottage at the disposal of the mission. With a little enlargement, at a cost of about £50, it can be made sufficiently commodious for the purpose. One of the clergy will reside at Lytton permanently, while the other journeys to and fro through the district. The one in residence will, in the first place, be responsible for the daily offering of the Sacrifice of praise and prayer, and, secondly, will combine with his spiritual ministrations the elementary instruction of young men and boys. This department of the Mission we propose gradually to extend by making provisions for the accommodation of pupils from distant villages, by the erection of workshops, and by associating with the Mission priests a lay brother competent to give instruction in the technical and industrial branches of education.

"When we shall have been allowed to accomplish this, we shall have wrought a social revolution in the land, for we shall have elevated the people from the servile condition of hewers of wood and drawers of water and given them an equal chance in the race of life. Whether they are capable of this is, of course, a question which we must expect to have raised. I have no doubt about it, or I should be less hopeful about making the experiment. There are already examples enough of self-improvement under the present very limited opportunities to warrant the highest expectations, and the opinion is shared by all who have brought unprejudiced observation to bear upon Indian character, amongst whom I may venture to include our late Governor-General. There is another branch of the work to speak of before I have done, and one, though second in order, by no means second in importance. If the men are to be raised socially, industrially, physically, *the women must be raised too.*

"The girls of the present generation will be the wives of the young men and boys we are going to educate, and, apart altogether from their right inherent to equal privileges, we must raise them mentally and spiritually if we would not have them unconsciously neutralize our efforts on behalf of the other sex. But there is a higher view than this to take, for if, amongst ourselves, the influence of woman is perhaps the strongest auxiliary for refining and purifying the nature of man, why may we not expect an equally happy result to follow the cultivation in these dusky maidens, of the more gentle and tender instincts and attributes of womanhood?

"And by the good Providence of God this auxiliary work has been placed within reach of accomplishment. A year ago a call to undertake it was heard at Ditchingham, and was immediately responded to, and three Sisters of the Community of All Hallows' are ready to come out as soon as we have provided the necessary premises. They come at their own expense, and maintain themselves, if necessary, for a year or more, and the cost to the

Church amounts to no more than the hire or erection of a suitable house, and the purchase of furniture. It is not yet decided whether to hire or to build. At the close of railway construction (that is, within twelve months), various buildings will be for sale which could easily be adapted for the purpose, though there are none such actually at Lytton. On the other hand, special buildings would be most convenient, and Lytton the most suitable site. The maintenance of pupils in the institution will be the most serious expense, for I cannot put the cost per head at less than £20 per annum, and the Indians themselves must not be depended on to contribute much.

"Now I have done. I have striven to write without exaggeration; I have even denied myself the expression of the enthusiasm I feel in the contemplation of this work (an enthusiasm warranted, I believe, by the grandeur of the possible results), because I would not risk the loss of a single practical mission helper by an apparently over-coloured picture. I know what I feel, and that the future will justify me.

"I ask only God's blessing; with that all we need besides will follow."

CHAPTER XV.

PROGRESS OF DIOCESAN ORGANIZATION.

1883–1884.

THE Bishop was fortunate throughout his episcopate in the possession of a strong Home Committee, which was ever at work presenting the claims of the diocese before the English public, and sending out help in men and means. In 1884 the work of the diocese had so increased in extent and interest that the Home Committee decided upon the printing and issuing of a quarterly paper, which should contain the latest news from the seat of work. To these quarterly papers for the history of the next few years the writer of this memoir is very largely indebted.

The visit of Archdeacon Woods to England in 1882, and his long tour of deputation work, were of the greatest service in arousing interest in New Westminster among the English parishes, and his return in 1883 left the committee without any one to carry on what had now become a necessary work, viz. that of pleading personally for the wants of the diocese. To quote the report—

"The committee had to face this difficulty, and, after careful consideration, came to the conclusion that it was necessary to employ a clergyman who should devote at least half the year to travelling as a deputation for the mission, and doing the other necessary work in connection with the Mission Guild."

The clergyman appointed to this important office, the Rev. H. H. Mogg, was, as a former worker in British Columbia, enabled to speak from personal observation, and to describe the needs of the diocese the more readily from having himself felt them.

It would be difficult to say to what an extent the work of this committee lightened the labours of the Bishop. Certainly there was ever the most loyal co-operation ; on the one hand, the single desire to carry out consistently and cheerfully the wishes of the head of the Mission ; on the other hand, the readiness to trust to the proved judgment and tried affection of friends at home. The Bishop's committee consisted of personal friends, and the friendship, which in many cases dated from before his consecration, continued unbroken till death—aye, and beyond.

While on this head, it may be mentioned that this year, mainly through the untiring energy of an English worker—Miss Lansdale—a mission-boat was sent out for conveying missionaries from place to place, and for visiting and holding services on board ships in the harbours. The funds had been collected in the autumn of 1884, and the boat was built at Bristol—a good, strong, seaworthy sailing-boat, about seventeen feet long, fitted with sails, oars, centre-board, and all the necessary gear, and manageable, if necessary, by one man.

While this important aid to the missionary work of New Westminster was on its way out, the Bishop was energetically engaged—although the winter was far from over—in the oversight of the districts immediately around the see city.

The Bishop paid an interesting visit to Surrey from the end of July to about August 9th.

Mr. Bell's parish was about twenty-seven miles long by about fifteen wide, and embraced two municipalities. Of Trenant, the western municipality, we have frequently heard already; the eastern portion was called Surrey—a poor district, but one in which the Church was making great advances. The services hitherto had been held in the Town Hall (let not the reader form his idea from the English equivalent of this), but, by dint of great self-sacrifice, the building of a church had at last become feasible, and one part of the Bishop's purpose in coming was to lay the foundation-stone.

This was done with full masonic rites, and Christ Church, Surrey, was auspiciously begun for a scattered flock, many of whom had not been inside a church for many years.

Baptisms and Confirmations were also administered by the Bishop, and when his visit was over, the people laboured so enthusiastically on their church that on September 29th—the Feast of S. Michael and All Angels—it was ready for opening, just seven weeks from the laying of the foundation-stone.

About this same time a desire, long entertained by the Bishop, was carried out in the inauguration of a Mission in the Spallumcheen and Kamloops district. The importance of the step had been pressed upon the S.P.G. from year to year, but at last the progress of railway construction compelled action, and the Rev. D. H. W. Horlock was removed from Yale, which was now a rapidly decaying place, with a daily diminishing population, to take charge of the Kamloops Mission.

The Mission extended from Clinton on the north to Okanagan on the south, and embraced

Cache Creek, Savona's, Grand Prairie, and Spallumcheen. One hundred miles in one direction, and seventy-five in the other, it was sufficiently large to fully task the energies of three men, especially as the railway was running through seventy or eighty miles of it. Kamloops was fixed upon as the head and centre of the Mission.

The first service was held in the temporary church at Kamloops on September 7th, when the Bishop officiated. Mr. Horlock entered upon the permanent duties of the mission a fortnight later, and his first coadjutor was found in the Rev. A. Shildrick, transferred from Maple Ridge. A new worker was also promised in the Rev. H. Irwin, expected early in 1885.

It will be seen that the diocese was gradually attracting to itself a staff of clergy more adequate for the work the Bishop had before him ; but in a diocese every day becoming more populous and important, and a hundred and sixty thousand square miles in extent, even thirteen clergy was not an extravagant provision.

Under these circumstances, it was a bright day for the Mission and the Bishop when, in October, the staff was reinforced by the arrival of the Rev. H. Edwardes for the Indian Mission, Lytton ; three Sisters from the Community of All Hallows', Ditchingham, for school work at Yale ; and Miss Boyce for school work at Nicola. The prospects of the Indian Mission now looked rosy indeed, and the new impetus given to it will be appreciated when we come to the Bishop's account of the Indian gathering this year at Lytton.

But in spite of the brighter outlook in many directions, financial anxiety had not ceased to paralyze, to a large extent, the Bishop's activities. The following letter addressed to the Secretary of the Home Committee will show the Bishop's position in this respect :—

"New Westminster,
"November 3, 1884.

"MY DEAR MOGG,

"For my own part I am afraid that my report this time must be a melancholy one. We held our quarterly Executive Committee meeting last week. Our bank balance amounts to £147, including all special donations, which of course ought to be reserved for their particular purpose. We required, however, £146 10*s.* for actual stipends, and the committee decided that it was better to appropriate the special funds rather than leave the stipends unpaid. We, therefore, paid the stipends in full, but bills to the amount of £75 had to be laid over. The simple fact, therefore, is that the diocese at this moment is insolvent. Understand particularly that I am not finding fault with *you.* I am aware of the circumstance that you have drawn no salary as organizing secretary during the year, and I require you to publish this circumstance with the rest of my letter. I am finding fault with no one except it be myself for not using my own pen to better purpose; but I abhor writing begging letters, especially to individuals, though I suppose I must descend to it, if money is not otherwise forthcoming.

"On December 31st a similar amount will be due for stipends, the bill will have to be paid, and we ought to replace the special donations which have been appropriated. Further than this, we are under engagements to pay £50 towards a church at Mud Bay now nearly completed, and £50 towards new buildings for Lorne College. I have exhausted local effort for this year, and must depend, therefore, wholly upon home contributions being remitted in time. . . .

"Ever yours sincerely,
"A. W. NEW WESTMINSTER."

Meanwhile, not only were those outside the diocese called upon to bestir themselves, but

Churchmen within the diocese were also invited to rise to the needs of the occasion. At the request of the Bishop, Archdeacon Woods undertook to organize what has since become a most important part of the diocesan machinery—the Diocesan Mission Fund. The Archdeacon put forth an appeal for prompt help, reminding Churchmen that grants from outside were only for a time, and might at any time fail or be withdrawn.

We may conclude this general review of the work of the year with a reference to the meeting of synod on November 20th. The Bishop preached a very able sermon at the opening of synod from the text, "Look not every man on his own things, but every man also on the things of others," and afterwards delivered his address, in which he dealt with the general condition of the diocese, the appointment of attorneys for S.P.G., the need of canons dealing with the solemnization of holy matrimony, the subject of periodical collections within the diocese for various public objects, such as S.P.G., S.P.C.K., and the Diocesan Fund, and the need for a proper arrangement of the boundaries of parishes. All these subjects were duly discussed, and such others as were brought up by individual members of the synod, various committees appointed, and a very good and useful session brought to a conclusion in one day.

From all these details of diocesan organization and work, which it was necessary to mention, we may now turn to the more interesting subject of the Bishop's journeys, in the spring and summer to Lytton for the great Indian gathering, in the autumn to Cariboo.

CHAPTER XVI.

THE INDIAN GATHERING AT LYTTON.

JUNE, 1884.

"AT length the night has passed away, and the dawn of a new and, we all hope, a more prosperous day has broken upon the long-neglected Indian Mission in this diocese."

So writes the Bishop in commencing an article to the *Mission Field* with regard to what was in some respects the most interesting diocesan event of 1884.

The Bishop continues—

"It was in July, 1882, that I announced to the S.P.G. the resignation of the Rev. J. B. Good, which took effect in September following. The officers of the Society will know the efforts that have been continually made ever since in the direction of a reorganization of the Mission, and I cannot hope for a better opportunity than this of acknowledging the sympathetic and patient consideration with which the Society has waited for the development of the plan of reorganization which I laid before it two years ago. To have hurried that plan to a premature execution would have been fatal to its success, but nevertheless to have been allowed so long a time for preparation demands a thankful acknowledgment. I would not have it supposed that during two years no work has been done. Far from that, for apart from the permanent residence at Lytton of the Rev. R. C.

Whiteway, I am much indebted to the Rev. G. Ditcham and the Rev. D. H. W. Horlock for the willing and valuable assistance they have rendered me, sometimes at the expense of much personal inconvenience. Still, the work has been necessarily desultory, and, in consequence, imperfect and unsatisfactory.

"With the greater thankfulness, therefore, I record the end of the interregnum and the happy inauguration of a new period in the life of the Mission. For two long years, and often with a desponding heart, I have been encouraging the Indians to look forward to the 'good time coming' when Church work, and specially education, would be resumed among them, and with greater earnestness than ever. And therefore, when the good time had come, it seemed fitting to usher it in with some amount of ceremony and observance. To this end, I summoned the Indians, far and near, as many as were able, to meet me in June, at a favourite camping-ground of theirs near Lytton, that I might introduce to them the Rev. R. Small, and publicly induct him into his office. I was desirous, too, of impressing upon their minds the reality of their fellowship with us in the Body of Christ, and therefore invited to be present the Archdeacon of Columbia and other clergy, engaged chiefly in white work, as well as a few representatives of the laity."

After describing the journey by steamer, rail, and road to Lytton, one of the party writes—

"On Friday, the 30th, we reached our camping-ground about 2 p.m., having ridden in from Lytton, a distance of about fourteen miles, a ride full of interest in every mile from the time we crossed the wooden bridge which spans the Thompson at its junction with the Fraser, and thence climbed up, on some surefooted Indian horses, hills which had literally in places to be *climbed* by the aid of steps cut in their sides; and as we rose higher and higher, we were able to look down on and trace for a considerable distance the course of the Thompson as

Photo: Thompson.]

HOPE PARSONAGE, AND INDIANS.

Photo: Thompson.]

ANOTHER VIEW OF INDIAN GATHERING.

it came down on our right to join the Fraser, which, facing us in our course, lay on our left. We could *see* for ourselves the geography of the land into which we were entering, how it lay in the fork between the two rivers. We passed in our ride two well-laid-out farms of no great extent, but rich to profusion through the fertility of the virgin soil, irrigated from some of the many cool, clear, rippling streams which crossed our trail every few miles.

"On reaching Pootanie we found our tents already pitched, and every preparation made for our comfort. Some few Indians came out to meet us, but there was no formal reception until later in the afternoon, after a short rest and such refreshment as cool water, grateful shade, and not unsubstantial 'tea,' were well calculated to afford. Having formally announced their intention, the Indians then came from their encampment towards the Bishop's reception-tent—a bell-tent pitched under the shade of a great pine tree—and marching past in single file, spoke to and shook hands with each member of our party, many of them, both men and women, recognizing Archdeacon Woods, who had visited the Hope, Yale, and Lytton Missions some years before the division of the diocese. The formalities of the reception over, there was little to be done until the next day, when there would be plenty of work for all. The Bishop announced the hours of the different Church services, the Sunday work was planned out, and other arrangements made clear, so that all should know what they had to do, and how far they were at liberty to follow their own devices. And now while we wait for the real work, which has brought us so far, to begin on Saturday morning, let us look round and observe the site of our camping-ground. Gentle swelling hills, covered with rich verdure—not grass in the sense in which the word is used in reference to cultivated pasture land, but yet every inch of the ground covered with a thick, rich, soft carpet of green, so thick and soft that to lie down on it was as restful as the most luxurious couch, so rich that the hundreds of horses belonging to the whole encampment, some tethered, but the greater part free, find ample pasture, while the wild flowers innumerable, and of so many various kinds, give an added beauty to what in itself is so lovely. On one small hill are two tents appropriated to the Bishop, Mrs. Sillitoe, and Miss Woods; on another are the tents assigned to the rest of the party; while the bell-tent stands midway between. Lower down, and on more level ground, is the awning—it cannot be called a tent—under which the table for meals is built. The word *built* is used advisedly, for the table consists of so many stout legs driven into the ground, and slabs laid on top; while benches run down each side, built after the same fashion as the table; the seat of honour at the head of the table being a round log sawn off so as to make a seat, and set up on end. The whole encampment is looped round by a stream of water of icy coolness and crystal clearness. Across a little valley stood the tents of the interpreter, Meshell, and his family and following, while the general camp of Indians was entirely out of sight, though close at hand, for one had but to walk a few hundred yards from the bell-tent and from the side of any of the low hills to look down upon a sight not easily, once seen, to be forgotten. A large low-lying plain, quite level throughout its whole extent, marked off from the forest and brush on its farthest border by the stream already described, was the place chosen by the Indians for their encampment. Our first view of it was after nightfall when the camp fires were lighted, and the work of the day being over, cooking, feasting, smoking, chatting, singing, or *rest,* pure and simple, varied the aspect of each group of tents.

"*The work of the day*—what was it? What had brought this crowd of Indians, men, women, and children, to the number of close on a thousand, from their different homes situated miles away in all directions? They were here to gather what was to them a valuable harvest of edible roots of various kinds, and the fact of their being thus assembled in one central spot afforded the Bishop his opportunity. Apart from the immediate proximity of both wings of our encampment stood the altar, with altar cross, flower vases, altar lights, and all that was needful for the due and reverent celebration of Holy Communion. The altar stood upon a slightly elevated platform, carpeted, as was the ground all round, with layers of young pine branches, the whole being under a screen, or, in ecclesiastical terminology, a baldachino, erected by the Indians before our arrival.

"On Saturday, the 31st, the greater part of the day was devoted to examining the credentials of those Indians who desired to present themselves for Holy Communion on Whit Sunday. Each Indian on being brought under Christian teaching is given a printed paper certifying that he is a catechumen belonging to a certain mission or section of a mission. When baptized, he is given another paper ruled for three separate entries, the first of which is filled in with the date and place of baptism. In due course, if all goes well, the second is filled in with the date of Confirmation, and the third with the date of his first Communion. These papers had to be examined one by one, the chief of a tribe, if a Christian, or the captain or watchman of a village being required to bear testimony that there was no charge against him. If all proved satisfactory, he was given a ticket signed by the priest who had examined his case. Among all who presented themselves as desirous of communicating, but two cases of any difficulty occurred. The examination of credentials occupied the three priests present a considerable part of the day. Throughout the afternoon and late into the evening new arrivals called for further examinations, so that the work may be said to have extended over the whole Saturday. In the course of the afternoon, the Bishop addressed the Indians on various subjects of interest and practical utility, suggesting to the men some questions (specially in relation to schools and education) for discussion by themselves in council. The women he addressed by themselves.

"Whit Sunday, June 1st, was indeed a glorious day,

one to be rememembered with thanksgiving by all who that day were gathered together in the secluded valley of Pootanie. It could not be but that one's mind was carried back to the first Whit Sunday, when 'the day of Pentecost was fully come.' True, there was no sound from heaven as of a rushing mighty wind, no cloven tongues like as of fire, but none the less there was the felt presence of God the Holy Ghost.

"The accredited messengers of God were there with the message of His Gospel and the Sacraments ordained by Christ Himself, to assure these Indians, many of them already Christians and inheritors of the kingdom of heaven, but many of them still heathen, yet with sufficient light and knowledge to comprehend the full meaning of the assurance that 'the promise is to you and to your children, and to all that are afar off, even as many as the Lord our God shall call.' When at the six-o'clock celebration—we believe the first in that place—*one hundred and eleven* Indians received the most comfortable sacrament of the Body and Blood of Christ, who could doubt but that a great and real work was being done among them? . . . On Whit Sunday there were three celebrations, the High Celebration being by the Bishop at 10.30. At the afternoon service the whole body of Indians was present, and Evensong having been said, the Rev. Richard Small, the Rev. G. Ditcham, and the Ven. the Archdeacon of Columbia gave short addresses—a plan adopted by request of the Indians themselves. At this service nineteen children were baptized by the Bishop.

"On Monday, June 2nd, the Bishop, the Rev. R. Small, and Mr. Cantell remained another day in camp to further certain details of work, the rest of the party, with the exception of Mrs. Sillitoe, turning their faces homeward, and reaching New Westminster on the evening of June 3rd."

The foregoing account may well be supplemented by some extracts from the Bishop's own description.

"On Friday, May 30th," he says, "we were all assembled in camp at a place called by the Indians Pootanie, about fifteen miles from Lytton, among the mountains, between the Thompson and Fraser rivers, about three thousand feet above the sea-level.

"I have not time for topographical word pictures, but I verily believe there are artists in England who would not think it too far to have come for one look at Pootanie. The first glance around was one of wondering admiration, the second afforded the fullest justification of our presence, for the extent of the Indian camp showed that large numbers had responded to my call, and a great opportunity was before us. The Indian camp was on a flat at the upper end of a narrow valley, and beyond it the ground rose suddenly in benches and terraces. On the first of these was Meshell's camp, and ours on the next, and between the two, in a little natural amphitheatre, was erected a canopy of evergreens, under which, on a raised platform, was the altar.

"A flag floated over nearly every tent, in most instances the diocesan flag, blue, with gold cross and mitre; and the whole scene was bright and picturesque and, to most of us, novel.

"A fifteen-miles' ride and two thousand six hundred feet altitude above our breakfast level made the dinner gong a pleasant sound, and the Indians were thoughtful enough to send us a message to the effect that they would not expect us to receive them until after we had rested; and having formed a procession in their own camp, we presently saw them approaching us from below, in Indian file, of course, with stately tread, the men coming first, the women following.

"They wound up the hill in zigzag lines, the men uncovering as they approached. We stood in a line, and shook hands with each as they passed by. There were about nine hundred of them, and the ceremony occupied just an hour. After the reception we had Evensong, and the Indians returned to their camp."

The Bishop goes on to describe the work of

Saturday, the examination of credentials, etc,, an account of which has been already given.

"In the afternoon," he resumes, "all the women and girls assembled under the shade of a gigantic pine, at the foot of which my tent was pitched. I addressed them on the subject of domestic life, the duties and responsibilities of their sex, and the cultivation of womanly virtues; and explained to them the object of the girls' school shortly to be established at Yale under a branch of the Ditchingham Sisterhood. Mrs. Sillitoe then distributed among them handkerchiefs, aprons, picture cards, etc., gifts for the purpose from friends in England.

"After this was held a meeting of chiefs, captains, and watchmen, to whom I explained the plan of the Mission as reorganized under Mr. Small and Mr. Edwardes and the Ditchingham Sisters, particularly insisting on the principle of self-support as regards both the church and education. I requested them to discuss the plan among themselves, and to report the result to me on Monday. It subsequently transpired that they sat in council over this discussion till three o'clock in the morning!

"They then presented me with a list of cases occurring within their several jurisdictions of delinquency in various forms, and I arranged to hold a court of inquiry on Monday. The Sunday services were then announced, and the meeting closed with a *potlatch*, or distribution of knives, fishhooks, pictures, and tobacco."

Omitting the account of the Sunday services, which have already been sufficiently described, let us come to the picture presented of a Bishop's court among the Indian converts.

"On Monday, after breakfast, . . . the whole throng ot men, women, and children gathered on the slope in front of my tent to 'assist' at the court of inquiry. The 'cause list' included two cases of matrimonial difficulty, one of drinking and gambling, one of practising 'medicine magic,' and a long-pending charge against the late catechist. It is creditable to the delinquents to say that they all put in an appearance, although, of course, they could not have been compelled to do so, nor were any of them under constraint.

"The matrimonial cases were easily arranged, and I had the happiness of restoring harmony to two wigwams. The drinking and gambling case was the more serious, inasmuch as the accused was no less a personage than the recognized chief of all the Thompson River tribes. It speaks volumes for the honesty and courage of these Church officers that they did not hesitate to present even their superior chief as an offender against the laws of morality.

"A lecture on the responsibility of his office and his Christian obligations was patiently listened to by the old chief. He then made a very humble, public acknowledgment of the justice of the charges, expressed his penitence, and only asked us to give him a little time in which to prove his sincerity. He then signed a written declaration to abstain both from whisky and gambling, and I told him I should require in two months' time certificates of his good behaviour in these respects.

"The charges against the catechist were fully proved, and he was deposed from his office. The 'medicine-man' proved the most difficult to deal with, chiefly because, as of old, his profession brought him 'much gain.' He denied ever receiving more than $10 for his work, and claimed that, after all, his work was chiefly one of prayer. There was evidence, however, that he had received as much as $50 in some cases, and I pointed out to him that on the ordinary occasions of prayer he did not find it necessary to strip himself naked, and dance and howl, as his custom was when officiating as medicine-man. He positively refused to abandon the practice, and there was no alternative, therefore, but to excommunicate him, and, further, to threaten with excommunication any who employed his services. I do not venture to hope that the remedy will be altogether effectual, but it will mitigate the evil. Another remedy, and a better one, I would like to be able to adopt, viz. the appointment of a medical missionary. . . .

"As the result of the Indian conference on school matters, they informed me that they were quite prepared to contribute to the support of schools, and wished me to say how much I expected them to give. . . . The appointment of a new chief, the registering of the baptisms of the previous day, and issue of certificates, together with some minor matters, concluded the day. Next morning, after a short farewell charge, I called for three cheers for the Queen—a name of mingled mystery and confiding love to Indian ears—to which they responded heartily in English fashion, and then we broke up camp and returned to Lytton."

One more account of this remarkable meeting must be given, coming as it does from one of the Indians present, and written after the Bishop's death.

"In June, 1884," the account runs, "our Bishop came up to Lytton with Mrs. Sillitoe to go to Pootanie. . . . Mr. Hughes and I went to Pootanie ahead of the Bishop's party to choose a good place for the camp. Mr. Hughes when he saw Pootanie was very glad, and said it was the best place the Bishop could come to. All the hills were covered with fine flowers, red, blue, white, and green. We had horses ready to meet the Bishop at Lytton, and we sent notice all round to the Indians belonging to the English Catholic Church. At once they came to Pootanie as fast as they could, some of them hardly taking time to bring their blankets and food.

"The first day in camp the Bishop rested quietly in his tent, being tired from the long journey. The following day all the Indians dressed up to go to his tent to shake hands with him. They walked in a straight line to his tent. When they had finished shaking hands we looked where they had been walking, and it was a very big trail, because the Indians were so many. The same day we built a rough church and altar, the clergy and Indians all working together. The church was built of green brush and flowers, and we hung up all our flags."

CHAPTER XVII.

THE REPORT FOR 1884.

IN the report issued at the end of 1884, the prevailing note is unmistakably that of disappointment—a disappointment all the keener inasmuch as it appeared to the Bishop that the gloominess of the outlook was attributable to causes within the control of Churchmen in the diocese.

There was disappointment with regard to the synod, which was poorly attended by the lay delegates, and the Bishop speaks out with great plainness and candour as to the failure of the laity to rise to their opportunities in this matter.

"Eighteen lay delegates," he says, "had been elected, but of this number only eight put in an appearance. . . . But further, with regard to the business transacted, it is the merest euphemism to say that expedition characterized the whole proceedings. The Committee on S.P.G. Attorneys recommended the Executive Committee to attend to the business. The Committee on Marriage Laws 'respectfully recommended' the Bishop to look into them and get them altered if he thought it necessary, and they added three other 'recommendations' to whom it might concern, extremely good as to the matter of them, but devoid of practical force. . . . Now, the question is pre-eminently a layman's question. The laity called for the synod in the first instance, and it was granted to them, although by many amongst us regarded as inopportune. It is, therefore, not unreasonable to require that the laity shall take an interest in the synod, and that the lay members shall cheerfully and patiently devote themselves to the business of the diocese.

"If the synod is simply to pass resolutions recommending the Executive Committee and the Bishop to do the work, we can do the work without such a recommendation at all. . . ."

A similar feeling of disappointment pervaded his lordship's remarks on Church schools, in the cause of which he had sacrificed so much time and money.

"It seems to be entirely ignored," he says, "that these institutions exist, not as private speculations, but for the promotion of religious education on Church principles. It is simply a question as to whether such an object is desirable or not. I established these schools because I believed that it is, and because I was encouraged to do so by the repeated solicitations of Church people. I am naturally, therefore, disappointed at finding Church children sent indiscriminately to Roman or to free schools, while our own are left to languish for want of support, and I myself am consumed with anxiety on their account."

Other subjects called for equally plain expressions of feeling, the uniform depression of the Bishop's statement being only broken by a more hopeful forecast of the prospects of the Indian work and schools.

The great anxiety which no doubt clouded the Bishop's estimate of the whole diocesan work was the serious financial outlook resulting from the decrease of offerings both in England and within the diocese. On this point the Bishop writes—

"While I would be the very last to regard the financial prosperity of the diocese as an absolute test of its success, nevertheless I am strongly of opinion that where a Church fails to attract the willing and hearty support of its members, the circumstance betokens a want of confidence and harmony for which there must be a cause, and for which it is the duty of all, and especially for those in authority, to seek a remedy."

One cause to which the Bishop called special attention, whether rightly or wrongly the present writer has no knowledge, lay in a direction upon which he speaks trenchantly and with characteristic courage.

"There is, however, another way of reading our financial embarrassment, and one which the solemn obligations of my office forbid me to overlook, viz. as affording an indication of the relationship existing between pastor and people. And herein, again, I must guard myself from being misunderstood. I do not for one moment allow that the personal relationship of any one to his parish priest is a lawful or proper measure of his obligation to support his Church. A man's duty in this respect belongs to a region far removed from all personal considerations. Nevertheless, unfortunately for human nature, we know only too well that personal relationship is the pivot on which a large proportion of our religious contributions turns, and the first and commonest indication of friction in the running of the parochial machine is often the failure or falling off of contributions. It would be childish to ignore that there is friction of a serious character in some of our parishes, and such friction as ought to be avoided, and could be avoided; for in every instance at present in my mind, self-will and no principle whatever is the originating cause of it. Self-will is equally unlovely, whether in priest or people, but it is undoubtedly less excusable in the former, who should have the more evenly balanced and more perfectly sanctified mind. 'It is impossible but that offences will come, but woe unto him through whom they come.' The responsibility, whether to priest or layman, is a terrible one, while the insignificance of the matter in dispute is an aggravation of the scandal and a wanton outrage to common sense.

"The shepherd is quick to complain if his flock do not follow him, but he complains also when they follow him in the path of self-will. He claims that to him is committed the cure of souls, and his conscience must not be fettered in the exercise of it. My brothers, there is a cure of souls of higher responsibility than yours, that is, your Bishop's, and his conscience is to him a matter as solemn as your own. You can, by submission, throw your responsibility on to him; he cannot dispose of his own. He may certainly err, but the blame is his, not yours, if you have yielded to his judgment; whereas your errors are his responsibility if he has suffered them to continue.

"And to my lay brothers may I not justly say that in their contentions there is more of self-will than of principle, more self-assertion than argument? 'We will not have these things so,' is neither convincing nor provocative of charity. It is possible to compel peace with a sword, but it is only the peace of a slumbering volcano, a breathing time for the vanquished to prepare again for the contest. A true peace is one for which both sides long, and for sake of which both sides are ready to yield."

Be the cause what it might, the Bishop had to bid the friends of the Mission at home and abroad to face the unpleasant fact that the diocese was practically bankrupt, and its chief pastor compelled to meet urgent liabilities out of his own private resources.

"It is not within the bounds of reasonable expectation," he writes, "that I should go on doing this, even if I were in a position, which I am not, to afford it. I am under no obligation to contribute more than one-tenth of my income for Church purposes, whereas during the last five years I have contributed more than one-fourth."

That this was a time of grievous anxiety to the Bishop was fully borne out at the time by the testimony of Mr. Justinian Pelly, treasurer to the Home Committee, then on a visit to the diocese, and who worked indefatigably to improve financial matters. He wrote as follows, under date of January 31, 1885:—

"... Since I arrived here I have occupied myself in making a complete investigation of the financial position of the Mission, and I now send you, under separate cover by book post, an abstract of the Mission accounts, from the time the Bishop entered upon his duties. I have endeavoured to put this abstract in such a form as shall be intelligible to persons not versed in accounts, as it is the opinion of the Bishop, subject to the concurrence of the English committee, that it would be expedient to have it printed and circulated among all interested in the diocese. ... There are some remarks regarding the several items of expenditure, which I venture to submit to the committee. 'Travelling Expenses' is necessarily a very heavy item. The cost of the journey of each employé coming from England was, until last year, £70. By arrangements with steamship owners in England, and with railroads in America, the cost has latterly been reduced to under £50, and negotiations are in progress for still greater reduction. Travelling expenses in the diocese are likewise very heavy. To those unacquainted with the condition of the country, it may be surprising to be told that the ordinary charges at the roadside inns, where only the very roughest accommodation is to be had, far exceed those of first-class hotels in England. The distances, moreover, from place to place are very great. With regard to the journeys of the Bishop, he has been treated with great liberality by the innkeepers and by the authorities of the railway company, who have given him a free pass over the line so far as completed, and have been equally liberal with regard to other clergy when travelling on ministerial duties. Moreover, the special donations and offertories which the Bishop has received in his journeys up-country have frequently exceeded and generally equalled his outlay. These contributions appear on the credit side of the account, under the head 'Offertories,' and are included in the sum of $5151 appearing there. I would here venture to remark on what appears to me the largeness of the sum so contributed by offertories, donations, and sales of work in the diocese, and for the general purposes of the Mission, as this does not include what was raised in the several parishes for church-building, maintenance of services, and clergy stipends. I find from the annual parochial returns that these in the four years, 1881–1884, amounted to $23,193.57.

"With regard to 'General Expenses,' I have looked through the several items charged under this head, and could not discover any outlay beyond what was absolutely necessary. Freight and duty on mission goods, included under this head, is either recouped by sales of work, or benefits the parishes for which the goods are destined, without appearing in the accounts.

"The finances of the Mission are managed by an Executive Committee of which the Bishop is president, and the strictest economy is exercised."

As the months went on the situation did not become less acute, and the quarterly paper issued in July, 1885, makes the following announcement:—

"Owing to the very unsatisfactory state of our funds, the Bishop has felt it his duty to come home next year and try to stir up more interest in his diocese. The necessity of this step comes at a most inconvenient time, for the completion of the C.P.R. especially demands his presence in the diocese to try to meet the fresh demands which will be made on the Church for her ministrations to the new settlers from England.

"More men will mean more money. At present some work will have to be given up, and though one of the saddest things in mission life is to give up work, yet it is better to do this than to get into debt. We are doing our best to avoid this, and to keep clear of owing money—though there are clergy out there now, hard-working men, who have not received the wretchedly small stipends due to them in full for the last six months. It is much better that our readers should know this. So many promised to collect for us and have given it up; so many were eager for boxes, but have become tired; so many clergy who gave offertories now say that they really cannot manage to give us a sermon once a year. Is it that the love of many is becoming cold? Is the interest in the welfare of our poor diocese so small that, at a critical time like the present, our old friends will not rally round us? . . . May God raise us up some helpers speedily, that the work may not fail."

It is a melancholy story, and by this time probably to the reader monotonous, but the reality was monotonous too, and it is just as well that this fact should be appreciated.

In the fall of the year came another letter from the Bishop, dated September 24, 1885, on the now too familiar subject. We quote this at length—

"My dear Mr. Mogg,

"My quarterly contribution to the paper cannot be a cheerful one. I am bitterly disappointed at the failure of support from home, and while I am cast down at the prospects of the Church here, I cannot help feeling some indignation as well at being left to do the best I can with obligations which home support, a year or two ago, encouraged me to incur.

"It would probably have been better had the money then given us been withheld. We certainly could not, in that case, have enlarged our borders as we wished to do, and as was really necessary to be done, but we should not have been in our present position of financial collapse. It is only another proof, were any needed, of the falsity of the principle of giving out of a temporarily excited interest, rather than out of a sense of duty and a love of God.

"I hope I shall be forgiven for writing somewhat severely, but it must be remembered that, on the strength of contributions in former years, I have opened up missions and brought men out from England to occupy them; I have established schools, and sent for teachers to superintend them; and then suddenly, and without one word of warning, contributions fail, and no alternative is left us but to abandon much promising and prosperous work.

"I am not exaggerating. Two churches are now closed, and a third will be closed at the end of a month; two have been reduced to fortnightly services. One school was closed last June, and another is to be closed at Christmas. We are in debt to the clergy for stipends, due on June 30th last, about £90, and we have about £20 in hand to meet this and the stipends falling due on the 30th inst.; and I have had to borrow money on the mortgage of Church property to meet liabilities which could not wait, and have made advances myself to the very utmost of my ability.

"I have no heart to write of work while this financial burden is weighing on me. A responsibility, heavy enough under any circumstances, becomes almost intolerable in such a case.

"'Why not come home and beg yourself?' say some people. I cannot afford to come home at present, but, further, it ought not to be necessary for me to come home. Where is the use of great missionary organizations like S.P.G. and C.M.S., or of the multitude of lesser 'committees,' 'councils,' and 'agencies,' if, after all, the Bishops have to do the begging? I maintain that we are *sent by the Church* to do her work, and our reports of the work doing and to be done ought to be sufficient. It is a degradation of our office to have to make 'appeals' to conjure pence out of people's pockets wherewith to do God's work.

"There is something wanting in a system that requires such appeals, but the supply of what is wanting is a subject altogether too big to be entered upon here, even if it were within my capacity to discuss it.

"I append a summary of the treasurer's statement, to show that (in the single item of stipends) we have in hand about £20 to meet about £220.

"Yours faithfully,

"A. W. New Westminster."

This has been a short and dull chapter, but it will not have been dull in vain if only Church people in England can be induced to think of the way in which our colonial Churches are starved in their tender infancy, rendered puny and weak for want of the nourishment a rich Mother Church has it in her power to give, and if they can be induced to think, too, of the way in which a Bishop's heart is crushed within him at the apparent indifference of those who have sent him forth.

Our dear old Church has had her martyr-bishops who have freely shed their blood in savage lands, but it has had, and still has, its martyrs also of another type—martyrs whose life-blood is pressed out of them drop by drop.

Still there was another side to the shield, and though the Bishop's heart was made sore within him by these and other trials, there were not wanting signs of great things, both achieved in the past and promised for the future. The opening of the C.P.R. during this year was a determining crisis in the history of the colony, and brought the Mission into closer touch with the rest of the Church work in Canada, while opening up the country more effectually to the ministrations of the Church. The Indian Missions went on apace at Yale and Lytton. In both places church-building proceeded rapidly, priests and people working enthusiastically together, and many converts were gathered into the fold by baptism. On every hand we see during this year that the influence of the Bishop's work was felt, and producing a far larger harvest of good than was at first sight apparent.

CHAPTER XVIII.

FROM KAMLOOPS TO THE COLUMBIA.

1885.

HERE is a narrative by Mrs. Sillitoe of an eventful journey.

"A new city having sprung up during the last few months on the Columbia river, where the C.P.R. crosses it the second time, the Bishop decided to take advantage of an opportunity which occurred to go up and pay Farwell a visit. On Friday, May 1st, we were up at 6 a.m., to be ready for the steamboat *Peerless*. We left Kamloops about 10 a.m., with a very large cargo on board, and a very rough crowd of passengers, numbering, Chinese included, nearly two hundred. The men were on their way up to work on different parts of the railway line. We spent a pleasant, lazy day, going slowly up the South Thompson river, often getting on the sand-bars—for the river was very low. Our progress was so slow that, instead of arriving at Eagle Pass at 10 p.m., it was six the following morning ere we arrived at that landing.

"It was 9 a.m. before we were able to 'hitch up' our horses and drive off. The morning had been misty, and so we were unable to see much of the Lesser Shuswap Lake, on the shores of which we had been landed. The day was very warm, and the sun scorching, yet all around snow lay on the ground, quite thick in the more sheltered places. The trees all along the road were wonderful. The timber of British Columbia is generally

Photo: Thompson.]

NELSON, IN THE KOOTENAY DISTRICT.

Photo: Thompson.]

KAMLOOPS.

very fine, in some places extraordinarily large, but never had we seen anything to equal this amongst which we now were—cedars for the most part so tall and straight that the tops were scarcely visible. About seven o'clock, when still three miles from our destination, we were stopped at a camp with the news that it would be impossible for us to proceed at present, as forest fires were raging ahead, and the road was blocked with fallen trees. They were expecting every moment the return of a party who had been engaged all day in clearing the road. Soon we met the 'boss,' who told us the fire was very bad, but that there were only a few more trees to clear away, and that he would send out a fresh gang of men and get us through if possible. We put-to the ponies, and, following the men, came up to them whilst they were chopping out the two last trees. It was by no means pleasant waiting in the midst of such fire and smoke, one's eyes streaming with tears, yet unable to withdraw them from the falling trees, which were liable to come down at any moment. Against one large cedar we were especially warned to be on our guard, and whilst watching this, down fell another between ourselves and the choppers, not many yards from either of us. How those men worked! Englishmen have little idea how, under ordinary circumstances, Canadian axemen can chop, but when working, as they then were, with almost superhuman efforts, it was a sight requiring to be seen to be believed.

"At last the road was clear, and the boss told the Bishop to whip the ponies 'all he knew how,' and gallop through. This he did, though at first it looked impossible, the bushes burning fiercely on either side, and the flames blowing right across the road, the dense smoke making everything else look dark. We did as we were told, and the ponies seeming fully to understand that this was a time for a special effort, galloped, and we, with our heads bent down, went through safely, the large cedar falling directly after. About 9 p.m. we reached Griffin Lake, and here we stopped for the night, being not sorry to have some rest, for we were thoroughly tired. Our start next morning was to be not later than six, for we had still seventeen miles to drive, and wished to reach the Columbia river in time at least for an afternoon service. Between Griffin Lake and the Columbia, four lakes have to be crossed on scows, and one's progress can be but slow.

"Griffin Lake is about a mile and a half wide, and this we got across all right, though the water had risen considerably during the night, making the landing very difficult. A short drive brought us to the second and largest, Three Valley Lake, three miles long, and here the unpleasant news reached us that a gale was blowing round the point, and it would be impossible to cross till the wind fell, which it might do about eleven o'clock. Our party was six in number, and we determined to go as far as the point and see for ourselves, but on each attempt to get round we were blown back, and so there was nothing else to be done but to tie the scow to a tree which had fallen into the lake, and to wait for the wind to abate. For two hours we remained tied up, and then made another effort, this time a successful one, and reached the end of the lake. Half a mile more brought us to Summit Lake. All these lakes are very beautiful, the two last with high rocky banks, and into Summit Lake a lovely waterfall comes tumbling from a great height. Our progress was so slow that it was 4 p.m. ere we reached the Columbia. Here we found a most kind hostess in Mrs. Wright, the wife of the contractor of the Eagle Pass Road, over which we had just travelled, which within the last two years had been made from Eagle Pass Landing to the Columbia river, a distance of forty-seven miles. During this day we had had to drive through several fires, the last being not half a mile from Mr. Wright's house. This being in the vicinity of a shed where a large quantity of charcoal was stored, required to be watched by a number of men, whose absence diminished the number of our evening congregation. Mr. Wright's house stands on the west shore of the Columbia. . . .

"Directly opposite, on the east shore, stands Farwell, the latest-born city in British Columbia, consisting of about eighty houses, some of them substantial log buildings, and gradually degenerating down to the shanty, built wholly of split cedar planks, and every kind of tent. Whisky selling was the principal trade, and hitherto a good deal of lawlessness had prevailed. The piers of the bridge over the Columbia are built, but the bridge itself is not finished, and the river is crossed in small boats, which, considering the swiftness of the current, is by no means a pleasure unmixed with danger. Boats are frequently swept down by the stream and swamped in passing the piers. Two days before our arrival, a boat with three men was swamped in going through the bridge, and the men left clinging to the piles. First one boat, then another, going to the rescue, met with the same fate, till seven men were all clinging on for dear life, whilst the rushing stream threatened every moment to carry them away. At last a boat succeeded in reaching them, and all were rescued twenty minutes after the first boat was upset. Three men out of five had that week been drowned whilst trying to get on board the steamer *Kootenay*, then making her first trip up the Columbia.

"On Monday we crossed to Farwell to see the place and visit a few people, and to make arrangements for a service to be held the following day. During the evening the fires approached so close to the house that, though no danger was anticipated, it was thought advisable to dig a trench and bury a quantity of powder kept in the storehouse. On Tuesday morning the men keeping watch over the fires came in to have a sleep. They had been on watch since Sunday morning, and were worn out; besides, the fire was thought to be well under control. Though only the beginning of May, the weather was intensely hot, and we were glad to stay in the cool log-house all the morning. About one o'clock a cry was raised that the fires were upon us, and running to the door, we found the bushes and trees blazing and roaring not eighty yards away. The house is closely surrounded on three sides by trees, no clearing having been made around, and it was very necessary to take prompt measures, or everything would soon be burnt up. Happily a large staff of men was at hand, and as there was no possibility of extinguishing the fire, it was thought best to burn the trees and brush immediately round the buildings, leaving a burnt space across which the forest fire would not be able to pass. Before doing this, however, the roofs were covered with blankets, which were kept wet with water 'packed' up from the river. Oh, the excitement of that afternoon and evening! And how thankful every one felt that the powder had been buried! It was, indeed, a grand, awful sight to see the fire catching tree after tree, running up the trunks like a flash of lightning, and bursting into a mass of flame as it caught the foliage at the top, roaring and crackling in the most deafening manner. From thirty to forty men must have been at work arresting the course of the fire, keeping it in check by shovelling on sand and snow (of which a quantity remained in the hollows), and by pouring on buckets of water. As night came on the danger to the house was lessened, as a space had by this time been burnt round it; but now the almost greater danger threatened from the trees, which by this time were burnt through, and were falling in all directions. Now it was that the wonderful skill of the axemen was noticeable. They marked every tree likely to fall on the house—though it is very difficult to know which way a burning tree will fall. Three men worked at felling each tree, two chopping and one sawing, till either the tree fell or they were obliged to give up on account of the intense heat. There was one tree leaning so much towards the buildings as to make it impossible for them to fell it so as to make it fall in another direction, so they decided it must fall between the houses, and to accomplish this they had first to fell a cotton-wood tree standing in the way.

"The tree was thirty-three inches in diameter, as I afterwards ascertained by measurement, and the three men took exactly seven minutes to fell it. They afterwards brought down the burning tree just where they intended, without the buildings being touched. Then on they went to another tree—a sound one, apparently, a puff of smoke only now and then issuing from the bark, showing that there was fire within. They chopped at it for awhile, when, all at once, a solid mass of flames burst out from the centre, and salamanders though the men seemed to be, they had quickly to get away. The scene was indeed weird, even more so than in the day-time, when the fire raged more fiercely. Fire on all sides as far as the eye could reach, each tree standing out clearly in the bright red light. Every minute a crash and a roar as one tree after another fell to the ground. I could not but admire the self-command of our hostess, who, in the absence of her husband, had so much extra anxiety and responsibility, but nevertheless did not for a moment lose self-possession and coolness, but was continually out and around watching how matters were going. The men worked hard during the whole of that night. The next morning broke on a scene of desolation, the coolness of night causing the flames to die down, leaving only the smouldering flame and thick smoke, with every minute the crash and roar of a falling tree. One tree in falling grazed the house, but happily did little damage. All that day the men worked, for the fires became fiercer as the sun waxed hot.

"In the afternoon we crossed the river to Farwell, and the Bishop held service at the hotel, recrossing the same evening. On the further bank of the Columbia the fire had been increasing all day, but no steps were taken to arrest its progress, because, first of all, it was nobody's business, and secondly, because the town was considered safe. Alas! for their supposed security! During the night a strong wind began to blow, increasing to a gale, and we were startled, while dressing, with a cry that Farwell was in flames. Rushing out, we saw that this was indeed the case, and from house to house the fire rushed with awful rapidity, driving out the inhabitants, who had not time to save any of their belongings, but had to fly for their lives. The strong wind was meanwhile bringing large pieces of burning wood across the river, and a look-out had to be kept on the buildings, which once actually took fire. In about half an hour the fire had burned itself out, leaving about thirty buildings standing out of eighty. During that day a scene of utter lawlessness prevailed, those who had saved anything having it appropriated by those who had nothing left, and the rescued whisky-kegs becoming common property.

"We had intended to leave the Columbia in time to catch the Saturday's boat from Eagle Pass, as we were due in Kamloops on Sunday. But this was not possible. The road was blocked with fallen trees, and men could not be spared to clear them away, the house being by no means out of danger. It was not, therefore, till midday on Sunday, after a morning service, that we said good-bye to our kind and hospitable hostess, and started, not knowing, indeed, how far we might be able to get without being stopped; for information had come that the fires were very bad along the whole road. For the first seven miles we had an escort with an axe, and very thankful we were for his help in unhitching the horses and getting the buckboard across two burnt-out culverts and some fallen trees.

"We crossed the lakes without trouble, reaching Griffin Lake about 7.30, where we found a number of teams waiting to get over the road. After an all too short night's rest, we started at 6 a.m., hoping, oh! so heartily, that the road might be clear, knowing with satisfaction that when we had accomplished the first ten miles, we should afterwards have one, or perhaps two, teams ahead. We, therefore, hurried on, as, being only our two selves in the buckboard, company would be very desirable in getting over our difficulties.

"Our hopes were, alas! futile. Hardly had we driven a mile before we found a tree fallen right across the road, with no possibility of getting round it, so we unhitched, and the Bishop chopped out the smaller branches. He then made the ponies jump over, and we proceeded to lift over the buckboard. Never had it seemed so heavy before, and, indeed, once or twice I felt almost hopeless. But time and perseverance accomplish most things, and so with this, though a number of bruises bore testimony that the task was by no means an easy one. Other logs we encountered, but were able to get round some, and we were fortunate in getting the help of men to get past others. The ten miles ended, we believed our troubles to have come to an end, and drove on with lighter hearts over the fresh wheel-tracks, but the first man we met informed us that the fires were so bad three miles further on that we should be stopped, and that a large bridge had been burnt during the night. This was not cheering; but thinking that where one team had gone another might follow, we proceeded, but were soon stopped by our friend, the overseer, who had conducted us through the first fire on our journey up. He recommended us to turn back, as we could not possibly get through until the next day. He said that not only was the bridge burnt, but the trees were falling so fast that it would be dangerous to go near where the repair party was already at work.

"Still, we pushed on, for the steamboat was to leave the landing that evening. Reaching the fire, the Bishop alighted, leaving me in the buckboard while he walked on. After a long, anxious wait, I heard his voice calling me to come on, and he brought the welcome news that the road was clear to the bridge if we could drive through very hot fires, and that the men would try and lift over the buckboard. Well, we got through, I know not how, and reaching the bridge, found quite an assemblage; for besides the repair party, there were two teams, a band of wild cattle, and a loaded pack-train, waiting on the other side. It seemed a big gap over which to lift the buckboard, but many hands make light work, and to cross the bridge did not take a quarter of the time it had taken us to cross some of the trees. Before the steamer had been many minutes at the landing, we had taken leave of our friends, and retired to a fairly comfortable cabin. I was soon asleep, or as much asleep as the case would admit, whilst the steamboat was going from one camp to another landing freight. A cry of 'Fire!' aroused me. At first I thought it must be a dream, but the cry being repeated again and again, I looked out and saw that we had returned to Eagle Pass, and the place was aglow with the flames of a burning shanty. I did not need the cry of a man from on shore to remind me that the steamboat was lying close to a shed where powder was stored. It seemed, indeed, as if our enemy were following us to the end of our journey. The night was calm, no wind blowing, so the fire burnt itself out, fortunately without spreading, no attempt being made to put it out. 'It's only a Chinaman's; let it burn,' I heard one white man say; though the agonized cry of the poor Celestial with his house on fire was dreadful to hear.

"After this our journey was uneventful, and we reached Kamloops in the afternoon of Saturday, with hearts full of thankfulness at having been safely brought through so many dangers."

CHAPTER XIX.

GENERAL SURVEY, 1885-1886.

ONE or two events of the year 1885 have been described at length, but the notice of interesting journeys and events has by no means been exhausted. For instance, we have an account of a nine hundred miles' drive into the Cariboo country undertaken by the Bishop and Mrs. Sillitoe from July to September. Inasmuch, however, as the ground has been covered once or twice before, and the narrative embraces only such now familiar incidents of up-country travel as forest fires, wash-outs, miry roads, and break-downs, together with the incessant recurrence of services, baptisms, and confirmations, which, of course, formed the primary object of the Bishop's visitations, we will leave the reader to imagine for himself this arduous, but no longer novel, journey.

Almost immediately after the return from this tour in Cariboo, took place the consecration of the new Indian church at Lytton on October 19th. We cannot do better than give Mr. Small's account of this festive event, cheering alike to the Mission priests, and to the Bishop, who was beginning to see his efforts on behalf of the Indians bearing fruit.

"You will be glad to hear," writes Mr. Small, "that our Indian church at Lytton—entirely rebuilt by the labour of the Indians themselves—was consecrated by the

Bishop on October 19th. I really never dreamed, when ministering in the old dilapidated church a year ago, that within twelve months it would be my happiness to find a bright, clean, waterproof building, with a sanctuary which in decency would compare with many, if not most, of the churches in which I have ministered at home. Meshell, our interpreter, and the chief agent in the whole matter, has been most faithful in following out the directions given by Mr. Edwardes's practical and tasteful mind, and in the final arrangements, the completeness was due to the personal help and instruction given by him and Mr. Clinton. On the Thursday previous to the consecration, the Governor-General, who was passing through Lytton, received a deputation and address from the Indians in the unconsecrated church. His excellency's reply was eminently grave and practical, and in it he promised the Indians an organ for their church, to be sent by the C.P.R. when the traffic is opened through. On the day of consecration we had Mattins, followed by the Consecration Service and Holy Communion at 9 a.m. Many services and a Confirmation took place; and in the evening, after the Bishop had left for Kamloops, the congregation gathered again in church, and at this service six infants and children were baptized."

The Bishop's report for 1885 also refers to a few other interesting items in the year's work.

1. Of Columbia College he has to report that, owing to the disadvantages of inadequate and unsuitable premises, of too frequent changes of lady principals, and the competition of the Government free schools, it had been found impossible to maintain the institution as then established, but with the help of S.P.G., and the kind promise of another Sister from Ditchingham, he felt that he might purchase commodious premises at Yale, and hand over the education of girls to the Sisters with every prospect of success.

2. Another matter referred to was the departure for England of Mr. Justinian Pelly, after a stay of some months in the diocese. During his visit Mr. Pelly was most assiduously engaged for the Bishop in lay work of the most valuable character. In alluding to his departure, the Bishop speaks of it as a terrible loss, both to himself personally and to the diocese at large.

However, it was a consolation to feel that Mr. Pelly was carrying his unequalled interest in the diocese with him to England, and would there continue to labour for the same ends. There was a further occasion for congratulation in the fact that his place as a visitor would be taken by Canon Thynne, a consistent friend of the Mission from the outset, and now desirous of strengthening his ties with the diocese by engaging in mission work for six months among the miners.

The effects of visits such as this was of considerable value to the diocese in keeping it in touch with sources of assistance in the old country. At this stage of the diocesan history, the home organization, carried on under the direction of Mr. Mogg, was doing excellent work. Centres of interest were formed in various parts of England, and guilds established for the deepening of zeal in the workers. It was to assist in this movement that the Bishop desired to visit England, but the same cause which impelled him to undertake the journey—viz. the necessity of raising funds—also seemed for a long time to bar the way, for he could not afford the journey.

Under date of March 10, 1886, the Bishop writes as follows:—

"My dear Mogg,

"I am sorry to say that I have been obliged to postpone my visit to England. I hoped to have been able to start next month, but I am so badly off that I could only come by borrowing the money for my travelling expenses, and this I am unwilling to do.

"I have had to pay out so much for public purposes that I cannot save a penny; and, indeed, if I come this year at all, it will have to be by stopping at home and economizing to the last degree. And yet I ought to go and visit the Granite Creek mines if I go nowhere else.

"The winter is probably a better time than summer for week-night meetings, but as regards Sundays, they are difficult to be had between Advent and Easter."

To make matters worse, the year 1886 was a year of considerable strain upon the diocese.

On Whit Sunday, June 13th, the city of Vancouver was visited by one of those disastrous conflagrations which seem at some time or other to visit all towns on the American continent, and practically the whole city was left in ashes. Only six houses, it is said, were left standing, and a thousand people were left homeless. The loss included the church of S. James', which was in the charge of the Rev. H. G. F. Clinton, who lost books, clothes, furniture, and everything, with nothing insured, while the church itself was only insured for the sum of $750. It was a strange coincidence, with perhaps some hidden sign of blessing, that the fire occurred on the day that the Church was celebrating the coming down of the Holy Spirit under the outward symbol of tongues of fire. The necessity for rebuilding this church came as an added anxiety to the already overburdened Bishop.

During the year it became imperatively necessary to place the position of the diocese prominently before the lay Church people. To every known Churchman an appeal was sent asking what each would give, not to his own parish, but to the general work of the diocese. In writing to meet some objections to the appeal raised by some, the Bishop remarks as follows:—

"Amongst the duties of the Bishop are some which involve expense, as, *e.g.* the management of property, the legal costs of which amount to a large sum annually. There are three ways of dealing with these expenses: (1) Let the Bishop pay them out of his own pocket; (2) Let the parishes generally contribute to the payment of them; (3) Don't pay them at all. I need scarcely say that they have been dealt with hitherto in the first mentioned way. There is a simplicity about this solution of the difficulty which quite accounts for the complacency with which the parishes have hitherto quietly acquiesced in the arrangement. I say the 'parishes,' because whatsoever help I have hitherto received in this direction has been altogether individual in its character, while my contention is that it should be parochial. . . . I firmly believe that the successful administration of a diocese, specially in regard to its finances, depends in a most important measure upon the full appreciation and practical observance of this principle. It admits of a simple illustration. A citizen of New Westminster is required to pay municipal taxes, but his payment in this respect does not exempt him from the payment of provincial taxes, nor do these again set him free from the imposts levied by the Dominion Government. The municipality corresponds with the parish, the province with the diocese, while the Dominion stands for the whole Church, especially in its mission field; and every Churchman is liable under these several ecclesiastical organizations, as is every citizen under the corresponding political ones."

The necessity for doing something above what had already been done was obvious enough. The completion of the C.P.R. was bringing large numbers of settlers into the province, and from every direction urgent and touching calls were being received for the ministrations of the Church—calls which considerations of distance made it peculiarly difficult and expensive to answer.

Here is one specimen letter received from a prominent and influential layman at Donald.

"June 2, 1886.

"RIGHT REV. AND DEAR SIR,

"I am induced to trouble you thinking that you would be pleased to learn what I have to communicate, and hoping you may have it in your power to meet the views of the people residing here, both as affects educational and religious matters.

"All last year there were quite a number of families with their children at this place, yet not once were they visited by a clergyman. It has been decided by the C.P.R. that Donald is to be the most important station this side of Winnipeg. Large machine shops and round houses are to be maintained, and some three hundred and fifty or four hundred men will be kept here by the C.P.R. Many of these fill important positions, and members of all classes coming in have families, but the superintendent tells me that they object to this place as being unfit as a dwelling-place for their families, there being no schools, no churches, nor any facilities for bringing up their children in the way they should go.

"That this place should be so neglected is the cause of much comment. Should you feel like running up here to see the country and people, what I can do I will freely do to make you comfortable.

"Yours very faithfully,
"A. W. VOWELL."

Unremitting efforts to meet such pressing wants were made throughout this year, and, as the statistics for the year show, not by any means unsuccessfully. The number of clergy shows a gratifying increase, and, by performing double duty, the clergy made themselves go a considerable way in supplying the lack of Church privileges. As an example of this, we may take the case of Mr. Croucher, who had charge of Maple Ridge and Ladner's Landing, two settlements twenty-four miles apart. To minister to these two localities, he had for some time to use a little skiff totally unsuited to breast the rapid flood of the Fraser river. In December, 1885, Mr. Croucher nearly lost his life in his efforts to perform this double duty. Returning from Ladner's Landing, the tide running swiftly out, and the wind blowing strongly against it, the boat capsized, and after struggling for three quarters of an hour in the deadly cold water, Mr. Croucher's cries were heard by the workmen in a salmon cannery near, during a stoppage of the machinery.

Good, however, came out of this perilous adventure, for by the kind efforts of friends of the Mission in England, a steam launch was bought and sent out from England for the use of Mr. Croucher and the Bishop in their visits to the settlers along the banks of the Fraser. The *Eirene*, as this new aid to the mission work was called, proved indeed a messenger of peace among the settlers, many of whom were living in a state of practical heathenism.

Moreover, what the *Eirene* effected on the water, namely, a saving in every direction of time and power, the C.P.R. was the means of effecting on the land; for in spite of the need of economy, the Bishop was obliged to pay Sunday visits up-country for the purpose of Confirmations. Take for example the week from March 30th to April 7th.

"Leaving home on March 30th, the Bishop reached

Yale the same afternoon, and at Evensong held a Confirmation in S. John's Church of three girls belonging to the Sisters' school, and five Indians, and later in the evening addressed a gathering of Indians in the Indian church. The next day he reached Kamloops, travelling by train as far as Savona's, and the remaining twenty-five miles by handcar. On Saturday, April 3rd, two persons were confirmed in the temporary church at Kamloops. The following morning the Bishop celebrated and preached, and left in the afternoon by handcar for Savona's, where he held service and preached in the evening. On Monday morning Lytton was reached at 9 a.m. Flags were flying, and people were dressed in their best and brightest garments. The Indians were found already gathered in church for a Confirmation, the watchmen representing the different tribes being present to receive the Bishop at the church door. Twelve men and six women were confirmed; and in the afternoon the Bishop, accompanied by the Rev. H. Edwardes and Mr. William Meshell, drove down to the S. Paul's Mission House, where he was received by the Rev. R. Small and the Rev. E. L. Wright. On Tuesday, the 6th, there was a Confirmation of three men and five women, and two infants were baptized. On Wednesday the Bishop baptized eighteen adults. Thursday was devoted to an inspection of the Mission premises and the examination of the pupils of the school. On Friday the whole staff of the Mission House, with the pupils, accompanied the Bishop down the river by canoe to Keefer's Station, where the Bishop took train, and reached home in the evening. During the journey the Bishop confirmed twenty men and sixteen women, and baptized eighteen adults and two infants."

In the year 1886 two meetings of the Diocesan Synod were held—one in March, and a second in November, previous to the Bishop's departure for England.

On the morning of November 3rd the Bishop

Photo: Notman.]

KICKING-HORSE PASS, NEAR GOLDEN.

celebrated Holy Communion in S. Mary's Church, Sapperton. A large number, both of clergy and laity, had assembled to say "Good-bye," and to pray for God's blessing on the journey. The parting, thus appropriately made, was soon over, and the Bishop sped on his way over that great highway of Canada, the C.P.R.

Thus the Bishop temporarily left his diocese, thinking anxiously of all he had to accomplish before seeing once more the glorious peaks and cañons of the Rocky Mountains.

Quebec was reached in time to sail by the *Parisian* on November 19th; and at length the welcome coast of England came in sight once more, and Liverpool was reached on the first Sunday in Advent, November 28, 1886.

The visit itself we must pass over, as every reader knows what the visit of a colonial Bishop is like—an endless series of appeals, sermons, and lectures, with but the merest fraction of time for rest. The great outstanding features of his stay were the annual meeting of the Mission in London, at which the Marquis of Lorne spoke, and the ever-memorable Jubilee Service at Westminster Abbey, at which the whole Empire lifted up its heart to God for our Queen's glorious and happy reign.

CHAPTER XX.

THE RETURN TO THE DIOCESE.

1887.

EVERYWHERE throughout the diocese, upon his return, the Bishop was warmly welcomed by his people.

At Donald an address, signed by some forty persons, was presented at the C.P.R. station, in the darkness of a stormy night, to greet the Bishop. The next day, being Sunday, the Bishop recommenced diocesan work by celebrating Holy Communion, and preaching morning and evening to crowded congregations in the new church—fitly called S. Peter's—the first church in the Rocky Mountains.

At Kamloops the visit was marked by a Confirmation on the Monday, and a conference with the clergy on the Wednesday. A parish conversazione was also held, and an address of welcome presented on behalf of the citizens of Kamloops.

The more official welcome was given in New Westminster, where a large number of friends, including the Executive Committee of the diocese, met the Bishop and Mrs. Sillitoe on October 17th. An address was presented, and, what was more, the affectionate greetings of all emphasized the gladness of heart with which the inhabitants of

New Westminster again saw their Bishop and his wife.

The year was marked by one other event deserving of notice.

On the Festival of S. Andrew an interesting ceremony took place in the church of the Holy Trinity, New Westminster, when a beautiful pastoral staff was presented to the Bishop in the name of the clergy and communicants of the diocese, as a token of personal love and esteem, and with the sincere hope that it would be many years before it passed into the hands of another.

The Bishop accepted the staff, and having laid it upon the altar, dedicated it to the service of God. He then gave a short address to the congregation, which gathered up in a few words the ideal he held of the episcopal office, and which he faithfully, to the best of his power, endeavoured to fulfil.

At least from the fourth century, he stated, the pastoral staff had been by all branches of the Church accepted as the symbol of episcopal rule—a rule, not autocratic as by a rod of iron, but as defined by the proper meaning of the word *regula*, a straight edge. A pastoral staff consisted of three portions, the central being the rod signifying the Bishop's rule over the flock committed to his charge by the Chief Shepherd, by drawing the straight lines of the Church's faith once delivered to the saints, so that his charge might stay in the old paths and walk therein. Another portion, the crook, typified the duty of the Bishop to seek the lost ones wandering from the fold, and with love and sympathy and tenderness draw them once more into the Church; and also to guide those who otherwise might stray away into the world without. The third portion, the point, symbolized the most painful portion of the episcopal duty, the exercise of Church discipline. As the clergy and laity, he concluded, had of their own accord presented him with this staff after eight years of episcopal rule, he judged that it was a sign that his rule had been commendable to them.

CHAPTER XXI.

STEADY PROGRESS.

1888–1889.

THE year 1888, like 1887, was broken into by a visit to England, and it is only necessary here briefly to indicate its leading events. The very first day of the year was marked by the consecration of S. James' Church, Vancouver, built in the place of the building swept away by the great Vancouver fire. The Bishop's Confirmation tours were as numerous as ever, though compressed into a smaller portion of the year, and, these over, a start was made for England immediately after the meeting of synod in April.

The object of this visit was to attend the Lambeth Conference, of which it is only necessary to say that to our Bishop, as to every Churchman, the spectacle of one hundred and forty-five Bishops, assembled together from the ends of the earth, united by the tie of a common faith and a common purpose, was deeply impressive, and furnished emphatic testimony to the vigorous growth and practical unity of the Anglican Communion.

With regard to the remainder of the stay the Bishop writes—

"I was occupied, as last year, in visiting as many as possible of the parishes from which we derive most of our support, and this occupied me continuously during the months of August, September, and October."

The diocese was reached once more on November 11th, when the mountain church of Donald came into view, and as it was Sunday morning, the party was able, while the train waited, to join in a service of thanksgiving and praise. Unhappily, the Bishop came back not in the best of health, and in fighting sickness ended the year.

The work of the year 1889 was of a perfectly unexciting, if not absolutely humdrum character. The tenth year of an episcopate could hardly be so full of varied interest as the first, and as the Bishop had learned by this time the exact amount of work of which he and his staff were capable, all that he had to do was to do it, as well as under the circumstances was possible. But humdrum work, sometimes called drudgery, is not the less valuable because it fails to appeal to men's love of the sensational, so that if we here give but the barest *résumé* of the work of 1889, it is not because it was less important than that of the preceding nine, but because the ground has already been covered in former chapters.

In one way the year was well marked—in the increase that took place both in the number of clergy and of churches in the diocese.

On Sunday, January 13th, an ordination was held in Holy Trinity Church, New Westminster, when the Rev. W. B. Allen, of Chilliwhack, was ordained priest, and Mr. Wright admitted to the diaconate.

With fresh clergy fresh churches were not long in springing up. The new church at Donald, built amid the bracing air of the mountains by men who seem to have inhaled with that air the spirit to become pioneers in the Church's work, was consecrated by the Bishop on Sunday, February 24th, at a service the impressiveness of which remained long after as a stimulus to those who took part therein. The Bishop seems to have spoken on this occasion on the sacredness of the House of God with more than his usual force and fervour.

At Kamloops, too, a new church had been erected, to the unfeigned gratification of those who had worshipped so long in a barn. The first service was held in the new edifice on the same Sunday as witnessed the Consecration Service at Donald, and the Bishop was able to be present and hold a Confirmation on the following Wednesday.

Again, in Vancouver, while the new parish of Christ Church was developing rapidly, the Rector of S. James', so far from feeling his work narrowed by the loss of a portion of his old parish, succeeded in building two Mission churches at some distance from the mother-church—S. Michael's on Mount Pleasant, and S. Paul's on Hornby Street.

Thus new work was pushed forward on every hand, and the character of the Bishop's work, during the first half of the year, was that of continual itinerancy, confirming the work already achieved, and inspiring the clergy to fresh efforts in the future.

Soon after reaching home, from an extended tour in the Okanagan country, the Bishop called together his synod, and in his address touched on many of the points raised in the Lambeth Conference, and committees were appointed to deal with several of them. In the matter of forming a Provincial Synod for the whole of British Columbia, no practical result was so far attained, the diocese of Caledonia being in practice more distant from the other dioceses than some of the eastern sees.

The great event of the year, and one which was fraught with far-reaching consequences—to the parish of New Westminster advantageous, to the Bishop personally physically ruinous—was the exchange effected between Archdeacon Woods, Rector of Holy Trinity, and the Bishop; whereby the former became rector of the little suburban church of S. Mary's, Sapperton, and the latter assumed the responsibilities of the parish of Holy Trinity. To the Archdeacon it was the means of obtaining a much-needed rest, to the parish it was the means of having the Bishop constantly in its midst, and the parish church recognized as a quasi-cathedral; but to the Bishop himself it was the undertaking of a burden far too heavy for his strength, even assisted as he was, for the greater portion of his incumbency, by a staff of two curates.

But, for the time, the impetus given to the parochial work was immense. The Bishop entered upon his new duties as rector on July 19th, and Mr. Irwin became assistant-curate a week later. The old rectory building was demolished, and the contract let for the building of a new house, which should be the official residence of the Bishop.

Mrs. Sillitoe writes at the time—

"The Bishop has now, in addition to his episcopal work, the charge of the parish of New Westminster, and this keeps him very busy—in fact, far too busy—for whilst we are living a mile and a half distant from the church, it is difficult to get through all the work. Our new house in New Westminster is being built, but we shall not be able to get into it till Christmas. As it is built of wood, we can move in as soon as it is finished. Sorry as I shall be to leave our present home, the knowledge that if we lived here the work would be too much for the Bishop, reconciles me to the change. It will be very nice to have a new house, but I fear it will have the effect of making my belongings look very shabby."

Meanwhile, the new work did not prevent the

Photo: Thompson.]
VANCOUVER, LOOKING OVER TO BURRARD'S INLET AND MOODYVILLE.

Chaplain: Rev. H. Irwin.

Photo: Thompson.] Dogs:
Chinese servant: Sing. Piper, Grip, and Jingo. Chinese servant: Gin.

THE BISHOP'S HOUSEHOLD.

accomplishment of the usual episcopal duties, and this year, for the first time in three years, he was able to be present at the annual gathering of the Lytton Indians at Pootanie.

On November 1st (All Saints' Day) a landmark in the Bishop's work was reached in the completion of the tenth year of his episcopate.

The occasion was fitly marked by a special service in Holy Trinity Church on All Hallows E'en, when the Bishop summed up the encouragements and lessons of his ten years' work in a striking sermon from the text, "Of myself I can do nothing." A few days later, in memory of the same interesting event, a reception was tendered to the Bishop and Mrs. Sillitoe in the Opera House, which was of more than parochial interest, since representatives from many of the outlying districts attended to offer their congratulations.

It is a significant comment on this tenth anniversary which is furnished in the statistics of the close of this year. The Bishop was able thankfully to chronicle the receipt of a material increase of funds. In the parish of Christ Church, Vancouver, no less than $7000 was raised during the year. And on every hand there were signs that Churchpeople, naturally so slow in such matters, were beginning to realize the part they were called upon to play in building up the Church in the West. Dr. Sillitoe's ten years' unremitting toil, although not spent to obtain dazzling or immediate returns, had not failed in bringing forth much fruit to the glory of God and the service of man.

CHAPTER XXII.

PAROCHIAL WORK.

1890.

THE record of 1890, to correspond with the Bishop's dual position as Bishop and Rector, must consist of two stories: the one, describing his progress with the parish work of Holy Trinity, New Westminster, the other, his efforts to perform his episcopal duties.

To secure a closer touch with his new parish, the Bishop had felt the need of building a See House in the city, and it was an event of no little local interest, when, on April 16th, the removal was made from S. Mary's Mount. The "flitting" was effected by dint of hard work in one day, although the interior fittings were as yet incomplete. A Benediction Service was held in the house on the evening of April 23rd, to which were invited all the members of the Parish Workers' Association, to the number of nearly seventy. The house was open to visitors on three afternoons and evenings in the following week, and a large number of friends availed themselves of the opportunity of inspecting it.

No sooner had the Bishop secured a house for himself, than he determined also to secure a home for the various organizations which the parochial work necessitated. The Sunday School, Trinity Church Club, Sewing Guild, etc., were all practically homeless until the Bishop planned the erection of a hall, which, with good acoustic properties, should give to all the manifold agencies of the Church "a local habitation."

The hall, dedicated to S. Leonard—was completed and opened on June 3rd, with an inaugural concert given by the Choral Union, of which the Bishop was the leading spirit. What might be called the parochial inauguration took place on June 5th, when the Bishop gave an address of welcome, and spoke hopefully of the future usefulness of the new hall.

Moreover, the quickening of the Church's vitality in the neighbourhood of Holy Trinity Church did not prevent the claims of other portions of the city from coming under consideration. New Westminster was at this time growing in size and population daily, and like many western cities where the "real estate" is in the hands of a not over-generous few, growing more on the outskirts, where the land was comparatively cheap, than at the centre, where the purchase of corner-lots demanded capital.

Consequently, the small beginnings of a future new parish were made by the commencement of service in the West End School-House, kindly lent for the purpose by the school trustees. But activity in the parish in no way interfered with the visitation of the diocese, as this year we find even more places visited than usual, though we must resist the temptation to describe any of them.

CHAPTER XXIII.

WORK IN THE INDIAN MISSIONS.

1891.

At the end of 1890, the Bishop felt considerable perplexity as to the way in which the work of the diocese would go on in face of the various changes which the year had brought about.

"My report for 1890," he writes, "will not be one of unmixed satisfaction. Though there has been much to rejoice at, in growth and prosperity, there has been much sadness, on the other hand, at the departure from among us of some of the most devoted of our labourers. The loss in one year of Mr. Croucher, Mr. Small, who went to Corea, and Mr. Edwardes, who joined the Universities Mission to Central Africa, whose faithful service has extended over half the life of our diocese, seems at first sight almost like the irremediable break-up of our staff, and yet it is, I suppose, with the diocese as with the world at large, one drops out and another takes his place; a gap appears in the ranks, it is noticed for a moment, and in a moment more it is filled, and things go on as before, and we learn to see how God hath so ordered life and His Church that no one of us is necessary to the accomplishment of His purpose and plan. That plan is one, embracing all; and while each has his little part to play, it is his part only and no more, and his part ended, another is forthwith raised up, and the one plan progresses unbroken and undisturbed."

But there was, nevertheless, progress along the

whole line. The clerical staff was seventeen, as compared with fourteen a year ago; an increase of three also appears in the list of lay-readers, and a corresponding increase in Church members, communicants, baptisms, marriages, and offertories. The only decrease was in the number of comfirmees—chiefly among the Lytton Indians, where the resignation of Mr. Small created a vacancy very difficult to fill.

Indeed, the Bishop's great anxiety this year was with respect to the Indian Mission and the finding of a suitable successor to Mr. Small.

"The history of our Indian Mission," the Bishop writes, "has been a very broken one this year. The loss of Mr. Small was a difficult one to repair in any case, but we have hitherto been unsuccessful in finding a successor at all. I gave notice of the vacancy, many months ago, to my representative, in England; but though many applications were received, there were none that Mr. Mogg could entertain, and, but for Mr. Wright's willing devotion, we should have been landed in a very serious difficulty. As it is, he is working single-handed, with the help that I have been able to afford him from New Westminster.

"The Indian school at Yale," the Bishop continues, "has not only made that progress, which we have now come to regard as a matter of course, but we have also been able largely to extend its accommodation, by the addition of a new building at a cost of over $3500, towards which a grant was made by the Dominion Government of $1500."

Of the opening of this new wing we have an interesting account in a letter written by one of the sisters. From this letter we take the following extract:—

"His Lordship and Mrs. Sillitoe arrived on Monday, December 29, 1890, and, as only two days could be spared for Yale, we had to crowd a good deal into Tuesday. About 6 p.m. a large number of Indians began to assemble, marshalled by 'George,' our mission servant and interpreter, and waited in perfect order till the procession had formed in the hall. From thence it started; the Bishop in cope and mitre, preceded by Aimie, a little half-breed girl of twelve, as crossbearer, dressed, like her confirmed companions, in white veil and red pinafore. Another child came after the Bishop, carrying the school banner, then four choir-children, then the remainder of the school, the sisters, and finally a troop of Indians. The last, nearly seventy in number, walked in couples and in reverent order and silence. Upstairs wound the long procession, numbering just a hundred in all, singing the 67th Psalm, going first to the children's dormitory and infirmary, then downstairs again to the refectory and schoolroom, suitable prayers and responses being said in each; ending with a short service in the little chapel, where there was hardly standing room. It had been arranged that the Benediction was to be followed by the annual Christmas tree for our children, in which this year their compatriots were to have a share. It was quickly lighted, and the presents were distributed by the good Bishop and other kindly helpers, and then the tree was removed, and the dusky crowd comfortably seated for the magic lantern—an exhibition of English cathedrals and abbeys—shown by the Bishop, and explained to the Indian spectators by the interpreter."

Thus progress at Yale was gratifying enough, but meanwhile Lytton was a sore trial of faith and patience. Every month the appeal was made, and still remained apparently unanswered.

"No suitable priest has yet been found for the Indian work. There never was a clearer-voiced call, 'Come over and help us,' than is contained in the appeals from the diocese for a really earnest, devoted man. There is really work for three men, and now only one is keeping it going.

Photo: Thompson.]

YALE.

Photo: Thompson.]

ALL HALLOWS' SCHOOL.

The Indians will be scattered, and, amid the enticements of the Romans on the one hand, and the denunciation of the Salvationists on the other, these poor, childish people are sore let and hindered. Midst the thousands of single priests in England, who are not specially tied by the circumstances of their lot, surely one can be found to go forth to this great work. It means self-denial and hard work—it does not mean good pay—but it means a great sphere for showing devotion to our blessed Lord."

The enforced return of Dr. Pearce, the medical missionary, to England, just when his work was beginning to tell, made the outlook still more gloomy.

Mr. Wright, in bad health, was doing his utmost to cope with the difficulties of his position, but with a district two hundred and twenty miles long, it was impossible to do much. Moreover, Indian work specially needed personal care, or it was liable to develop in unexpected and undesirable directions. On one occasion Mr. Wright wrote—

"I have just heard of an Indian woman, who was supposed to have died and has come to life again just as she was being put into a coffin. I suppose, some trance. When she came to, she said she had been to a place where some people were miserable and some happy, and all the happy ones belonged to the Church of England! This has had a great effect upon the unbaptized Indians, who now say they are all coming to us. Great care will have to be exercised about their preparation for Baptism under such circumstances."

At last the welcome announcement was made, though not until near the close of the year—

"The senior priest's vacancy at Lytton is filled. God has answered our prayers, and in a way we least expected. The Rev. R. Small has offered to return to his old work, and the Bishop has readily accepted his offer.

Christmas, at latest, will see him back among the Indians, who so dearly love him. This is joyful news indeed, and let us not forget to thank God for His goodness. Mr. Small offered, of himself, to come back, as he heard his post was not filled, and the Bishop of Corea would not stand in his way. This action on the Bishop's part is most generous, and demands our gratitude. Thus the difficulty in regard to *one* vacancy is at an end. We still have to send out an earnest, devoted assistant to Mr. Small, either priest or deacon. He would have to live in the Mission House, and be ready to enter into the system of community life, which means some roughness and self-discipline."

To compensate for the lack of regular pastoral visitation from which the Lytton district suffered this year, the Bishop gave a considerable part of his own time to this particular branch of work.

A few extracts from letters will give some idea of what the work was.

Of the developments of the Mission and up-country districts, the Bishop writes—

"A railway is now being constructed from Sicamous to Enderby, and on past Lansdowne to Vernon on Lake Okanagan. This railway is bringing all these places into prominence, and opening up a district which, from a missionary point of view, is at the present moment as interesting as any we have. Enderby and Vernon are about twenty-five miles apart, Lansdowne lying between the two.

"At Lansdowne we have a church and a small parsonage; at Enderby the people are prepared to build, but have not determined which site to accept out of the several that have been offered; at Vernon the people are taking steps to obtain a site.

"Churches in these places are very unpretentious buildings, costing not more than £250, with a seating capacity of about a hundred, but even this apparently small amount is a considerable tax upon the few Church people who have to provide it, especially when it is remembered that they already contribute to the stipend of their clergy as well. . . .

"An incident of missionary life to close with. I heard of a dying man who wished to see a clergyman. He was in a hut or cabin eleven miles down the track. There was no train, nor any road, but the chief engineer of the line, who happened to be there, procured me a handcar and a crew to take me down and back. A handcar on a single line of railway, where freight trains run independently of time-tables, and where curves are as sharp as they have to be in this gorge of the Fraser river, is an exciting kind of travelling. In many places the track overhangs the river at a height of several hundred feet; at others it is carried over deep gullies or ravines on wooden trestles, of which our friends have seen illustrations in our lantern show, and the platform of a handcar, without a rail to hold on by, and five men occupying the space of about five feet square, is a position from which one can appreciate without effort the 'chances of this mortal life.' Without misadventure, however, my 'crew' covered the eleven miles in an hour.

"The sick man was a Churchman from the north of Ireland, who has been twenty years in this country, and has naturally lost sight of all old-country relations and friends. He is suffering from heart disease, and may be taken at any moment, and being dependent entirely upon chance visits of trackmen passing up and down the line for help, he more than probably will be alone at his death. I helped him as well as I could, and tried to persuade him to allow himself to be taken down to the coast, but he said he would rather die where he was than in a 'charity hospital,' and I am afraid he probably will."

"Temmelch Creek Camp,
"August 15, 1891.

"My dear Mogg,

"I shall not have time to send you a full account of our visit to the Indian district for publication in the

September *Record*, but you shall have a few lines by way of summary. This is our last camp, and I am waiting to commence work while the people are building a stone altar in the church tent. This is the first time we have had to revert to the ancient type of altar. Hitherto we have had a village church within reach, or have been able to procure a few boards for an altar table.

"Our camp here is three miles from the nearest village church or Indian ranch, but the rock about is all of a slaty character, and slabs of it are very convenient for our purpose. I have endeavoured to cover as much ground as possible in the trip, my first object having been to impress upon the Indians generally the fact that we had not abandoned them. . . . Consequently, we have 'gone forward' every two or three days, halting at convenient places for assembling the flock. At each camp we have had congregations of from fifty to sixty. Most days we have commenced with a celebration at 6.30 and taken three services during the day, for instruction, baptism, confirmation, etc. Once or twice the afternoons have been too hot to sit out in places where shade was not procurable, and our evening sessions have been prolonged by the light of the camp fire until long after dark.

"It is impossible to speak in terms of exaggeration of the attention and patience of these people. They simply never tire of instruction. Such responsiveness is the great charm of the work, and gives it an attraction which is certainly too often wanting in the missionary's experience among white people.

"All the more strongly, therefore, is borne in upon me the necessity for supplying the vacancy—the necessity for finding *the man* ordained of God to take up the work. . . ."

Here, too, are some extracts from Mrs. Sillitoe's vivid description of the same visitation.

"I am writing under difficulties, with a tiny gold pencil and my paper on my knee, under the shadow of the church. We are camped out near an Indian village on a dry, dusty, and exceedingly barren flat, under a burning sun, with not a tree nearer than on the steep mountain sides which surround us. I am hardly correct in calling this a barren flat, for on it thrives a vigorous growth of cactus, and with the utmost care one cannot go many yards without getting one's shoes full of the sharp prickles. One night in rolling over in bed I got my side full of them.

" . . . On Wednesday, July 29th, we drove down the waggon-road about fifteen miles, and after crossing the Thompson river in an exceedingly ramshackle canoe, and climbing the steep bank, we arrived at this our first camp, Pakyst. Meshell was there already, and had our tents pitched. As it was getting dusk, I lost no time in unpacking our blankets, and as on account of the great heat we needed none for covering, we had a less hard bed than would otherwise have been the case. After that we had our supper of bread and marmalade by the light of a candle, the candlestick consisting of three nails in the top of a piece of wood driven into the ground. After supper we retired to bed rather than to sleep, for a strong gale had sprung up, which threatened to carry our tent away, and in the course of the following day the threat was carried out, and I had to fly about in all directions gathering up my scattered belongings. We have stayed three whole days in this camp, and the programme has been much the same as at Ashcroft. . . .

"Pakyst was a comfortless, hot camp, and it was without any regret that we left it on Saturday, August 1st, walking three miles down the railway track to Spatsum station, while the tents and pack were sent on horses over the trail. The west-bound train was due at Spatsum at 3 a.m. on Sunday, and the long, weary night did we spend sitting on the platform; and as if that were not enough, the train was an hour and a half late, so not till 4.30 did we get away. Spatsum is only a flag station, and about ten o'clock the man in charge brought us a lantern, telling us to wave it, and he then retired. It was 6.30 on Sunday morning before we reached Lytton. . . . It seems impossible that animals on four legs can walk as slowly as these Indian horses do. Arrived in camp, we found lots of Indians ready to help, and in a wonderfully short time the tents were pitched, a thick carpet of brush laid, and it was just getting dusk when we sat down to our supper, spread on the ground in front of our tent. After supper the Bishop arranged for the next day's proceedings with the Indians, while I made up the bed. Then we sat down over the camp fire, admiring the dim outline of the surrounding mountains, and the picturesque encampment about two hundred yards away in a grove of large pine trees, everything looking weird and ghostlike in the light of three camp fires. Then the stillness was broken by the sound of a bell summoning to prayer, and the whole camp gathered, and the low monotony of the voices sounded not unmusical, and wonderfully solemn and impressive, borne to us on the evening breeze. The Indians are most regular in their attendance at the daily offering of prayer and praise, both morning and evening, but are not as diligent as they might be in teaching the prayers to their children and to those adults who have not managed to pick them up, and the Bishop has had to speak very seriously to them about this. At 10 p.m. we turn in, but alas! there are many disturbances. First of all, the camp fire spreads, a most dangerous proceeding during the dry, hot weather, and it has to be beaten out, and later on there is an ominous pitter-patter on the tent, increasing to a steady downpour, and the Bishop has to go outside and loosen the ropes. Then a careful look round is necessary, for if anything is touching the tent, in comes the wet; even the cabin bags had to be taken down.

"It was still raining at six o'clock next morning, and the celebration had to be postponed, as our second tent, used as a church tent, is only big enough for the altar, and the congregation has to be in the open. About ten o'clock the rain cleared off, but it had lost us a day, as we had intended moving on that afternoon. All the day the Bishop spent with the Indians, giving instruction, catechizing the children, conferring with the chiefs and watchmen, and there was besides the interesting ceremony of the election of two new watchmen.

"The following day, August 5th, we commenced with a celebration at 6.30, after which the horses were hunted up; but with all the haste possible we did not get away till 11.30, too late to allow of our reaching the next rendezvous, N'chakup Camp, the same day. So we rode about twelve miles, passing on our way an Indian lying in his tent, ill from the bite of a rattlesnake. These reptiles are said to be very numerous in these parts, but from the fact that recovery from the bite is possible if the right remedy be used in time, I imagine they are not so deadly as in other countries. I am afraid I shall shock you if I describe the remedy; but remember it is a case of life or death. The bite is usually on the foot or leg, and a tight string is at once tied above the wound to prevent as far as possible the circulation of the poison in the blood. After that the patient is dosed with raw spirit until the system becomes saturated. The poison causes intense pain, and it takes a long time for it to work its way out. As there is a strict law in force in British Columbia forbidding the sale of liquor to Indians except on an order from a clergyman, doctor, or J.P., it is no easy matter for them to obtain the required remedy in time. It is curious that the Indians, who are skilled in the use of herbs, should not yet have discovered an antidote. Our camping-ground on the night of the 5th was a most unpromising one—near the bed of the creek, with nothing but rocks and sand, and it was too late to allow of much brush being collected, so our bed was none too soft, and the tent was badly pitched, so did not entirely keep out the rain which fell during the night. Towards six o'clock in the evening we reached N'chakup Camp, leaving the proper trail about half a mile back. Oh, if you could have seen that last half-mile I think your hair would have stood on end! First we skirted round a sandy, gravelly bluff—the trail was, I am sure, not more than six inches wide, and at every step the horses sent the stones and sand rolling down the precipice. Then we started zig-zagging down the mountain side, and it was no easy matter to stick on the horses' backs. My contempt for Indian horses on a good road is unbounded, but in dangerous places and broken-away trails, my contempt changes to confidence and admiration.

"For grandeur of scenery N'chakup Camp is unrivalled; in other ways it was not well chosen. There was no shade and the ground was sandy. Certainly the Indians did their best for us, covering the sand with brush, and bringing cottonwood trees and planting them around, but the shade these threw was a very poor apology for the real article, and the inside of the tent during the day was like a furnace. Happily, the surrounding mountains are high, and the sun disappears at 5.30 p.m. It rises, however, at 6.30 a.m., and it is well to clear out of the tent as soon as possible after that.

"At N'chakup Camp we spent three whole days, and every moment of the Bishop's time, except what was grudgingly snatched for meals, was devoted to the Indians. . . . One afternoon we crossed the river in order that the Bishop might visit a sick child. The Fraser is extremely swift, and the boat had to be towed a long distance up the shore before the crossing was attempted. I have pretty strong nerves, and like being in a canoe; but this craft was an exceedingly cranky and leaky flat-bottomed boat, and was besides overloaded, and two or three times I thought we should have capsized. The sick child was lying under a kind of shelter made of rush mats. She was about seven years old, and did not look ill, but was lying quietly sleeping; and in this way her parents said she had been lying for the past three weeks, taking nothing but an occasional spoonful of cold water. We could give them but little advice, but sent them from the camp some condensed milk to mix with the water. Near the sick child sat an old Indian, stone blind, who was led forward to shake hands with us by his equally ancient spouse. A decrepit old pair they were, and not pleasant to look at. Our return journey across the river was not beset with so many dangers, as we were the only passengers, and pleasanter, as the sun had set.

"On Monday we were up early so as to start before the sun got hot; but although we breakfasted at 6.30, we did not get away till nine, and then rode on till 3 p.m. in such heat as I do not care to recall. Not wishing to repeat the experience, we started next day directly after breakfast, leaving the pack to follow, and succeeded in reaching Lytton at midday. Here, by a curious coincidence, we met the Sister Superior on her way back from England. We were four days late in returning to Lytton, and the Sister seven hours late, yet we arrived within ten minutes of each other. It was but poor hospitality we had to offer, as the house had been shut up for over a week, and we could not expect the pack for an hour or two, but in our delight everything else was forgotten. The afternoon, however, was not entirely devoted to talk, as there was plenty to be done. The camp kitchen had to be gone through and stores replenished, clothes had to be washed, and callers to be received.

"Next morning we were up at four so as to start the Sister off by the five-o'clock train, and by eight o'clock we were jogging down the road. We had now two additions to our party—Mali, one of the Indian girls from Yale, who was spending her holidays at Lytton; and Philip, the Lytton church servant, whose duty it was to shepherd the horses. His work proved no sinecure, for the horses were always trying to run home. In recommending him, Meshell said that although not very young, he was a capital worker, and could stay awake all night if we wished. As we had never curtailed the night's rest of any of our Indians, we considered the recommendation uncalled for. When, however, I found what an intense desire the horses evinced to return home, I could see that Philip had a good deal of staying awake to do;

and, poor man, he was not even allowed the peaceful enjoyment of the services, for every now and then there would be a stampede, and off would fly Philip in pursuit. Our camp that night and the following was at Staziani, at the foot of Jackass Mountain, not a hundred yards from the old Mission House. When the headquarters of the Indian Mission was moved to Lytton, the place was sold to an Indian, and looked well cared for. There was not time to get through all the work before midday on Friday, August 15th, when we left for our next camp, so the five couples to be married followed the Bishop down the road. On the way one of the watchmen met us to ask the Bishop to baptize a dying child, a little mite of three months old. Such a disappointment we had that day: we were riding a short distance ahead of the pack, and a bear crossed the road behind us, but in front of them, and we never saw it. Temmelch Creek was our last camp, where we stayed till the 19th. The ground was rough and rocky, but it was near a lovely creek full of delicious trout, which we greatly appreciated. We had intended breaking up camp on the 18th, but the Indians required so much instruction and preparation that we were obliged to stay an extra day. Very unfortunate it was for us, as all Monday it rained, and it was most troublesome work getting everything dry before packing up. We left behind a memorial of our camp in the altar which the Indians had built with the flat stones out of the creek. We had a most pleasant trip in the canoe across the Fraser, and then a steep climb up the bank on the other side brought us back to civilization in the shape of the C.P.R. Hotel at North Bend. On August 20th the Bishop, accompanied by Meshell only, went down to Spuzzum, and his day there brought the trip to a conclusion."

Of the other events of the year, the daily tasks at New Westminster and the routine of Confirmations in the country parishes, there is no need now to speak. Suffice it to say that, all things considered, the diocese was now in a condition to excite admiration and astonishment among those who knew the difficulties which had been encountered. The Rev. Allan Pitman, who stayed for some months of 1891, expresses in the *Mission Field* his delight in the work he saw proceeding. In concluding his article, he says—

"I cannot help it if these remarks seem too laudatory; they ought to have shown me something I could criticize. Or perhaps it is that the sun of that land, where it is always shining, where the air is always fresh, where the sound of the water falling, rushing, gliding, is ever within hearing, where all life seems freer, where the sadness of the Indian past is altogether obscured by the promise of a golden future—perhaps it is this and things like this which have made me strike the 'major' with never a note from the 'minor.' That I must leave to those who can play the whole piece; but I guarantee that any one who visits the diocese of New Westminster will be as startled and delighted as I was with the amount of work and love which must have been poured out on the diocese, and the rich return it has yielded."

CHAPTER XXIV.

ILLNESS AND WORK.

1892.

It was in this year that the illness began from which the Bishop never fully recovered. Just as the prospects of the diocese looked brighter than at any time since the foundation of the see, and all were looking forward to greater progress still, the mysterious *la grippe*, which had wrought such havoc in other lands, made its presence known in this distant western diocese, and violently attacked among the very first the Bishop, one of those who could least be spared from active life.

The Bishop's illness commenced at the beginning of February, and though he was able to be out two or three days at the beginning of March, he broke down again on March 5th, and was sent to bed again. He forced himself through a visit to Yale, and an ordination at S. James', Vancouver, on March 27th, and then got away again till April 8th for a few days' rest.

From this time onward, although the Bishop was by no means strong, the record of work shows little if any diminution from that of preceding years. Indeed, the Bishop seems to have gone over the greater portion of the diocese, including three visits to Nelson.

Of visits to Kamloops, Lytton, Ashcroft, Donald,

Golden, Vernon, Penticton, Surrey, and other places, it will not be necessary to say more than that they resembled the past visits which have already been described.

An interesting visit was also paid to Nelson, where the Bishop introduced the Rev. A. J. Reid to his new flock, and where vigorous signs of Church life showed themselves. Nelson is an important centre of a large and growing mining district.

The Bishop, later in the year, paid two other visits to this remote portion of his diocese, and had the satisfaction of seeing his plans rapidly and successfully developing.

One other incident in the itinerary of this year deserves more than passing mention, viz. the great Indian gathering at Hope. In itself the gathering was similar to those which took place at Pootanie in preceding years, but it had a special interest through the presence of the venerable Bishop of Columbia, Dr. George Hills, then on the eve of departure from the diocese he had ruled so indefatigably for thirty-five years, and of the Rev. J. B. Good, who was the Indian missionary in charge at the time of Bishop Sillitoe's appointment. Not only was it a great delight to the Bishop and Mr. Good to renew acquaintance with their old friends of the interior, but it was a great source of both delight and profit to the Indians to see once more among them those who had been in very truth their first fathers in God. It was a witness to them and to all of the continuity of the Church's work, and of that unity of faith which binds men together in every land in one "Communion of Saints."

It was shortly after this that the Bishop went out to meet Bishop Hills at Mission to speak on behalf of the diocese of New Westminster the words of farewell to its former chief pastor, and present him with an album, which would bring some of the old faces from time to time before his eyes.

It was a great comfort to the Bishop at this time to feel that his efforts in supplying ministrations to every part of the unwieldy diocese had not been altogether unproductive. Although by no means over-manned, the diocese was at this time better equipped with clergy than at any time since its formation.

The return of three former workers in the diocese, in the persons of Mr. Small, Mr. Edwardes, and Mr. Croucher, was a telling instance of the magnetic attraction possessed by New Westminster. Two new clergy were also admitted to the priesthood on March 27th, the Revs. E. F. Lacey and F. Yolland. Besides these, the Rev. A. J. Reid (as we have seen) came to take up the new work at Nelson, the Rev. A. R. Macduff from Lahore to work at Ashcroft, the Rev. A. A. Dorrell to fill the long-vacant vicarage of Trenant, and the writer of the present sketch to work at the cathedral and do other work in the city of New Westminster.

This other work included two new efforts upon which the Bishop had long set his heart, the evangelization of the Chinese and the establishment of a new district church in New Westminster.

The work among the Chinese, difficult and slow as it necessarily is, had been long crying out for support. In Vancouver and New Westminster the placid, persevering, long-suffering Celestials had been gathered in considerabe numbers, and scattered in smaller communities over the province, working in the cities as laundrymen, cooks, market-gardeners, and store-keepers, in the country places as miners, and along the Fraser taking their part in the important industry of catching and canning the salmon. There was, perhaps, on their part no consciousness of the need for mission work—indeed, there was little visible sign of their belief in any religion whatever—nor was there any great enthusiasm among the Church people of the diocese on behalf of a mission. Rather, sad it is to say, there was a sort of unchristian conviction that such a mission was a mistake and a needless waste of money. But, nevertheless, upon the Bishop's heart the responsibility weighed heavily, and he was glad indeed to find some one ready to take up the work.

Of that work it is not needful to write at length. Disappointing in some respects, small and feeble, perhaps, it has nevertheless done something to teach Church people the practical value of missionary work, to make known among the Chinese that the Church cares for *their* souls as well as for those of whites and Indians, and, at any rate, to be a kind of standing protest in the face of the world against a Christianity which regards the Chinaman as outside the pale of evangelistic work.

The centre of this work naturally gravitated to Vancouver, where the Chinese most do congregate. Here a school, for which the nucleus already existed in a class established by the Rev. H. Hobson, Rector of Christ Church, was organized, from which a Chinese catechist from Honolulu, Mr. S. Ten Yong, worked in a large circle, including the two principal cities of the mainland.

The work in connection with the West End Mission in New Westminster was easier and more immediately productive. The ground had lain as it were fallow, and the response of the people to the efforts made on their behalf was spontaneous and generous. Twice this year the Bishop came up to the little church to administer the rite of Confirmation. By the end of the year the necessity for enlargement had become pressing. To complete the mention of the work now, we may add that by the Easter of 1893 the church had been enlarged to three times its former size. By the end of 1893, from paying half the stipend of the clergyman in charge, it undertook the whole; and at Easter, 1894, only a month or two before the Bishop's death, it was constituted a new parish, under the name of S. Barnabas'.

To go back to 1892, we find the Bishop making one other effort towards supplying a religious education for boys. New premises were secured in Vancouver, and energetic efforts made to ensure success. But, apparently, success was not to be. So far the history of the diocese has shown that until the people generally care a great deal more for religious education than they do at present, it is hopeless to attempt to compete with the public school system. Perhaps some other way will have to be found to make religion a part of an ordinary education, which need not involve the costly experiment of separate schools.

At any rate, this effort shared the fate of its predecessors, and died a natural death in the course of a few months.

Another matter, however, which had long been on the Bishop's mind, was brought to a satisfactory consummation. This was the constitution of Holy Trinity Church, New Westminster, as the Cathedral Church of the diocese.

A committee had been appointed in October, 1891, to draw up the constitution and agreement between the Bishop and the Vestry of Holy Trinity Parish. After long and thoughtful discussion, and much labour in studying the constitution of other cathedrals, the task was brought to a happy conclusion, and on September 28, 1892, the Vestry of Holy Trinity Church passed the following resolution, accepting the conditions laid down by the Bishop:—

"RESOLVED that this vestry consents to the said constitution and ordination of Holy Trinity Church as the Cathedral Church of this Diocese; and agrees to the conditions set forth in the said agreement, and authorizes the Rector and Churchwardens to sign the same on its behalf."

The following is a copy of the deed of constitution:—

"To all to whom these presents shall come,

"ACTON WINDEYER, by Divine permission, Bishop of New Westminster, in the Name of the Father, and of the Son, and of the Holy Ghost, greeting.

"Whereas it hath ever been by authority of Holy Scripture and of the Primitive Church, an ancient custom to establish new Bishoprics in populous cities, more easily resorted to by the inhabitants of the Dioceses, or in the seats of civil governments, or ancient capitals, of states or provinces,

"And whereas, upon the division of the Diocese of British Columbia, a new see was created under the name or title of New Westminster, which said city of New Westminster was then the sole city within the limits of the new diocese, and was, and still is, the seat of the County Government of the District of New Westminster, and the original capital of the Colony of British Columbia,

"And whereas Her Majesty, by and with the advice and consent and Vestry, they hereunto consenting, appropriate and attach to the see and Bishopric of New Westminster, the Rectory and Rectorship of the said parish church of the Holy Trinity, reserving always to us and our successors our Episcopal rights,

"Moreover, it is hereby expressly provided, that certain conditions contained in the resolution of the vestry meeting held on the 28th day of September, one thousand eight hundred and ninety-two beforementioned, shall be formulated in an agreement, which shall be signed by us, and by the Rector and Churchwardens of the parish of the Holy Trinity, before thirty days next ensuing from the date of these presents shall have expired and the said conditions shall be faithfully observed and performed at all times hereafter, otherwise these presents shall be void and have no effect.

"In witness whereof we the said Bishop have hereunto set our hand and Episcopal seal on the fourteenth day of October, in the year of our Lord, one thousand eight hundred and ninety-two, and of our consecration the thirteenth.

"(Signed) A. W. New Westminster.

"E. M. N. Woods }
E. A. Jenns } Witnesses." [Seal.]

Of this year's meeting of synod there is nothing which calls for special mention. It was held in New Westminster on November 16th and 17th, was largely attended, and harmoniously conducted. The principal reference in the Bishop's address was to the constitution of the cathedral which is described above.

It was a subject of congratulation to the Bishop that in spite of the drawback of his illness the diocese had made such progress both in the number of its clergy and the results of their work. This thought finds emphatic expression in the Bishop's summary of the year's work.

Profiting by this knowledge, and by the desire to make the diocese and its needs better known to the Dominion of Canada generally, the Bishop accepted an invitation from the Domestic and Foreign Missionary Society of Canada to visit in the following spring the principal cities in the eastern provinces, to lecture upon the work and needs of the Church in the Far West. Of this visit we shall speak briefly in the next chapter.

CHAPTER XXV.

TOUR IN EASTERN CANADA AND GENERAL SYNOD.

1893.

THE first day of 1893 saw the Bishop enthroned in his newly constituted cathedral. The ceremony took place after the *Te Deum* at Mattins, and was conducted by the Archdeacon of Columbia, who at the same time was installed as Canon in the chair of St. Nicolas. The episcopal throne was subscribed for by the ladies of Holy Trinity Church, and is a beautiful piece of work, of oak, and nicely carved.

As mentioned in the last chapter, a promise had been given by the Bishop to visit Eastern Canada on behalf of the Domestic and Foreign Missionary Society. The tour commenced in weather such as, fortunately, British Columbia does not often see, but a letter of Mrs. Sillitoe's, dated April 13th, will give a fair outline of the trip:—

"MY DEAR FRIENDS,

". . . When we left on February 4th there was, beside the cold, a heavy snowfall, and we had not proceeded many miles on our journey before we began to be delayed. We were, in spite of all delays, comparatively fortunate, for before we had been twenty-eight hours on the road we had caught up with the trains which had left the day before and the day but one before us. At Donald we were all moved into the first train, and instead of being almost the sole occupants of the Pullman, we had rather a crowded car. From Donald we made slow progress, the train having to be sent on in sections, in spite of our having two engines, and by breakfast-time on Monday morning we were only at Field, which we should have reached on the previous evening in time for supper. From Field up to the summit of the pass to the Rockies, a distance of seven miles up a very steep grade, we had four engines, one of which, 'Jumbo' by name, is an unusually powerful one, used for pushing the trains up this grade. But, although we had four engines and only six cars on the train, the cold was so intense that the wheels would not grip the rails, and it took us over an hour to make the ascent. The scenery was never seen to better advantage; there had been an unusually heavy snowfall, and the sun was shining brightly, the sky of an unclouded and dazzling blue. We spent all day in the Rockies, being delayed at every station with thawing out frozen pipes, and also in repairing the mail car, the back of which had been pushed out in the struggle up the steep ascent. Tuesday morning found us steaming over the plains of the North-West, which look terribly monotonous in an unbroken expanse of snow as far as the eye could see. Our only excitement was caused by herds of antelope, which were often seen quite close to the line. Swift Current, where we stayed for twenty minutes, was the coldest place I have ever been in; indeed, so cold was it that, although we went out for a walk, we had to hurry back again to the car, not being able to stand it. I do not know what the temperature was the day we passed through, but for several days before the thermometer had stood at 65° below zero, and with a blizzard blowing at the time it was impossible to venture out. One poor man who went a short distance to report a train snowed up got frozen to death, and was found stiff in an upright condition. To give you an idea of what such cold is, going out in it makes one's eyes water, and each tear immediately becomes solid ice. In

Winnipeg we were delayed five hours in order to be joined with the train that left Vancouver twenty-four hours after us. We walked up to the hotel for dinner, a distance of about one and a half miles; and although it was only 35° below zero, I got my cheeks very sore. From Winnipeg on nothing of importance happened. As we were bound for Toronto, we had to change cars at North Bay, and, unfortunately, instead of the change taking place at 6 p.m., as it should have done, it came at 4 a.m. We reached Toronto at 2 a.m. on Saturday, thirty-three hours late, and we had been travelling since 2.30 p.m. on the previous Saturday. We were the guests of the Bishop and Mrs. Sweatman, and as we had been expected early the previous morning they had arranged for a large 'At Home' from four to six that afternoon. Happily we reached the house in time for it. The next day the Bishop preached in the morning at St. Thomas', and in the evening at St. Alban's Cathedral, holding meetings during the week both in Toronto and Guelph. The second Sunday we spent in Hamilton, returning again to Toronto for more meetings. In Canada there is a wonderfully useful organization of women called the Women's Auxiliary to the Domestic and Foreign Mission Board, a branch of which is to be found in almost every parish. The wonderful organization of this body makes it a very powerful auxiliary to the Church. Wherever we went I addressed meetings of the Women's Auxiliary, so as in some measure to relieve the Bishop. Our third Sunday was spent in London, Ontario. It is most amusing how they have tried to copy in every way the older namesake. The Bishop, for instance, preached in the morning at St. Paul's Cathedral, on Monday we drove through Piccadilly, and over the River Thames across Westminster Bridge. During the week we visited Brantford and Port Hope, and by Sunday reached Montreal.

"From Montreal we went to Richmond, Quebec, Lennoxville (the Church boys' school and college for the diocese of Quebec), Sherbrooke, Kempville, and finally

Ottawa. We should have visited three more towns, but in Ottawa the Bishop became so ill that the doctor forbade further work, and he was obliged to cancel his three last engagements. We stayed nearly a week at Ottawa, and at the end of that time got permission from the doctor to start off home. Unfortunate permission, as it proved, for either the Bishop was worse than the doctor realized, or else he caught fresh cold leaving. He was very ill all the journey home, and on arriving our doctor pronounced him to be suffering from pneumonia, and sent him straight off to bed, where he still is, though that is more than a fortnight ago; and although he is now on the mend, his progress is very slow."

From the effects of this illness the Bishop never really recovered, and although with indomitable will he persisted in rising to the call of duty, it was obvious that every effort was made painfully and laboriously.

These efforts, however, were by no means few or far between. The combined labour as Bishop and as rector of Holy Trinity was enough to take the strength of the most vigorous of men, yet the Bishop's illness was not permitted to interfere with the arrangements for Confirmations made in all parts of the diocese. A visit to the Kootenay country is, under no circumstances, an easy one to take, yet in order to introduce the Rev. H. S. Akehurst—who had come to succeed Mr. Reid—to his flock, the Bishop once again made the acquaintance of Nelson, at the beginning of August. The following account is given in the *Gazette:*—

"The Bishop left home on Monday, August 7th, and travelled direct to Field, the most easterly point in the diocese, on the railway line, exactly five hundred miles from New Westminster. The Rev. J. C. Kemm met the

Bishop at Field, and a service had been arranged for the evening of the 8th, which was held in the C.P.R. Reading Room, and was well attended. ... While the Bishop was at Field, the Rev. H. S. Akehurst arrived from Qu'Appelle, and after a stop over of a day, proceeded with the Bishop by way of Revelstoke and the Columbia river to Nelson, where the party arrived on the evening of the 10th. Friday and Saturday were occupied in calling upon members of the congregation in Nelson, and on Sunday services were resumed for the first time since the departure of Mr. Reid. The Bishop celebrated Holy Communion at 8 a.m., and preached both morning and evening, Mr. Akehurst taking the rest of the service. Nelson maintained its reputation for excellent choir singing, and the services, especially in the evening, were very hearty. On Monday evening a social meeting was held, at which the Bishop formally introduced Mr. Akehurst, and an address of welcome was presented to him on behalf of the congregation. . . . After five days spent at Nelson, the Bishop with Mrs. Sillitoe and Mr. Akehurst started to visit other points on Kootenay Lake. Numerically these 'points' are many, for the real estate fiend has blocked out town sites every few miles without regard to anything but his own aggrandisement, a feat in which he is only too successful, for it is no exaggeration to say that one-tenth of the money sunk by the unwary investor in those embryo cities that will never be born could have accomplished such a development of mineral resources of the district as would have advanced by many years the prosperity both of the country and of the investors themselves. There are, for example, largely advertised 'towns' on the lake which consist of a shack and a tent or two. There are 'towns' where instead of new buildings going up, the existing buildings are being torn down to be removed elsewhere. And yet the maps of these 'towns' are to be seen posted in every real estate office throughout the land, and lots are being sold at prices which will certainly never be warranted during the present century. It is waste of breath probably to preach caution to the man to whom the hope is held out of cent per cent on the purchase of a town lot, but it would be largely in his interest if a fee, say of $1000, were required for the registration of a map of a new town site. Such a fee would have relieved the country of most of the *bogus* town sites that exist, and would have saved many thousands of dollars to the pockets of a too-confiding public.

"Kaslo, however, forms an exception to this criticism. It has taken hold, and has evidently 'come to stay.' The site itself is convenient and spacious, the buildings substantial, and the stores furnished in a manner equal to any in the province. The growth of this town has been phenomenal. In June, 1892, it had no existence, in October it had a population of 3000. Since then it has been overshadowed by the cloud of the 'silver question,' and having been caught in the very bud of its youthfulness, it has felt the check more seriously than older places have done. Nevertheless its very youthfulness, when the reaction sets in, will give it opportunities of vigorous revival above places of maturer development. . . .

"Friday and Saturday were employed in visiting the people and making arrangements for Sunday's services. The only church at present is one built for the Presbyterians, which was kindly placed at the disposal of the Bishop. A celebration of Holy Communion was held in a private house, and services in the church at 11 and 7.30. A large congregation attended in the morning, but in the evening the building was packed with over two hundred people, many having to stand throughout the service. It was impossible to estimate the proportion of Church people present, but there is good ground for believing that they form the most numerous body in the town. At a business meeting presided over by the Bishop, the vestry was organized, and an undertaking given that $30 a month could be contributed to the stipend fund. For the present a room will be hired for the use of the congregation, and no attempt will be made to build before next year. The Town Site Company have made an offer of one hundred feet square for a church, but no selection has as yet been made. A further offer was made to the Bishop of a five-acre block for hospital or school purposes, objects which must be delayed until church accommodation is provided.

"On the return journey Lytton was visited again."

This visit to Lytton had a special object, which was nothing less than the consummation of a three years' endeavour to provide a Church hospital for Indians.

As long ago as 1890 Miss Rosetta Lansdowne of Manchester, a devoted friend of the Mission, had appealed for funds for such an institution. In the course of this appeal she wrote—

"On being admitted to Christ's religion in Holy Baptism an Indian is required to renounce many of his old customs; among these, and perhaps the hardest of all, is to give up the medicine-man. These men are supposed to possess supernatural powers. He pretends to go in search of the spirit of the sick person in order to fetch it back. Having succeeded in this, he places it in the body of the patient, after which he is expected to recover. The mode of proceeding is to cover his head with a piece of rush matting to prevent his seeing, then to use the incantations—dancing, howling, and singing. When he has found the spirit he replaces it, dipping his hands into a basin of cold water, and then passing them round the face of the sick person, keeping up a continual muttering. In cases of extreme danger three or four men act together, on the principle that unity is strength. I suppose what we should call 'public opinion' is on the side of the medicine-man, and we all know the strength of that in England. When therefore we are told that 'the first adult publicly baptized by the Bishop, though prostrated by sickness for several months, has resolutely refused the offers of the medicine-man and the solicitations of his friends,' we may feel that it has been 'a triumph of faith.' A fully qualified medical man, Dr. A. Pearse, went out as medical missionary, November, 1888, the S.P.C.K. having promised the Bishop a stipend for him of £150 for the first year, and £100 for the second and third. He writes, 'The Indians are subject to many of the worst constitutional diseases, more particularly to consumption, which often runs a rapid course; and from the same causes, together with dirt and injury, the eyes frequently suffer. During the past five months I have attended about a hundred and fifty cases of illness, and the result of my efforts so far gives me great encouragement. They have no idea of cleanliness, or of making a poultice or dressing a wound, though they are quite willing to submit to treatment. A small hospital placed at some central point would help our work very much.'"

Miss Lansdowne gradually accumulated a sum of $500, to which the Bishop added $100 collected during his eastern tour, and a grant of $500 obtained from the Indian department at Ottawa. This amount covered the cost of building, while various friends in the diocese contributed sums towards the furnishing, and Sister Frances, of S. Luke's Home, Vancouver, gave valuable help in superintending the furnishing and supplying a nurse.

It was, therefore, a source of great gratification to the Bishop, so familiar with the trials of sickness himself, to declare open this House of Refuge for the sick Indians of the district, who, however superstitious, ignorant, and uncivilized, were yet members of the same great family of the All-Father.

The opening took place on August 26th, and is thus described—

"A large gathering of the white and Indian inhabitants of Lytton and the neighbourhood took part

Photo: Thompson.]

LYTTON

S. PAUL'S MISSION HOUSE AND INDIAN HOSPITAL, LYTTON.

in the opening of the new Indian hospital on Saturday evening in the Mission grounds. The Benediction of the building was performed by the Lord Bishop of New Westminster, assisted by the clergy of the Mission and the Rector of Esquimalt. A procession, consisting of the clergy, acolytes, the Bishop, vested in cope and mitre, and the visitors, passed round the hospital, singing Ps. xviii., after which the various wards and offices of the house were visited, and special prayers said in each. Subsequently the visitors were entertained at the hospital in a most pleasant way by Sister Frances, who has kindly consented to undertake the work in connection with the hospital for some time. The little building is an ornament to Lytton, and reflects great credit upon all who have so generously given help towards its construction and support, both in money and kind, and also upon Mr. E. Disney, the builder.

"In one day Sister Frances, assisted by a band of willing helpers, had converted the empty building into a model cottage hospital."

No sooner had the Bishop arrived home from Lytton than it was time for him to leave again to attend the General Synod of the Canadian Church in Toronto. After the trying journey in the spring, and the exertions necessary after his recovery, it was really more than the Bishop should have undertaken, but his energy deceived not only all around him, but himself also, and he went.

The following letter and its prefatory note from the *Monthly Record*, published in England, shows this to have been the case:—

"Since the last publication of the *Monthly Record*, the Bishop's health has been gradually restored, and, with great thankfulness to Almighty God, a complete recovery can now be announced to his friends.

"It appears to have been a far more serious attack than we at home thought it to be, and it makes us all the more thankful that he has been spared to carry on the important work of the diocese at a very critical time. From all accounts, there seldom, if ever, has been a more depressed state of commerce in the colony; and the Church suffers. An extract from a letter lately received from the Bishop gives a graphic account of the present situation—

"'New Westminster, B.C.,
"'September 7, 1893.

"'MY DEAR MOGG,

"'Before I leave for Toronto, to attend the meeting of the General Synod, I must get a letter written for the October meeting of the committee. I cannot sufficiently thank you all for many kind expressions of sympathy, as well as for the forbearance which spared me the trouble of letter writing when I was unequal to it.

"'This year has been quite the most trying of my episcopate, personally and officially. My terrible journey through the eastern provinces in February, March, and April was in itself labour enough for a year, as my subsequent illness testified. In that time I travelled nearly ten thousand miles, preaching every Sunday twice, and sometimes three times, and lecturing afternoons and evenings nearly every day but Saturday. There was little wonder I came home a wreck. That God granted me recovery is, I venture to hope, a sign that my work for Him is not yet done.

"'But apart from personal labour and trial, the year has been throughout the province the most disastrous in its history. There has been, comparatively, no business done. The lumber trade is at a standstill; mining is unprofitable on account of the silver crisis; large numbers of people have been compelled to leave, being unable to gain a livelihood. In every town in the province there are hundreds of houses unoccupied and stores unlet. To give you an illustration—the Endowment Fund of the Bishopric includes five stores or shops in New Westminster. Two are empty, the tenant of one has paid no rent this year as yet, and I have had to reduce the rent of the other two to $35 a month, in place of $60 they were paying two years ago. .

"'Happily the salmon-canning industry has had a good year—a better one, indeed, than has ever been known. The fish have been running prodigiously, and kept running during the whole open season. But we must wait for a general revival of trade before we can expect a general improvement. Meanwhile, the Church is the first to suffer. Offertories have diminished one half, and there is not a parish in the diocese which has not difficulty in meeting expenses. I have collected literally nothing this year for the Diocesan Fund, and but for what I collected in the east, our Chinese work must have been suspended. I worked chiefly for that and the Indian hospital. . . . The question of maintenance now arises.'"

To reach Toronto in time for the General Synod, which opened on September 13th, the Bishop had to hurry his up-country visits; but he reached the synod in time, and took an important part in its deliberations.

It is impossible yet to estimate rightly the importance of this historic gathering. The attainment of the consolidation of the whole Church in Canada, from the Atlantic to the Pacific, the creation of the two Archbishoprics of Canada and Rupertsland, are in themselves sufficient to mark an epoch in the Colonial Church. That men of varying and even opposing schools of thought should alike sink their differences and hail consolidation was a notable sign of the times in Canada. A deadlock was indeed threatened on one occasion, and it is to the credit and honour of the Bishop of New Westminster that he played no small part in composing the differences that threatened to render the meeting of the synod a failure.

At the thanksgiving service held at the close of the synod the sermon was preached by Bishop Sillitoe from Eph. iii. 20, 21, and in a few words at the beginning of his discourse he well gathered up the reasons for thankfulness as to the past and joyful anticipation as to the future.

"What," he asked, "is the work that we have accomplished? We call it the consolidation of the Church in the Dominion of Canada. Three years have been spent in preparation for this—three years of patient deliberation and communion of minds and hearts, consummated in the act of the past week, which has welded together the scattered fragments of which the Church in the Dominion has been hitherto composed. And we are here to praise and thank our God for what He has enabled us to do. And rightly and properly so. But the thought that is in my heart at the present moment, and with which I desire to inspire your minds as well, is a thought of the insignificance of that which we have accomplished in comparison with the possibilities of the grace and power of the Holy Spirit. It is a fault of our nature to be satisfied in spiritual attainment, and the fault is equivalent to a limiting of Divine grace and power. Search the universe, and you will never find a halting-place. Forward! Onward! is the eternal law, and it is the law of the unseen world as much as of the seen. It is a law of the spiritual world as much as of the natural. It is a law of Christ, it is the law of the individual soul. Human ends may be attained, human aims may be accomplished, but myriads of efforts could not exhaust the immeasurable grace of God. 'God is able to do exceeding abundantly above all that we ask or think, according to His power that worketh in us.' What a limitless field is opened to us here! What an expanse of opportunity! How is it possible for the thought of attainment to enter in? Here is association with the Infinite, association with the Omnipotent! We marvel at the achievements of scientific research in the application of steam and electricity to the uses of men. What are these in comparison with the power of grace which God has given us by the Spirit through the Church?"

The Archbishop of Rupertsland, in addressing his synod a year or two ago, spoke gratefully of the assistance Bishop Sillitoe had rendered in word and action towards bringing the first General Synod of the Canadian Church to a successful issue.

In a similar manner, the Bishop of Nova Scotia bore testimony before his synod at Halifax.

"Well do I recall," said the Bishop, "his strenuous endeavour to avoid not only the impending deadlock, but the threatened failure to consummate the consolidation of the Church, when the Bishops and elected delegates met in the city of Toronto in September last; for it was largely owing to his pleading with his fellow-Bishops, and his advocacy of a conciliatory attitude towards those whom some of us looked upon as taking a position unwarranted by facts, that harmony was restored, and peace came to cement and perfect our union."

Commenting on this, the Canadian *Church Guardian* says—

"We feel sure that every one who took part in that historic meeting will be glad to find this now open tribute paid to the late Lord Bishop of New Westminster, whose strong personality and wise judgment, as well as winning manner, impressed itself upon all who were present, and won so great a benefit for the Church in Canada."

And had the Bishop done nothing more for Christ and His Church, he would not have departed this life with scanty sheaves of harvest for the Master's garner.

But the labour went on, in spite of almost continuous sickness. Confirmations at Penticton and Vernon were held on his way home. Arrived home, there was a meeting of the Diocesan Synod to be faced, with all its attendant anxieties.

It met, the Bishop's last synod, on November 15th and 16th, but, owing to the Bishop's illness and inability to leave his room, the session was constituted by a *quorum* meeting in the Bishop's library. This being done, the synod resolved itself into committee of the whole to debate the subjects set down upon the agenda paper. After the discussions were completed, the reports were presented again to the Bishop in his room, and the synod adjourned, many feeling that the Bishop had bravely and from a sense of duty subjected himself to a strain which was physically beyond his powers. But his willingness thus to endure enabled the diocesan business to be carried on, and the votes of sympathy and thanks passed to him and Mrs. Sillitoe were no mere formal expressions of feeling.

Thus concluded the practical work of a year which the Bishop may well have felt to be the most laborious in his episcopate, including, as it did, two difficult and tiring journeys to the east in the interests, not of his own diocese alone, but of the whole Church of Canada, and indeed of the whole Church of God.

Photo: Alfred Ellis and Walery.]

A LATER PORTRAIT OF THE BISHOP.

CHAPTER XXVI.

IN HARNESS TO THE LAST.

1894.

AT the beginning of this year the Bishop was hopeful that his illness was over and that the opportunity of vigorous work had returned.

But others were not so hopeful, and even the English committee, though far away from him, were not reassured by the bright optimism of his letters. In February Mr. Mogg writes—

"The committee, knowing the state of things, begged him to give up for some months, and an offer was made to meet the expenses attending an entire rest. His answer overflowed with gratitude; he pointed out the difficulties of leaving, and continued, 'I cannot go away until I have given the parishes the opportunity of Confirmations. . . . We must try and make up for the falling off last year. Again, I do not think I *need* go away for six months. I am now very well, my only trouble some symptom in my heart, which last year's attacks seem to have left rather shaky; but quiet, and, above all, peace of mind, are the best relief for this.' He felt, whether wisely or unwisely, he could *not* give in. God had placed him in his responsible position, and as long as any strength remained, he would be at his post and fight on with undiminished hope. This was emphatically his character."

So, weak as he was, he started out on his round of Confirmations.

First of all, he visited Trenant to hold Confirmation there. This passed off happily, and the Bishop greatly cheered the vicar in his difficult work during the short stay he made before proceeding to Victoria. Immediately after this, with completest self-forgetfulness, he went off to Tacoma, Washington, to officiate at the funeral of his old friend, Bishop Paddock. He little dreamed that in three months Bishop Paddock's successor would act in a similar capacity beside his own grave.

On returning home to New Westminster he had at once to leave for a Confirmation at Kamloops, arriving early in the morning after a whole night's travelling, and returning again the night following. On Palm Sunday, though feeling very ill, he took the early celebration at the cathedral, and morning service with sermon, and then went over to Vancouver for a Confirmation at S. Paul's. Here he broke down, and was compelled to omit the usual address after the laying on of hands. Taking the Rector of S. Paul's back with him, to officiate for him in his stead at the cathedral (for at this time the Bishop was taking the cathedral services almost single-handed), he returned to New Westminster, and was at once ordered to bed. Here he remained over Easter, and was prevented from fulfilling various Confirmation engagements for Holy Week.

But as soon as he was the least bit stronger he moved up to Lytton, believing that the bracing air, which he had always found so beneficial before, would suffice to restore him. Lytton had always been a favourite resting-place for him.

The Rev. H. Edwardes, writing of this visit, says—

"It was my privilege to have the Bishop and Mrs. Sillitoe as my guests shortly before his death. He came to Lytton, which place he always loved, despite its evil winds, hoping to build up his health again, but day by day we could see there was no improvement, and that he was growing weaker and more nervous and sleepless. But he still struggled daily with the work of his diocese, and with miserable worrying difficulties which would follow him, dictating his letters to me when he was utterly unfit for any worry, or work, or correspondence at all."

Meanwhile, he had determined upon the cutting off of one great source of labour and worry in the resignation of his post as Rector of Holy Trinity, New Westminster. That post he had accepted under circumstances which entitled him to believe that it would be to the great advantage of the parish. This it undoubtedly proved, but the double work, and its attendant worry, was fatal to himself, and for some time his resignation had appeared inevitable.

Early in the year he had written in his report—

"It is already, I think, generally known that I have determined to divest myself of the office of rector of the parish. I had anticipated that it would be possible to hold the office nominally, while the duties should be performed by a deputy, but I have learned that there is more in a name than I had thought; and having convinced myself that the parish could be better served by an actual rector permanently resident, I am now about making such an appointment. What little hesitancy I may feel in taking what appears to be a retrogressive action in this matter is amply compensated for by the satisfaction of having accomplished the work of establishing so successful a mission in the parish as St. Barnabas', the consummation of which work I still hope to see in the elevation of the Mission into independent parochial life before I lay down my office."

Both these wishes were realized at Eastertide, when the Rev. A. Shildrick, late incumbent of Kamloops, was licensed to the Rectory of Holy Trinity, and the Mission district of S. Barnabas' was constituted a separate parish under the present writer.

Leaving Lytton on May 5th, the Bishop once more set out for the coast for Confirmations at Vancouver and New Westminster. The journey was managed better than had been expected, but a very bad night followed with no sleep. The Confirmation at S. Michael's, Vancouver, was successfully administered, and a second one at Christ Church, although the Bishop's voice sounded very weary. In the evening he left for New Westminster, and again a sleepless night followed, with a sense of weakness in the morning. Several hours' rest during the next day enabled him to confirm at the cathedral in the evening for the two parishes of S. Mary's, Sapperton, and S. Barnabas', New Westminster, and on the 8th he left again for Lytton.

Mr. Edwardes writes—

"He returned to Lytton decidedly worse after the excitement and exertion of services, confirmations, and worrying meetings in New Westminster. A number of Indians had been prepared for Confirmation, and so again he braced himself up to give them the precious Gift. On Whit Sunday we had all ready for him at the Indian Church by 8.50 a.m., when he came to the door supported by Mrs. Sillitoe. The Indian churchwardens and sidesmen received him, and the big congregation rose as he entered. It was a touching and anxious service for all of us, a service full of self-sacrifice, for he could hardly get through it, and his words to the confirmed Indians were very brief and to the point. We are proud and thankful that his last public act of service was for the poorest and most ignorant, but by no means least loved, of his scattered flock.

"He had intended to celebrate the Holy Eucharist later that morning in the Lytton Chapel for the white people, but was utterly unable to do so. . . . The last time he celebrated the Holy Mysteries was at the altar in the little Mission Chapel on Ascension Day. On Monday in Whitsuntide he left us for Yale by the doctor's orders, and the end came rapidly after that. Compared with the terrible time of suffering which clouded his last days, the time at Lytton was for him a season of rest and peace, and for that we are thankful indeed."

Removed to Yale, he became decidedly worse, with sickness off and on during the day, followed by sleepless nights. It was, says an account written shortly afterwards—

"A time of terrible sufferings, a literal fighting for breath. His almost ceaseless cry was, 'O God, help me!' At other times he would be whispering prayers, and at one of the worst attacks he repeated aloud a psalm of praise. This continued till Sunday, May 27th, and his delirious condition seemed hopeless. The parsonage at Yale, where the Bishop stayed, is close to the church, and on Trinity Sunday, as he sat in his bedroom with Mrs. Sillitoe, he followed Mattins and Evensong, joining in all the responses. During some of the periods of delirium the only thing that soothed him was the reading of psalms and chapters of Holy Scripture by the hour together. The doctors had now ascertained the real cause of his malady, which they held to be incurable. With their consent, Mrs. Sillitoe telegraphed to Victoria for the Bishop's old friend and medical attendant, Dr. Hanington. He came and remained several days, during which he fought the terrible blood-poisoning, superintending the nursing himself. After five days an improvement manifested itself, and there was a return to consciousness. Again the doctor's untiring efforts brought him through a collapse from extreme weakness which had all but taken him away. It was during this time that accounts reached New Westminster of his serious condition. The Archdeacon thus writes of it: 'Then there came a time of almost unbearable anxiety to us all here. The river rose in a few days, owing to the rapid melting of the snow on the mountains, to such a height that railway bridges, permanent way, telegraph lines were so injured that traffic was interrupted and telegrams could not be forwarded; so that, though we knew of his illness, we could get no definite intelligence as to his actual state.'

"The whole of the lower part of Yale was under water. At Ruby Creek steamers took the place of the train, carrying passengers to New Westminster, and then by train to Vancouver. Entire places were under water, and it was no uncommon sight to see wooden houses sailing down the Fraser at a great speed. The realization of what this would mean to a colony already suffering from failure of trade, without doubt added to the anxiety of the Bishop, and hastened his end. Still, there seemed real improvement, and on Friday, June 1st, he was considered strong enough to start for his home. He was carried to the train by Doctors Hanington and McGuigan, attended by Mrs. Sillitoe and a nurse. They were astonished at the way in which he stood the journey, and felt quite hopeful about him, holding out prospects of his being in time able to get away for complete change. He reached New Westminster on board one of the river steamers, which had been sent by the C.P.R. to connect the broken links of the railway. Mr. Abbot, general superintendent of the line, had sent his private car to bring him down; but, though the car reached Yale, it was unable to return because of the floods. Towards night on Saturday the pains returned, and the laboured breathing. All Sunday he was growing worse, and in the afternoon the doctor's verdict was given that there was no hope. His first thought, when he was told, was for Mrs. Sillitoe. 'My poor little wife,' he said, 'this comes very hard upon you.' He then said how he trusted she would be an example to others, showing how a Christian should bear sorrow. Then he spoke of the affairs of the diocese as being left, he hoped, fairly in order. His domestic chaplain, Mr. Croucher, who had given the Bishop unfailing attendance since the time of his coming to Yale, and had accompanied him to New Westminster, suggested his receiving the Holy Sacrament. The Bishop at first demurred, thinking a communion in the evening inconsistent with the practice and teaching of his life, but upon the chaplain's urging the immunity of the sick from the Church's rule, and the desire he and others felt to receive the Communion with him, he consented. He made immediate preparation, and joined devoutly in the responses all through the service. This was the last act he performed in full consciousness. On this Sunday notice was given in more than one church that the daily celebration would be with special intention on behalf of the Bishop, and in five of the churches arrangements were made to have ceaseless intercessions offered from 6 a.m. to midnight each day. The circle of the whole twenty-four hours could have been easily completed had it been possible to communicate with outlying parishes. As it was, New Westminster, Sapperton, and Vancouver shared the sad yet blessed and hopeful privilege between them. Describing this period, the Archdeacon writes—

"'We all knew he whom we loved so dearly, and so deservedly valued, had entered the borderland, but none could tell whether it was to be for *life* or *death*. We asked (if it might be God's will) life, and "Thou grantedst him a long life, even for ever and ever." Once during that anxious week I saw him for a few minutes, but he did not seem to know me. When I stood beside him and laid my hand on his head to give him my blessing, he bent his head reverently, was silent for a few moments, his delirious talk ceasing, and then raised his eyes to mine, but still, so far as I could judge, not knowing who I was.'

"Monday and Tuesday during this week were days of pain, but on Wednesday the Bishop was restful. It was during the closing half-hour of the last two hours' watch that was being kept at S. James', Vancouver, on the Saturday night, that he quietly breathed his last, and entered, on the Lord's day, the blessed and more lasting joy of Paradise."

Expected as the departure had been, it came that Sunday morning with a great shock, not only upon those who were numbered among his flock, but to all of every class and every creed who admired and reverenced the man and his work.

A day or two before his death one of the Vancouver papers had the following words in its editorial :—

"The very deepest interest is taken in the condition of his lordship, Bishop Sillitoe. Beloved by those to whom he especially ministers, he has endeared himself to all creeds, and has formed a large part of the highest and best life of this portion of the province. The cutting short of so useful a career would be deplorable. At this time, when cant and fanaticism seem to be holding their carnival, broad-minded men like his lordship are wanted to teach the lesson of charity that is of the very essence of religion. Prayers are being offered up in the various Episcopal churches for the Bishop's recovery, and all his friends are asked to participate in the services." (*The World*, June 5th.)

And immediately after the sad event had become known another secular paper stated as follows :—

"The death of Bishop Sillitoe is an event which will be regretted by many besides those who are members of the Church to which the late Bishop belonged.

In his death the Church of England in this province loses not merely one of its chief pastors, but also one of its most energetic leaders. Zealous for the interests of his Church, Bishop Sillitoe set a worthy example to the clergy and laymen of his diocese. The welfare and prosperity of the Church was a sentiment which pervaded every action of his life. In a vast diocese like that of New Westminster even the ordinary performance of the duties of the Episcopal office is sufficient to absorb all the energy which the incumbent of it may possess. But Bishop Sillitoe did not remain satisfied with the carrying out of the mere perfunctory obligations imposed upon him. 'To spend and be spent' in the service of the Church was his motto. The necessities of the diocese, the need for more clergy and Church buildings, in order that the widely scattered settlements might be afforded spiritual ministrations, were ever before Bishop Sillitoe. Not merely did he strain every effort to make the Church more effective for the end for which it was founded; there is every reason to believe that the anxieties and disappointments which he suffered as the result of his perception of the inadequacy of the means at his disposal had also a serious effect on a frame not robust. But he has laid well the foundations, and those who may come after him will find their abilities and zeal taxed to the utmost, if they carry out to the full those works to the planning of which Bishop Sillitoe devoted the best efforts of his life. His example will remain, though he has passed away."

Owing to the floods, which cut New Westminster for a time completely off from Eastern Canada, the news travelled slowly; but it evoked a unanimous outburst of sorrow and regret, all the more sincere, perhaps, because but a year before Churchmen there had seen him at work actively among them, lecturing and preaching, from city to city, in order that he might disseminate knowledge respecting his distant diocese. From the many notices in Canadian Church papers that from the *Church Guardian* may be quoted here as representative of all:—

"The sad news of the severe loss which has fallen upon the whole Church of England in Canada through the death of the Right Rev. the Lord Bishop of New Westminster, on the 9th of June, only reaches us on the 22nd instant, owing, doubtless, to the interruption of mail and telegraphic communication through the late floods in British Columbia. We cannot express how deeply we feel the loss which has befallen the Church. It is not our custom to write words of eulogy of the dead, great or small, but there are occasions when expression of loss through the removal, in God's providence, of *leaders* is not only expected, but is just. And this is one of such occasions, for the late Lord Bishop of New Westminster was a Bishop in every sense of the word—apostolic, self-denying, laborious, and devout, and one who in his short episcopate (as we reckon time) has built securely, and must have left behind him an undying record. We feel, too, that the Church in Canada owes him a debt of gratitude, for we think that it was, under God's good guidance, largely through his influence that a direct conflict was avoided in regard to the formation of the General Assembly of the Church in Canada, and that that important event was finally carried through. The loss, humanly speaking, is appalling; but faith looks beyond the present, and realizes that God overrules as well the destiny of individuals as that of the Church, and that He can and will provide a worthy successor for the first good, able, and devoted Bishop of this now bereaved See."

And in England, where, however, the Bishop was less known, the regret was real and profound. The Home Committee announced the sad news in the following appropriate words:—

"'Grant them grace to witness to the Faith'—thus have

ever prayed the members of our Guild; and God, in a special way, has answered the prayer in the case of our first Bishop. It has been granted to him to witness to the Faith even unto death. In all our sorrow, in the bitter personal grief which so many of us feel that we shall no more welcome him home amongst us, we would first try and thank God for thus allowing him the lofty privilege, at times permitted to the saints, to die rather than give up his work and the fulfilment of his duty to His Holy Church. The words of the telegram received on June 11th have a touching, simple pathos seldom found in such messages: 'Bishop asleep.' A brief sentence, but the essence of a lengthy statement full of information. 'Asleep' after that toiling life of activity, never sparing himself, refusing to leave his post, though pressed to do so, and warned by medical opinion of the probable result. Others wanting rest were encouraged to go back to the old country, but, thoughtless of himself, he stayed on, not only weakened by repeated attacks of pneumonia, but worried by the effect on the Church of the commercial depression under which the Colony has for some time been suffering."

And, last to be mentioned, but by no means least prized by Mrs. Sillitoe, I place the following letter, received from the Lytton Indians, who had received so much love from the departed Bishop:—

"June 10, 1894.

"The Indians very sorry because the Bishop is die, because he loves them very much and takes care of them. They awful sorry Bishop die, because they all feel they belong to him. The people hear he die last night, and that what they are awful sorry for. From to-day they will pray all the time for his happiness in Paradise. They want these three days to say prayers for him till the funeral. They are sorry they have lost their things through the water, but more sorry the Bishop is die. They want Mrs. Sillitoe to let them know if she is well or not, because we love the Bishop very much, and we love Mrs. Sillitoe too, and they will all pray to God that He will comfort her in her sorrow."

CHAPTER XXVII.

AT REST.

THE tolling of the cathedral bell early on that Sunday morning informed the outside world that the first Bishop of New Westminster had completed his labours on earth. Within the See House loving hands dressed the dead Bishop in his robes, and gathered around the private altar to find comfort in the Communion of Saints realized through Communion with Christ in the Sacrament of His Body and Blood.

All day the bereaved parishioners and citizens came to have one last look at him whose loving presence they had lost.

The body lay thus in simple state till it was borne by the priests of the diocese to the cathedral, after Evensong on the Tuesday. At the gate of the cathedral grounds the little procession was met by the Archdeacon of Columbia, who, with the impressiveness which came from knowing himself a dying man (he did not survive the Bishop long), recited the opening sentences of the Burial Service.

The body was then laid in the chancel immediately before the altar, and a watch service, which, like the other arrangements for the funeral, had been long before provided for by the Bishop himself, was commenced by the Archdeacon, and kept up all through the night and following morning.

At 7.30 a.m. there was a plain celebration of the Holy Communion, and at nine o'clock a full Choral Celebration exactly like those at which the Bishop had so often officiated and had taught his people to love. With eyes closed to shut out the sight of the flower-laden coffin, it was difficult to believe the Bishop was not there in the living flesh. Indeed, the choir he had trained with so much enthusiastic self-sacrifice must have felt him present. The celebrant was the Bishop of Columbia, Dr. Perrin, and a very large number of people, both clergy and laity, communicated.

Immediately after the celebration, about 11.30, the Burial Service was resumed by Bishop Perrin, and with deep feeling the psalms chanted and the two hymns sung. The hymns were, "The Saints of God! their conflict past" and "For all the Saints who from their labours rest." Then, many being moved to tears, the body, borne by the clergy, was carried for the last time from the church, while the strains of the "Dead March" pealed forth from the organ.

The funeral cortège was, perhaps, the largest the city of New Westminster ever beheld. The body was carried by relays of bearers, representing the three city parishes of Holy Trinity, S. Barnabas', and S. Mary's, Sapperton, and the churches of Vancouver. The choir, members of the Women's Auxiliary and other parochial organizations followed. Then came delegations from the Westminster Bar, the Grand Lodge of Freemasons (of which the Bishop had been an influential member), the City Council, and other public bodies. Finally came the mourners and a long line of private carriages containing friends of the deceased Bishop.

When the grave was reached, it was found to be already almost covered with floral offerings of all kinds, tokens of respect laid by many hands, while at the head of the grave there shone in the sun a large cross twelve feet in height, made entirely of golden blossoms of the broom.

The service at the grave was said by Bishop Barker of Colorado, U.S.A., and at the close the hymn "Now the labourer's task is o'er" was impressively sung by the choir. The filling in of the grave was done by the clergy, each one present taking a turn, and then the newly raised mound was covered with the beautiful flowers brought from the church.

So the tired body was left in peace while the thoughts of the bereaved ones went out in thankfulness to God for a noble life worthily ended, and a noble labour worthily rewarded.

* * * * *

But "dead, he yet speaketh;" and the diocese, under the new ruler given her by God, will go forward inspired and heartened by the memory of him who was called upon to lay the foundations.

Men of all types and schools of thought were ready to bear testimony to the value of the work he had done.

On the Sunday following the Bishop's death, the Rector of Christ Church, Vancouver, in the course of his sermon, thus summed up the loss the diocese had sustained:—

"I cannot let this opportunity pass without saying at least one feeble word as to the loss which this diocese has sustained in the death of Bishop Sillitoe. Called to preside over it at a time when it was little more than a vast and virgin forest, like a wise master-builder he laid its foundations broad and deep—foundations that are likely to stand the test of time. For years he toiled in this laborious field with a zeal and devotion and self-denial that are beyond all praise. And he toiled to the very last. It is scarcely more than a month since he was in our midst administering to our candidates the rite of Confirmation. It is not too much to say that he died in harness—even to say that he died a martyr to his deep sense of duty. No one, I am sure, could know Bishop Sillitoe intimately without being charmed by his genial and friendly manner, and without being impressed by his zeal, earnestness, and manliness. Such qualities—the gifts of the Eternal Spirit—are not likely soon to die or to be forgotten. Through them, though dead, he yet speaketh, and will speak for many years to all who knew him. . . ."

And one who knew the Bishop still more intimately, the Rev. H. Edwardes, of Lytton, has written a testimony which I cannot forbear quoting—

"Speaking for myself," he writes, "it is difficult to know what to say. But throughout the 'Upper Country' the Bishop was appreciated very highly indeed for his manly qualities and his indefatigable travel and work. Every man on the road—hotel-keepers, farmers, teamsters, roadmen—knew him and respected him as a friend and as a man. It was the same on the railway, few men being so familiarly known, and withal so respected as the Bishop throughout the rough days of construction.

"How well I remember when I first met him at the old S. Paul's Mission House in the depths of the Fraser Canon in 1884, and the kind brotherly manner in which he bade me welcome, and made me feel that he was not only my Bishop, but my brother.

"And how patiently and laboriously he took his part in our Indian work whenever he could visit us there or at Lytton! We generally had a large number of Indians ready for him to baptize and confirm, and administer discipline to—oh! such a dense, stupid, apparently brainless crowd—and hour after hour the

Bishop would patiently teach and catechize them when my own little stock of patience had run dry hours before, and my temper had grown rusty. I remember one night, as he was deep in such a class of catechumens, a lamp in the kitchen adjoining burst, and in a moment the room was in flames, which were making their way through the roof of cedar shakes. There was immediately a scene of excitement and confusion, no one quite knowing what to do until the Bishop's common sense came to the rescue, and he set us to throw earth over the flames. He was very soon back at his teaching and examining, as though nothing had happened.

"No man was so popular up the Cariboo Road and amongst the Cariboo people as the Bishop. He and Mrs. Sillitoe were always welcome guests, and everywhere made themselves at home with the people they visited. Very rough times they often had on the road, sometimes driving in great danger through raging forest fires, and sometimes unharnessing the horses, and themselves lifting the well-known buckboard over fallen trees. In all kinds of places the Bishop was ready to hold service for the benefit of any handful of men he came across, in bar-rooms, stores, hotels, stations, on the roadside, in railway camps and cars, anywhere where his message would be received. Often he carried a concertina, and would himself accompany the Canticles and hymns at these impromptu services. . . . May I say in conclusion that I know no man I loved more truly, no man more generously forgiving and more ready to *forget* also.

"It was that which made one love him so, I think. His manly courage, his ready sympathy, his delightful unselfishness, his keen sense of humour, his quiet dignity, combined with higher qualities still, made up a splendid character. We have not only lost our Bishop, but our *friend*. British Columbia has been fortunate in the possession of a Bishop of such powers and character as Bishop Sillitoe, and so say hardheaded business and working men of all creeds wherever I go in my travels in British Columbia. . . . God grant him eternal rest and peace."

Of other and similar personal testimony from both Indians and whites, from both cultured and unlearned, there is no lack.

One writes to Mrs. Sillitoe—

"It may seem selfish to obtrude my own thoughts and feelings at such a time, and yet I feel that you will care to know that I can never cease to thank God for the Bishop. His wise and loving direction at a time when my mind was most unsettled regarding religious questions has without doubt saved my life from shipwreck, and it is to him I owe my present happiness in God's service."

And another—

"Our dear Bishop was always considerate for the views and perhaps the prejudices of others. I can never forget the kindness and courtesy with which he always received me, even when asking him to do things with which he could not agree. . . . It may surprise you to know that he was the only clergyman to whom I ever went for consolation when in trouble."

And another—

"As one who has received from Bishop Sillitoe much spiritual assistance, much for which there must be always very deep thankfulness, I can assure you that I must always bear a very grateful remembrance of him."

Once again—

"No one knows, dear Mrs. Sillitoe, what he has been to us, how lovingly he has led us on to higher things."

And for the Church at large no words can more fitly sum up the Bishop's character and work than the following passage from the address of the Bishop of Nova Scotia to his synod:—

"A man of solid learning and many gifts, he never spared himself in any way if he might do or say something which would further the work committed to his trust, the establishing and extending of the Church in the newly created diocese, including all the southern half of the mainland of British Columbia, and containing an area of one hundred and eighty-six thousand square miles, a territory about eight times the size of this diocese. Is it any wonder that fourteen years and a half of such work, in such a field, should have quite sufficed to cut short, before its time, a life full of great blessing, and to arrest a career which contained the elements of greatness? Another warm heart has ceased to beat; another encouraging presence has been withdrawn; another cheering voice has been hushed; another workman's task is ended; another leader of God's host is fallen. 'They shall enter into peace; they shall rest in their beds, each one walking in his uprightness.'"

* * * * *

There are many aspects of the Bishop's life which this imperfect memoir has not touched. If it were a record of the Bishop's life, rather than the story of a Bishop's work, these pages would be incomplete without separate chapters telling of Bishop Sillitoe's work as musician, his work as Mason, his work as citizen. So full of charm as a host was he, that we should have had to tell of that unfailing humour which made his table a feast of mirth, and his home the attraction of so many varied types of men.

But these things live in the memory of many, and are not to be reproduced in any written word.

So we bring to an end this chronicle of an Episcopate characterized by unceasing toil, if not by romantic adventure, and fruitful to all time in the lesson of duty heroically done in face of obstacles innumerable.

With such a Bishop's grave amongst us the

diocese can never be poor. As we gaze upon it under the shadow of the mighty trees of the Western forest it speaks to us of the continuity of a cause which marches on victoriously, though every standard-bearer fall in the fight. We know that while God has given rest to His servants, their work is not done, nor can their graves be cold.

> "Cold graves, we say? It shall be testified
> That living men, who burn in heart and brain,
> Without the dead were colder. If we tried
> To sink the past beneath our feet, be sure
> The future would not stand.
> Who dared build temples without tombs in sight?
> Or live without some good man's benison?
> Or seek truth, hope for good, and strive for right,
> If looking up, he saw not in the sun
> Some angel of the Martyrs all day long
> Standing and waiting?"

APPENDIX

Mr. Gowen has referred in the foregoing chapters to the important part taken by Bishop Sillitoe in the organization of a General Synod of the Church in Canada, so successfully accomplished in September, 1893.

An extract from the summary of the Bishop's sermon at the Thanksgiving Service on that occasion has been quoted. His concluding words are so full of faith, and hope, and thankfulness, and so characteristically clear and to the point, that we feel sure they will interest our readers, and we here append them—

"'God is able to do exceeding abundantly above all that we ask or think.' Graft these words inwardly in your hearts. Read, mark, learn, and inwardly digest them. Then ask and think, not according to the limited horizon of our own senses, but according to the infinitude of Divine will and power. What can we learn herefrom respecting the work that we have accomplished? Well, looking into the past, perhaps we have accomplished much. But, looking forward to the future, what is left to be done? The Church is one from east to west. Now she can speak with one voice from ocean to ocean. Now, at length, she has become a power in the land. Praise be to God for the manifestation of His grace! Praise be to Him for that! He hath given abundantly of His blessing! But He can give exceeding abundantly above all that we ask or think. So let our demands go up fearlessly for more grace and blessing; so let our thoughts expand in the realms of faith, unwavering, unsatisfied, till we be filled with all the fulness of God, till His whole power be manifested in His Church and in each individual soul.

"Let us believe in the mission of the Church and in the mission of each individual Churchman; let us believe in the real indwelling of the Holy Spirit in the Church and in each one of us. An indwelling of power, an indwelling of responsibility. Above all, let us believe in the possession of the Truth of God—a sacred trust in behalf of all that are in error, as well as all that are in ignorance. While we rejoice in the unity wherewith God has blessed us, let us never forget that it is not we only that are to be one, but that all are to be one, according to His will. This is our mission, and we may not be satisfied so long as it is unattained. All that we have done is not enough, so long as God has more for us to do. We have touched the outer circle of organic unity amongst ourselves. We have drawn a circumference of united action. At the centre is God, the Father, Son, and Holy Ghost. At the centre only is perfect unity. There alone is our end; there only is the full accomplishment. Now towards this centre must every diocese converge, and every Churchman in every diocese, each one a separate ray, sparkling and bright with holy endeavour and unselfish aim, hastening on by the attractive power of the indwelling Spirit, until all shall be absorbed in the eternal being of God, and He shall be all in all."

We also gladly insert a letter from Mrs. Jephson, of Ayot St. Peter Rectory, Welwyn, which speaks for itself of the good and lasting influence left by the Bishop in this little Hertfordshire village.

The Rev. Henry Jephson and his people have for many years, with their prayers and intercessions, sent an extraordinary amount of help and sympathy to New Westminster, and have helped to cheer the hearts of many clergy and workers in that distant diocese.

Mrs. Jephson says—

"Although it is nearly twelve years since Bishop Sillitoe first spoke on Foreign Missions at Welwyn, his words are still graven on my memory, and have been the means of guiding all sorts and conditions of people, who have desired to help our missions in some way, but yet were held back by the thought that their offerings might be too small and poor.

"He always explained so well what is meant by the true 'spirit of missions,' and how useless large sums given spasmodically were, compared with a little, done earnestly and with quiet conviction.

"Although he was always most grateful for the least thing done for his diocese or himself, he did not believe much in money given from a personal interest in himself, or in the particular part of the country in which he worked. He used to say that at first, in the early days of the diocese, he had positively suffered from such gifts, for they gradually diminished, and at last ceased. Having a most trustful and hopeful nature, he unfortunately believed that these large subscriptions would always be forthcoming, and would embark on some cherished scheme on the strength of them. But he found that subscriptions often gradually diminish as interest flags, and the elements of novelty and romance become too familiar to attract. Direct personal appeal was only possible at long intervals.

"The Bishop gave offence several times by refusing to preach about his own diocese and its needs.

"'The pulpit is not the place,' he said, 'from which to plead any cause but the great one of the Christian's duty. *That* I *will* tell you about.'

"It was only at meetings he would enter into details of his needs, and he never thought any gathering too unimportant for his very best efforts.

"We all in Ayot remember a Sunday evening on the village green, after a hard day's work, how he stood under one of the trees surrounded by the poor people and the children, all listening eagerly to every word he spoke to them.

"His pleading tone, when speaking of his Master's work, quickly drew out the sympathies of his audience—

not to himself—but to the importance and seriousness of their duty to spread the knowledge of salvation.

"He had a way of effacing himself whenever he spoke of missionary work, and I can only account for his lasting influence in this place by the very fact that he put duty and high motive so conspicuously in front of everything else. It made us all feel ashamed of anything less than heart and soul work.

"The first time he came to the Rectory, his sunny, cheery manner, and his simple ways and habits, made every one feel at home with him at once.

"Always dignified in, and conscious of, his high office, nothing could be simpler than the manner of his life. He carried usually a small valise containing just a few necessaries, and a neat case with his robes of office, which he tried to have of the very best he could afford, but for his own personal use not a luxury of any kind.

"These are perhaps but little things, but surely an index of the character of the man who laid down his life for his Master's work.

"With his dying lips he commended to us a certain part of his Indian work which he had much at heart, and which he had hoped to see started and flourishing before he was called away.

"We must always thank God for what he was allowed to do here, and *is doing*, for, as his teaching was not of the sort that passes away with the teacher, we may surely venture to say this."

THE END.

PRINTED BY WILLIAM CLOWES AND SONS, LIMITED, LONDON AND BECCLES.

A Selection of Works
IN
THEOLOGICAL LITERATURE
PUBLISHED BY
MESSRS. LONGMANS, GREEN, & CO.

London: 39 PATERNOSTER ROW, E.C.
New York: 91 and 93 FIFTH AVENUE.
Bombay: 32 HORNBY ROAD.

Abbey and Overton.—THE ENGLISH CHURCH IN THE EIGHTEENTH CENTURY. By CHARLES J. ABBEY, M.A., Rector of Checkendon, Reading, and JOHN H. OVERTON, D.D., Canon of Lincoln. *Crown 8vo. 7s. 6d.*

Adams.—SACRED ALLEGORIES. The Shadow of the Cross—The Distant Hills—The Old Man's Home—The King's Messengers. By the Rev. WILLIAM ADAMS, M.A. *Crown 8vo. 3s. 6d.*

The four Allegories may be had separately, with Illustrations. *16mo. 1s. each.*

Aids to the Inner Life.

Edited by the Venble. W. H. HUTCHINGS, M.A., Archdeacon of Cleveland, Canon of York, Rector of Kirby Misperton, and Rural Dean of Malton. *Five Vols. 32mo, cloth limp, 6d. each; or cloth extra, 1s. each.*

OF THE IMITATION OF CHRIST. By THOMAS À KEMPIS.

THE CHRISTIAN YEAR

THE DEVOUT LIFE. By ST. FRANCIS DE SALES.

THE HIDDEN LIFE OF THE SOUL.

THE SPIRITUAL COMBAT. By LAURENCE SCUPOLI.

Barnett.—THE SERVICE OF GOD: Sermons, Essays, and Addresses. By SAMUEL A. BARNETT, Warden of Toynbee Hall, Whitechapel; Canon of Bristol Cathedral; Select Preacher before Oxford University. *Crown 8vo. 6s.*

Bathe.—Works by the Rev. ANTHONY BATHE, M.A.

A LENT WITH JESUS. A Plain Guide for Churchmen. Containing Readings for Lent and Easter Week, and on the Holy Eucharist. *32mo, 1s.; or in paper cover, 6d.*

AN ADVENT WITH JESUS. *32mo, 1s.; or in paper cover, 6d.*

WHAT I SHOULD BELIEVE. A Simple Manual of Self-Instruction for Church People. *Small 8vo, limp, 1s.; cloth gilt, 2s.*

Bathe and Buckham.—THE CHRISTIAN'S ROAD BOOK. 2 Parts. By the Rev. ANTHONY BATHE and Rev. F. H. BUCKHAM.

Part I. DEVOTIONS. *Sewed, 6d.; limp cloth, 1s.; cloth extra, 1s. 6d.*
Part II. READINGS. *Sewed, 1s.; limp cloth, 2s.; cloth extra, 3s.; or complete in one volume, sewed, 1s. 6d.; limp cloth, 2s. 6d.; cloth extra, 3s. 6d.*

Benson.—Works by the Rev. R. M. BENSON, M.A., Student of Christ Church, Oxford.

THE FINAL PASSOVER: A Series of Meditations upon the Passion of our Lord Jesus Christ. *Small 8vo.*

Vol. I.—THE REJECTION. 5*s.*
Vol. II.—THE UPPER CHAMBER.
Part I. 5*s.*
Part II 5*s.*
Vol. III.—THE DIVINE EXODUS. Parts I. and II. 5*s.* each.
Vol. IV.—THE LIFE BEYOND THE GRAVE. 5*s.*

THE MAGNIFICAT; a Series of Meditations upon the Song of the Blessed Virgin Mary. *Small 8vo.* 2*s.*

SPIRITUAL READINGS FOR EVERY DAY. 3 *vols. Small 8vo.* 3*s. 6d. each.*

I. ADVENT. II. CHRISTMAS. III. EPIPHANY.

BENEDICTUS DOMINUS: A Course of Meditations for Every Day of the Year. Vol. I.—ADVENT TO TRINITY. Vol. II.—TRINITY, SAINTS' DAYS, etc. *Small 8vo.* 3*s. 6d. each; or in One Volume,* 7*s.*

BIBLE TEACHINGS: The Discourse at Capernaum.—St. John vi. *Small 8vo.* 3*s. 6d.*

THE WISDOM OF THE SON OF DAVID: An Exposition of the First Nine Chapters of the Book of Proverbs. *Small 8vo.* 3*s. 6d.*

THE MANUAL OF INTERCESSORY PRAYER. *Royal 32mo.; cloth boards,* 1*s.* 3*d.*; *cloth limp,* 9*d.*

THE EVANGELIST LIBRARY CATECHISM. Part I. *Small 8vo.* 3*s.*

PAROCHIAL MISSIONS. *Small 8vo.* 2*s. 6d.*

Bickersteth.—YESTERDAY, TO-DAY, AND FOR EVER: a Poem in Twelve Books. By EDWARD HENRY BICKERSTETH, D.D., Lord Bishop of Exeter. *One Shilling Edition, 18mo. With red borders, 16mo,* 2*s. 6d.*

The Crown 8vo Edition (5s.) may still be had.

Blunt.—Works by the Rev. JOHN HENRY BLUNT, D.D.

THE ANNOTATED BOOK OF COMMON PRAYER: Being an Historical, Ritual, and Theological Commentary on the Devotional System of the Church of England. *4to.* 21*s.*

THE COMPENDIOUS EDITION OF THE ANNOTATED BOOK OF COMMON PRAYER: Forming a concise Commentary on the Devotional System of the Church of England. *Crown 8vo.* 10*s. 6d.*

DICTIONARY OF DOCTRINAL AND HISTORICAL THEOLOGY. By various Writers. *Imperial 8vo.* 21*s.*

DICTIONARY OF SECTS, HERESIES, ECCLESIASTICAL PARTIES AND SCHOOLS OF RELIGIOUS THOUGHT. By various Writers. *Imperial 8vo.* 21*s.*

THE REFORMATION OF THE CHURCH OF ENGLAND: its History, Principles, and Results. 1574-1662. *Two Vols. 8vo.* 34*s.*

Blunt.—Works by the Rev. JOHN HENRY BLUNT, D.D.—*contd.*

THE BOOK OF CHURCH LAW. Being an Exposition of the Legal Rights and Duties of the Parochial Clergy and the Laity of the Church of England. Revised by Sir WALTER G. F. PHILLIMORE, Bart., D.C.L., and G. EDWARDES JONES, Barrister-at-Law. *Crown 8vo.* 7*s.* 6*d.*

A COMPANION TO THE BIBLE: Being a Plain Commentary on Scripture History, to the end of the Apostolic Age. *Two Vols. small 8vo. Sold separately.*

THE OLD TESTAMENT. 3*s.* 6*d.* THE NEW TESTAMENT. 3*s.* 6*d.*

HOUSEHOLD THEOLOGY: a Handbook of Religious Information respecting the Holy Bible, the Prayer Book, the Church, etc., etc. *Paper cover, 16mo.* 1*s.* *Also the Larger Edition,* 3*s.* 6*d.*

Body.—Works by the Rev. GEORGE BODY, D.D., Canon of Durham.

THE LIFE OF LOVE. A Course of Lent Lectures. *16mo.* 2*s.* 6*d.*

THE SCHOOL OF CALVARY; or, Laws of Christian Life revealed from the Cross. *16mo.* 2*s.* 6*d.*

THE LIFE OF JUSTIFICATION. *16mo.* 2*s.* 6*d.*

THE LIFE OF TEMPTATION. *16mo.* 2*s.* 6*d.*

THE PRESENT STATE OF THE FAITHFUL DEPARTED. *Small 8vo. sewed,* 6*d.* *32mo. cloth,* 1*s.*

Boultbee.—A COMMENTARY ON THE THIRTY-NINE ARTICLES OF THE CHURCH OF ENGLAND. By the Rev. T. P. BOULTBEE, formerly Principal of the London College of Divinity, St. John's Hall, Highbury. *Crown 8vo.* 6*s.*

Bright.—Works by WILLIAM BRIGHT, D.D., Regius Professor of Ecclesiastical History in the University of Oxford, and Canon of Christ Church, Oxford.

SOME ASPECTS OF PRIMITIVE CHURCH LIFE. *Crown 8vo.* 6*s.*

THE ROMAN SEE IN THE EARLY CHURCH: And other Studies in Church History. *Crown 8vo.* 7*s.* 6*d.*

WAYMARKS IN CHURCH HISTORY. *Crown 8vo.* 7*s.* 6*d.*

LESSONS FROM THE LIVES OF THREE GREAT FATHERS. St. Athanasius, St. Chrysostom, and St. Augustine. *Crown 8vo.* 6*s.*

THE INCARNATION AS A MOTIVE POWER. *Crown 8vo.* 6*s.*

Bright and Medd.—LIBER PRECUM PUBLICARUM ECCLESIÆ ANGLICANÆ. A GULIELMO BRIGHT, S.T.P., et PETRO GOLDSMITH MEDD, A.M., Latine redditus. *Small 8vo.* 7*s.* 6*d.*

Browne.—WEARIED WITH THE BURDEN: A Book of Daily Readings for Lent. By ARTHUR HEBER BROWNE, M.A., LL.D., Rector of St. John's, Newfoundland. *Crown 8vo.* 4*s.* 6*d.*

Browne.—AN EXPOSITION OF THE THIRTY-NINE ARTICLES, Historical and Doctrinal. By E. H. BROWNE, D.D., sometime Bishop of Winchester. *8vo.* 16*s.*

Campion and Beamont.—THE PRAYER BOOK INTERLEAVED. With Historical Illustrations and Explanatory Notes arranged parallel to the Text. By W. M. CAMPION, D.D., and W. J. BEAMONT, M.A. *Small 8vo.* 7*s.* 6*d.*

Carter.—Works by, and edited by the Rev. T. T. CARTER, M.A., Hon. Canon of Christ Church, Oxford.

THE TREASURY OF DEVOTION: a Manual of Prayer for General and Daily Use. Compiled by a Priest.
18mo. 2*s.* 6*d.*; *cloth limp*, 2*s.* Bound with the Book of Common Prayer, 3*s.* 6*d.* Red-Line Edition. *Cloth extra, gilt top.* *18mo,* 2*s.* 6*d.* *net.* Large-Type Edition. *Crown 8vo.* 3*s.* 6*d.*

THE WAY OF LIFE: A Book of Prayers and Instruction for the Young at School, with a Preparation for Confirmation. Compiled by a Priest. *18mo.* 1*s.* 6*d.*

THE PATH OF HOLINESS: a First Book of Prayers, with the Service of the Holy Communion, for the Young. Compiled by a Priest. With Illustrations. *16mo.* 1*s.* 6*d.*; *cloth limp*, 1*s.*

THE GUIDE TO HEAVEN: a Book of Prayers for every Want. (For the Working Classes.) Compiled by a Priest. *18mo.* 1*s.* 6*d.*; *cloth limp*, 1*s.* *Large-Type Edition. Crown 8vo.* 1*s.* 6*d.*; *cloth limp*, 1*s.*

THE STAR OF CHILDHOOD: a First Book of Prayers and Instruction for Children. Compiled by a Priest. With Illustrations. *16mo.* 2*s.* 6*d.*

SIMPLE LESSONS; or, Words Easy to be Understood. A Manual of Teaching. I. On the Creed. II. The Ten Commandments. III. The Sacrament. *18mo.* 3*s.*

A BOOK OF PRIVATE PRAYER FOR MORNING, MID-DAY, AND OTHER TIMES. *18mo. limp cloth*, 1*s.*; *cloth, red edges*, 1*s.* 3*d.*

NICHOLAS FERRAR: his Household and his Friends. With Portrait engraved after a Picture by CORNELIUS JANSSEN at Magdalene College, Cambridge. *Crown 8vo.* 6*s.*

MANUAL OF DEVOTION FOR SISTERS OF MERCY. 8 parts in 2 vols. 32mo. 10*s.* Or separately:—Part I. 1*s.* 6*d.* Part II. 1*s.* Part III. 1*s.* Part IV. 2*s.* Part V. 1*s.* Part VI. 1*s.* Part VII. Part VIII. 1*s.* 6*d.*

HARRIET MONSELL: A Memoir of the First Mother Superior of the Clewer Community. With Portrait. *Crown 8vo.* 2*s.* 6*d.*

PARISH TEACHINGS. First and Second Series. *Crown 8vo.* 4*s.* 6*d.* *each sold separately.*

SPIRITUAL INSTRUCTIONS. *Crown 8vo.*

THE HOLY EUCHARIST. 3*s.* 6*d.*
THE DIVINE DISPENSATIONS. 3*s.* 6*d.*
THE LIFE OF GRACE. 3*s.* 6*d.*
OUR LORD'S EARLY LIFE. 3*s.* 6*d.*
OUR LORD'S ENTRANCE ON HIS MINISTRY. 3*s.* 6*d.*
THE RELIGIOUS LIFE. 3*s.* 6*d.*

THE DOCTRINE OF THE PRIESTHOOD IN THE CHURCH OF ENGLAND. *Crown 8vo.* 4*s.*

THE DOCTRINE OF CONFESSION IN THE CHURCH OF ENGLAND. *Crown 8vo.* 5*s.*

THE DOCTRINE OF THE HOLY EUCHARIST, drawn from the Holy Scriptures and the Records of the Church of England. *Fcp. 8vo.* 9*d.*

VOWS AND THE RELIGIOUS STATE. *Crown 8vo.* 2*s.*

[*continued.*

Carter.—Works by, and edited by the Rev. T. T. CARTER, M.A., Hon. Canon of Christ Church, Oxford—*continued.*

COLLECTS, EPISTLES, AND GOSPELS, Suggested for Use on certain Special Occasions and Holy Days. *Crown 8vo.* 1*s.* 6*d.*

FAMILY PRAYERS. 18*mo.* 1*s.*

RETREATS, with Notes of Addresses. *Crown 8vo.* 5*s.*

Conybeare and Howson.—THE LIFE AND EPISTLES OF ST. PAUL. By the Rev. W. J. CONYBEARE, M.A., and the Very Rev. J. S. HOWSON, D.D. With numerous Maps and Illustrations.

LIBRARY EDITION. *Two Vols.* 8*vo.* 21*s.* STUDENTS' EDITION. *One Vol. Crown 8vo.* 6*s.* POPULAR EDITION. *One Vol. Crown 8vo.* 3*s.* 6*d.*

Creighton.—A HISTORY OF THE PAPACY FROM THE GREAT SCHISM TO THE SACK OF ROME (1378-1527). By Right Hon. and Right Rev. MANDELL CREIGHTON, D.D., Lord Bishop of London. *Six volumes. Crown 8vo.* 6*s. each.*

DAY-HOURS OF THE CHURCH OF ENGLAND, THE. Newly Revised according to the Prayer Book and the Authorised Translation of the Bible. *Crown 8vo. sewed,* 3*s.*; *cloth,* 3*s.* 6*d.*

SUPPLEMENT TO THE DAY-HOURS OF THE CHURCH OF ENGLAND, being the Service for certain Holy Days. *Crown 8vo. sewed,* 3*s.*; *cloth,* 3*s.* 6*d.*

Devotional Series, 16mo, Red Borders. *Each* 2*s.* 6*d.*

BICKERSTETH'S YESTERDAY, TO-DAY, AND FOR EVER.
CHILCOT'S TREATISE ON EVIL THOUGHTS.
THE CHRISTIAN YEAR.
HERBERT'S POEMS AND PROVERBS.
KEMPIS' (À) OF THE IMITATION OF CHRIST.
LEAR'S (H. L. SIDNEY) FOR DAYS AND YEARS.
FRANCIS DE SALES' (ST.) THE DEVOUT LIFE.
WILSON'S THE LORD'S SUPPER. *Large type.*
*TAYLOR'S (JEREMY) HOLY LIVING.
* ——— ——— HOLY DYING.

* *These two in one Volume.* 5*s.*

Devotional Series, 18mo, without Red Borders. *Each* 1*s.*

BICKERSTETH'S YESTERDAY, TO-DAY, AND FOR EVER.
THE CHRISTIAN YEAR.
KEMPIS' (À) OF THE IMITATION OF CHRIST.
HERBERT'S POEMS AND PROVERBS.
WILSON'S THE LORD'S SUPPER. *Large type.*
FRANCIS DE SALES' (ST.) THE DEVOUT LIFE.
*TAYLOR'S (JEREMY) HOLY LIVING.
* ——— ——— HOLY DYING.

* *These two in one Volume.* 2*s.* 6*d.*

Edersheim.—Works by ALFRED EDERSHEIM, M.A., D.D., Ph.D.

THE LIFE AND TIMES OF JESUS THE MESSIAH. *Two Vols. 8vo.* 24*s.*

JESUS THE MESSIAH: being an Abridged Edition of 'The Life and Times of Jesus the Messiah.' *Crown 8vo.* 7*s.* 6*d.*

HISTORY OF THE JEWISH NATION AFTER THE DESTRUCTION OF JERUSALEM UNDER TITUS. 8*vo.* 18*s.*

Ellicott.—Works by C. J. ELLICOTT, D.D., Bishop of Gloucester.

A CRITICAL AND GRAMMATICAL COMMENTARY ON ST. PAUL'S EPISTLES. Greek Text, with a Critical and Grammatical Commentary, and a Revised English Translation. *8vo.*

GALATIANS. 8s. 6d.
EPHESIANS. 8s. 6d.
PHILIPPIANS, COLOSSIANS, AND PHILEMON. 10s. 6d.
THESSALONIANS. 7s. 6d.
PASTORAL EPISTLES. 10s. 6d.

HISTORICAL LECTURES ON THE LIFE OF OUR LORD JESUS CHRIST. *8vo.* 12s.

ENGLISH (THE) CATHOLIC'S VADE MECUM: a Short Manual of General Devotion. Compiled by a PRIEST. *32mo. limp,* 1s.; *cloth,* 2s.

PRIEST'S Edition. *32mo.* 1s. 6d.

Epochs of Church History.—Edited by Right Hon. and Right Rev. MANDELL CREIGHTON, D.D., Lord Bishop of London. *Small 8vo.* 2s. 6d. *each.*

THE ENGLISH CHURCH IN OTHER LANDS. By the Rev. H. W. TUCKER, M.A.

THE HISTORY OF THE REFORMATION IN ENGLAND. By the Rev. GEO. G. PERRY, M.A.

THE CHURCH OF THE EARLY FATHERS. By the Rev. ALFRED PLUMMER, D.D.

THE EVANGELICAL REVIVAL IN THE EIGHTEENTH CENTURY. By the Rev. J. H. OVERTON, D.D.

THE UNIVERSITY OF OXFORD. By the Hon. G. C. BRODRICK, D.C.L.

THE UNIVERSITY OF CAMBRIDGE. By J. BASS MULLINGER, M.A.

THE ENGLISH CHURCH IN THE MIDDLE AGES. By the Rev. W. HUNT, M.A.

THE CHURCH AND THE EASTERN EMPIRE. By the Rev. H. F. TOZER, M.A.

THE CHURCH AND THE ROMAN EMPIRE. By the Rev. A. CARR, M.A.

THE CHURCH AND THE PURITANS, 1570-1660. By HENRY OFFLEY WAKEMAN, M.A.

HILDEBRAND AND HIS TIMES. By the Rev. W. R. W. STEPHENS, M.A.

THE POPES AND THE HOHENSTAUFEN. By UGO BALZANI.

THE COUNTER REFORMATION. By ADOLPHUS WILLIAM WARD, Litt.D.

WYCLIFFE AND MOVEMENTS FOR REFORM. By REGINALD L. POOLE, M.A.

THE ARIAN CONTROVERSY. By the Rev. H. M. GWATKIN, M.A.

EUCHARISTIC MANUAL (THE). Consisting of Instructions and Devotions for the Holy Sacrament of the Altar. From various sources. *32mo. cloth gilt, red edges.* 1s. *Cheap Edition, limp cloth.* 9d.

Farrar.—Works by FREDERICK W. FARRAR, D.D., Dean of Canterbury.

THE BIBLE: Its Meaning and Supremacy. *8vo.* 15s.

ALLEGORIES. With 25 Illustrations by AMELIA BAUERLE. *Crown 8vo.* 6s.

CONTENTS.—The Life Story of Aner—The Choice—The Fortunes of a Royal House—The Basilisk and the Leopard.

Fosbery.—Works edited by the Rev. THOMAS VINCENT FOSBERY, M.A., sometime Vicar of St. Giles's, Reading.

VOICES OF COMFORT. *Cheap Edition. Small 8vo.* 3*s.* 6*d.*

The Larger Edition (7s. 6d.) may still be had.

HYMNS AND POEMS FOR THE SICK AND SUFFERING. In connection with the Service for the Visitation of the Sick. Selected from Various Authors. *Small 8vo.* 3*s.* 6*d.*

Geikie.—Works by J. CUNNINGHAM GEIKIE, D.D., LL.D., late Vicar of St. Martin-at-Palace, Norwich.

HOURS WITH THE BIBLE: the Scriptures in the Light of Modern Discovery and Knowledge. *New Edition, largely rewritten. Complete in Twelve Volumes. Crown 8vo.* 3*s.* 6*d. each.*

OLD TESTAMENT.

In Six Volumes. Sold separately. 3*s.* 6*d. each.*

CREATION TO THE PATRIARCHS. *With a Map and Illustrations.*

MOSES TO JUDGES. *With a Map and Illustrations.*

SAMSON TO SOLOMON. *With a Map and Illustrations.*

REHOBOAM TO HEZEKIAH. *With Illustrations.*

MANASSEH TO ZEDEKIAH. With the Contemporary Prophets. *With a Map and Illustrations.*

EXILE TO MALACHI. With the Contemporary Prophets. *With Illustrations.*

NEW TESTAMENT.

In Six Volumes. Sold separately. 3*s.* 6*d. each.*

THE GOSPELS. *With a Map and Illustrations.*

LIFE AND WORDS OF CHRIST. *With Map.* 2 *vols.*

LIFE AND EPISTLES OF ST. PAUL. *With Maps and Illustrations.* 2 *vols.*

ST. PETER TO REVELATION. *With 29 Illustrations.*

LIFE AND WORDS OF CHRIST.

Cabinet Edition. With Map. 2 *vols. Post 8vo.* 7*s.*

Cheap Edition, without the Notes. 1 *vol. 8vo.* 5*s.*

A SHORT LIFE OF CHRIST. *With Illustrations. Crown 8vo.* 3*s.* 6*d.*; *gilt edges,* 4*s.* 6*d.*

OLD TESTAMENT CHARACTERS. *With Illustrations. Crown 8vo.* 3*s.* 6*d.*

LANDMARKS OF OLD TESTAMENT HISTORY. *Crown 8vo.* 3*s.* 6*d.*

THE ENGLISH REFORMATION. *Crown 8vo.* 3*s.* 6*d.*

ENTERING ON LIFE. A Book for Young Men. *Crown 8vo.* 2*s.* 6*d.*

THE PRECIOUS PROMISES. *Crown 8vo.* 2*s.*

GOLD DUST: a Collection of Golden Counsels for the Sanctification of Daily Life. Translated and abridged from the French by E.L.E.E. Edited by CHARLOTTE M. YONGE. Parts I. II. III. Small Pocket Volumes. *Cloth, gilt, each* 1s. Parts I. and II. in One Volume. 1s. 6d. Parts I., II., and III. in One Volume. 2s.

*** The two first parts in One Volume, *large type*, 18mo. *cloth, gilt*. 2s. 6d. Parts I. II. and III. are also supplied, bound in white cloth, with red edges, in box, price 3s.

Gore.—Works by the Rev. CHARLES GORE, M.A., D.D., Canon of Westminster.

THE MINISTRY OF THE CHRISTIAN CHURCH. *8vo.* 10s. 6d.

ROMAN CATHOLIC CLAIMS. *Crown 8vo.* 3s. 6d.

GREAT TRUTHS OF THE CHRISTIAN RELIGION. Edited by the Rev. W. U. RICHARDS. *Small 8vo.* 2s.

Hall.—Works by the Right Rev. A. C. A. HALL, D.D., Bishop of Vermont.

THE VIRGIN MOTHER: Retreat Addresses on the Life of the Blessed Virgin Mary as told in the Gospels. With an appended Essay on the Virgin Birth of our Lord. *Crown 8vo.* 4s. 6d.

CHRIST'S TEMPTATION AND OURS. *Crown 8vo.* 3s. 6d.

Hall.—THE KENOTIC THEORY. Considered with Particular Reference to its Anglican Forms and Arguments. By the Rev. FRANCIS J. HALL, D.D., Instructor of Dogmatic Theology in the Western Theological Seminary, Chicago, Illinois. *Crown 8vo.* 5s.

Harrison.—Works by the Rev. ALEXANDER J. HARRISON, B.D., Lecturer of the Christian Evidence Society.

PROBLEMS OF CHRISTIANITY AND SCEPTICISM. *Crown 8vo.* 7s. 6d.

THE CHURCH IN RELATION TO SCEPTICS: a Conversational Guide to Evidential Work. *Crown 8vo.* 3s. 6d.

THE REPOSE OF FAITH, IN VIEW OF PRESENT DAY DIFFICULTIES. *Crown 8vo.* 7s. 6d.

Hatch.—THE ORGANIZATION OF THE EARLY CHRISTIAN CHURCHES. Being the Bampton Lectures for 1880. By EDWIN HATCH, M.A., D.D., late Reader in Ecclesiastical History in the University of Oxford. *8vo.* 5s.

Heygate.—THE MANUAL: a Book of Devotion. Adapted for General Use. By the Rev. W. E. HEYGATE, M.A., Rector of Brighstone. *18mo. cloth limp*, 1s.; *boards*, 1s. 3d. *Cheap Edition*, 6d. *Small 8vo. Large Type*, 1s. 6d.

Holland.—Works by the Rev. HENRY SCOTT HOLLAND, M.A., Canon and Precentor of St. Paul's.

GOD'S CITY AND THE COMING OF THE KINGDOM. *Cr. 8vo.* 3*s.* 6*d.*

PLEAS AND CLAIMS FOR CHRIST. *Crown 8vo.* 3*s.* 6*d.*

CREED AND CHARACTER: Sermons. *Crown 8vo.* 3*s.* 6*d.*

ON BEHALF OF BELIEF. Sermons. *Crown 8vo.* 3*s.* 6*d.*

CHRIST OR ECCLESIASTES. Sermons. *Crown 8vo.* 2*s.* 6*d.*

LOGIC AND LIFE, with other Sermons. *Crown 8vo.* 3*s.* 6*d.*

Hollings.—Works by the Rev. G. S. HOLLINGS, Mission Priest of the Society of St. John the Evangelist, Cowley, Oxford.

THE HEAVENLY STAIR; or, A Ladder of the Love of God for Sinners. *Crown 8vo.* 3*s.* 6*d.*

PORTA REGALIS; or, Considerations on Prayer. *Crown 8vo. limp cloth,* 1*s.* 6*d. net*; *cloth boards,* 2*s. net.*

MEDITATIONS ON THE DIVINE LIFE, THE BLESSED SACRAMENT, AND THE TRANSFIGURATION. *Crown 8vo.* 3*s.* 6*d.*

CONSIDERATIONS ON THE SPIRITUAL LIFE. Suggested by Passages in the Collects for the Sundays in Lent. *Crown 8vo.* 2*s.* 6*d.*

CONSIDERATIONS ON THE WISDOM OF GOD. *Crown 8vo.* 4*s.*

PARADOXES OF THE LOVE OF GOD, especially as they are seen in the way of the Evangelical Counsels. *Crown 8vo.* 4*s.*

ONE BORN OF THE SPIRIT; or, the Unification of our Life in God. *Crown 8vo.* 3*s.* 6*d.*

Hutchings.—Works by the Ven. W. H. HUTCHINGS, M.A. Archdeacon of Cleveland, Canon of York, Rector of Kirby Misperton, and Rural Dean of Malton.

SERMON SKETCHES from some of the Sunday Lessons throughout the Church's Year. *Vols. I and II. Crown 8vo.* 5*s. each.*

THE LIFE OF PRAYER: a Course of Lectures delivered in All Saints' Church, Margaret Street, during Lent. *Crown 8vo.* 4*s.* 6*d.*

THE PERSON AND WORK OF THE HOLY GHOST: a Doctrinal and Devotional Treatise. *Crown 8vo.* 4*s.* 6*d.*

SOME ASPECTS OF THE CROSS. *Crown 8vo.* 4*s.* 6*d.*

THE MYSTERY OF THE TEMPTATION. Lent Lectures delivered at St. Mary Magdalene, Paddington. *Crown 8vo.* 4*s.* 6*d.*

Hutton.—THE CHURCH OF THE SIXTH CENTURY. Six Chapters in Ecclesiastical History. By WILLIAM HOLDEN HUTTON, B.D., Birkbeck Lecturer in Ecclesiastical History, Trinity College, Cambridge. *With* 11 *Illustrations. Crown 8vo.* 6*s.*

Hutton.—THE SOUL HERE AND HEREAFTER. By the Rev. R. E. HUTTON, Chaplain of St. Margaret's, East Grinstead. *Crown 8vo.* 6*s.*

INHERITANCE OF THE SAINTS; or, Thoughts on the Communion of Saints and the Life of the World to come. Collected chiefly from English Writers by L. P. With a Preface by the Rev. HENRY SCOTT HOLLAND, M.A. *Seventh Edition. Crown 8vo.* 7*s.* 6*d.*

Jameson.—Works by Mrs. JAMESON.

SACRED AND LEGENDARY ART, containing Legends of the Angels and Archangels, the Evangelists, the Apostles. With 19 Etchings and 187 Woodcuts. 2 *vols.* 8*vo.* 20*s. net.*

LEGENDS OF THE MONASTIC ORDERS, as represented in the Fine Arts. With 11 Etchings and 88 Woodcuts. 8*vo.* 10*s. net.*

LEGENDS OF THE MADONNA, OR BLESSED VIRGIN MARY. With 27 Etchings and 165 Woodcuts. 8*vo.* 10*s. net.*

THE HISTORY OF OUR LORD, as exemplified in Works of Art. Commenced by the late Mrs. JAMESON; continued and completed by LADY EASTLAKE. With 31 Etchings and 281 Woodcuts. 2 *Vols.* 8*vo.* 20*s. net.*

Jennings.—ECCLESIA ANGLICANA. A History of the Church of Christ in England from the Earliest to the Present Times. By the Rev. ARTHUR CHARLES JENNINGS, M.A. *Crown 8vo.* 7*s.* 6*d.*

Jukes.—Works by ANDREW JUKES.

THE NEW MAN AND THE ETERNAL LIFE. Notes on the Reiterated Amens of the Son of God. *Crown 8vo.* 6*s.*

THE NAMES OF GOD IN HOLY SCRIPTURE: a Revelation of His Nature and Relationships. *Crown 8vo.* 4*s.* 6*d.*

THE TYPES OF GENESIS. *Crown 8vo.* 7*s.* 6*d.*

THE SECOND DEATH AND THE RESTITUTION OF ALL THINGS. *Crown 8vo.* 3*s.* 6*d.*

THE ORDER AND CONNEXION OF THE CHURCH'S TEACHING, as set forth in the arrangement of the Epistles and Gospels throughout the Year. *Crown 8vo.* 2*s.* 6*d.*

THE CHRISTIAN HOME. *Crown 8vo.* 3*s.* 6*d.*

Knox Little.—Works by W. J. KNOX LITTLE, M.A., Canon Residentiary of Worcester, and Vicar of Hoar Cross.

THE PERFECT LIFE: Sermons. *Crown 8vo.* 7*s.* 6*d.*

CHARACTERISTICS AND MOTIVES OF THE CHRISTIAN LIFE. Ten Sermons preached in Manchester Cathedral, in Lent and Advent. *Crown 8vo.* 2*s.* 6*d.*

SERMONS PREACHED FOR THE MOST PART IN MANCHESTER. *Crown 8vo.* 3*s.* 6*d.*

THE MYSTERY OF THE PASSION OF OUR MOST HOLY REDEEMER. *Crown 8vo.* 2*s.* 6*d.*

THE LIGHT OF LIFE. Sermons preached on Various Occasions. *Crown 8vo.* 3*s.* 6*d.*

SUNLIGHT AND SHADOW IN THE CHRISTIAN LIFE. Sermons preached for the most part in America. *Crown 8vo.* 3*s.* 6*d.*

Lear.—Works by, and Edited by, H. L. SIDNEY LEAR.

FOR DAYS AND YEARS. A book containing a Text, Short Reading, and Hymn for Every Day in the Church's Year. 16*mo.* 2*s.* 6*d.* *Also a Cheap Edition,* 32*mo.* 1*s.*; *or cloth gilt,* 1*s.* 6*d.*; *or with red borders,* 2*s.* 6*d.*

FIVE MINUTES. Daily Readings of Poetry. 16*mo.* 3*s.* 6*d.* *Also a Cheap Edition,* 32*mo.* 1*s.*; *or cloth gilt,* 1*s.* 6*d.*

WEARINESS. A Book for the Languid and Lonely. *Large Type. Small 8vo.* 5*s.*

JOY: A FRAGMENT. With a slight sketch of the Author's life. *Small 8vo.* 2*s.* 6*d.*

CHRISTIAN BIOGRAPHIES. *Nine Vols. Crown 8vo.* 3*s.* 6*d. each.*

MADAME LOUISE DE FRANCE, Daughter of Louis XV., known also as the Mother Térèse de St. Augustin.

A DOMINICAN ARTIST: a Sketch of the Life of the Rev. Père Besson, of the Order of St. Dominic.

HENRI PERREYVE. By PÈRE GRATRY.

ST. FRANCIS DE SALES, Bishop and Prince of Geneva.

THE REVIVAL OF PRIESTLY LIFE IN THE SEVENTEENTH CENTURY IN FRANCE.

A CHRISTIAN PAINTER OF THE NINETEENTH CENTURY.

BOSSUET AND HIS CONTEMPORARIES.

FÉNELON, ARCHBISHOP OF CAMBRAI.

HENRI DOMINIQUE LACORDAIRE.

[*continued.*

Lear.—Works by, and Edited by, H. L. SIDNEY LEAR—*continued.*

DEVOTIONAL WORKS. Edited by H. L. SIDNEY LEAR. *New and Uniform Editions. Nine Vols.* 16mo. 2s. 6d. *each.*

FÉNELON'S SPIRITUAL LETTERS TO MEN.

FÉNELON'S SPIRITUAL LETTERS TO WOMEN.

A SELECTION FROM THE SPIRITUAL LETTERS OF ST. FRANCIS DE SALES. Also *Cheap Edition*, 32mo, 6d. *cloth limp*; 1s. *cloth boards.*

THE SPIRIT OF ST. FRANCIS DE SALES.

THE HIDDEN LIFE OF THE SOUL.

THE LIGHT OF THE CONSCIENCE. Also *Cheap Edition*, 32mo, 6d. *cloth limp*; and 1s. *cloth boards.*

SELF-RENUNCIATION. From the French.

ST. FRANCIS DE SALES' OF THE LOVE OF GOD.

SELECTIONS FROM PASCAL'S 'THOUGHTS.'

Lepine.—THE MINISTERS OF JESUS CHRIST: a Biblical Study. By the Rev. J. FOSTER LEPINE, Curate of St. Paul's, Maidstone. *Crown 8vo.* 5s.

Liddon.—Works by HENRY PARRY LIDDON, D.D., D.C.L., LL.D.

LIFE OF EDWARD BOUVERIE PUSEY, D.D. By HENRY PARRY LIDDON, D.D., D.C.L., LL.D. Edited and prepared for publication by the Rev. J. O. JOHNSTON, M.A., Principal of the Theological College, and Vicar of Cuddesdon, Oxford; the Rev. R. J. WILSON, D.D., late Warden of Keble College; and the Rev. W. C. E. NEWBOLT, M.A., Canon and Chancellor of St. Paul's. *With Portraits and Illustrations. Four Vols.* 8vo. *Vols. I. and II.*, 36s. *Vol. III.*, 18s. *Vol. IV.* 18s.

SERMONS ON SOME WORDS OF ST. PAUL. *Crown 8vo.* 5s.

SERMONS PREACHED ON SPECIAL OCCASIONS, 1860-1889. *Crown 8vo.* 5s.

EXPLANATORY ANALYSIS OF ST. PAUL'S FIRST EPISTLE TO TIMOTHY. 8vo. 7s. 6d.

CLERICAL LIFE AND WORK: Sermons. *Crown 8vo.* 5s.

ESSAYS AND ADDRESSES: Lectures on Buddhism—Lectures on the Life of St. Paul—Papers on Dante. *Crown 8vo.* 5s.

EXPLANATORY ANALYSIS OF ST. PAUL'S FIRST EPISTLE TO TIMOTHY. 8vo. 7s. 6d.

EXPLANATORY ANALYSIS OF PAUL'S EPISTLE TO THE ROMANS. 8vo. 14s.

SERMONS ON OLD TESTAMENT SUBJECTS. *Crown 8vo.* 5s.

SERMONS ON SOME WORDS OF CHRIST. *Crown 8vo.* 5s.

THE DIVINITY OF OUR LORD AND SAVIOUR JESUS CHRIST. Being the Bampton Lectures for 1866. *Crown 8vo.* 5s.

ADVENT IN ST. PAUL'S. *Two Vols. Crown 8vo.* 3s. 6d. *each. Cheap Edition in one Volume. Crown 8vo.* 5s.

[*continued.*

Liddon.—Works by HENRY PARRY LIDDON, D.D., D.C.L., LL.D.—*continued.*

CHRISTMASTIDE IN ST. PAUL'S. *Crown 8vo.* 5s.

PASSIONTIDE SERMONS. *Crown 8vo.* 5s.

EASTER IN ST. PAUL'S. Sermons bearing chiefly on the Resurrection of our Lord. *Two Vols. Crown 8vo.* 3s. 6d. *each. Cheap Edition in one Volume. Crown 8vo.* 5s.

SERMONS PREACHED BEFORE THE UNIVERSITY OF OXFORD. *Two Vols. Crown 8vo.* 3s. 6d. *each. Cheap Edition in one Volume. Crown 8vo.* 5s.

THE MAGNIFICAT. Sermons in St. Paul's. *Crown 8vo.* 2s. 6d.

SOME ELEMENTS OF RELIGION. Lent Lectures. *Small 8vo.* 2s. 6d. [*The Crown 8vo. Edition* (5s.) *may still be had.*]

SELECTIONS FROM THE WRITINGS OF. *Crown 8vo.* 3s. 6d.

MAXIMS AND GLEANINGS. *Crown 16mo.* 1s.

Luckock.—Works by HERBERT MORTIMER LUCKOCK, D.D., Dean of Lichfield.

THE HISTORY OF MARRIAGE, JEWISH AND CHRISTIAN, IN RELATION TO DIVORCE AND CERTAIN FORBIDDEN DEGREES. *Crown 8vo.* 6s.

AFTER DEATH. An Examination of the Testimony of Primitive Times respecting the State of the Faithful Dead, and their Relationship to the Living. *Crown 8vo.* 3s. 6d.

THE INTERMEDIATE STATE BETWEEN DEATH AND JUDGMENT. Being a Sequel to *After Death. Crown 8vo.* 3s. 6d.

FOOTPRINTS OF THE SON OF MAN, as traced by St. Mark. Being Eighty Portions for Private Study, Family Reading, and Instruction in Church. *Crown 8vo.* 3s. 6d.

FOOTPRINTS OF THE APOSTLES, as traced by St. Luke in the Acts. Being Sixty Portions for Private Study, and Instruction in Church. A Sequel to 'Footprints of the Son of Man, as traced by St. Mark.' *Two Vols. Crown 8vo.* 12s.

THE DIVINE LITURGY. Being the Order for Holy Communion, Historically, Doctrinally, and Devotionally set forth, in Fifty Portions. *Crown 8vo.* 3s. 6d.

STUDIES IN THE HISTORY OF THE BOOK OF COMMON PRAYER. The Anglican Reform—The Puritan Innovations—The Elizabethan Reaction—The Caroline Settlement. With Appendices. *Crown 8vo.* 3s. 6d.

THE BISHOPS IN THE TOWER. A Record of Stirring Events affecting the Church and Nonconformists from the Restoration to the Revolution. *Crown 8vo.* 3s. 6d.

MacColl.—Works by the Rev. MALCOLM MACCOLL, M.A., Canon Residentiary of Ripon.

CHRISTIANITY IN RELATION TO SCIENCE AND MORALS. *Crown 8vo.* 6*s.*

LIFE HERE AND HEREAFTER: Sermons. *Crown 8vo.* 7*s.* 6*d.*

Mason.—Works by A. J. MASON, D.D., Lady Margaret Professor of Divinity in the University of Cambridge and Canon of Canterbury.

THE CONDITIONS OF OUR LORD'S LIFE UPON EARTH. Being the Bishop Paddock Lectures, 1896. To which is prefixed part of a First Professorial Lecture at Cambridge. *Crown 8vo.* 5*s.*

THE PRINCIPLES OF ECCLESIASTICAL UNITY. Four Lectures delivered in St. Asaph Cathedral. *Crown 8vo.* 3*s.* 6*d.*

THE FAITH OF THE GOSPEL. A Manual of Christian Doctrine. *Crown 8vo.* 7*s.* 6*d.* *Cheap Edition.* *Crown 8vo.* 3*s.* 6*d.*

THE RELATION OF CONFIRMATION TO BAPTISM. As taught in Holy Scripture and the Fathers. *Crown 8vo.* 7*s.* 6*d.*

Maturin.—Works by the Rev. B. W. MATURIN, sometime Mission Priest of the Society of St. John the Evangelist, Cowley.

SOME PRINCIPLES AND PRACTICES OF THE SPIRITUAL LIFE. *Crown 8vo.* 4*s.* 6*d.*

PRACTICAL STUDIES ON THE PARABLES OF OUR LORD. *Crown 8vo.* 5*s.*

Medd.—THE PRIEST TO THE ALTAR; or, Aids to the Devout Celebration of Holy Communion, chiefly after the Ancient English Use of Sarum. By PETER GOLDSMITH MEDD, M.A., Canon of St. Alban's. Fourth Edition, revised and enlarged. *Royal 8vo.* 15*s.*

Mortimer.—Works by the Rev. A. G. MORTIMER, D.D., Rector of St. Mark's, Philadelphia.

JESUS AND THE RESURRECTION: Thirty Addresses for Good Friday and Easter. *Crown 8vo.* 5*s.*

CATHOLIC FAITH AND PRACTICE: A Manual of Theological Instruction for Confirmation and First Communion. *Crown 8vo.* Part I., 7*s.* 6*d.* Part II., 9*s.*

HELPS TO MEDITATION: Sketches for Every Day in the Year.

Vol. I. ADVENT to TRINITY. *8vo.* 7*s.* 6*d.*

Vol. II. TRINITY to ADVENT. *8vo.* 7*s.* 6*d.*

STORIES FROM GENESIS: Sermons for Children. *Crown 8vo.* 4*s.*

THE LAWS OF HAPPINESS; or, The Beatitudes as teaching our Duty to God, Self, and our Neighbour. *18mo.* 2*s.*

THE LAWS OF PENITENCE: Addresses on the Words of our Lord from the Cross. *16mo.* 1*s.* 6*d.*

SERMONS IN MINIATURE FOR EXTEMPORE PREACHERS: Sketches for Every Sunday and Holy Day of the Christian Year. *Crown 8vo.* 6*s.*

NOTES ON THE SEVEN PENITENTIAL PSALMS, chiefly from Patristic Sources. *Fcp. 8vo.* 3*s.* 6*d.*

THE SEVEN LAST WORDS OF OUR MOST HOLY REDEEMER: with Meditations on some Scenes in His Passion. *Crown 8vo.* 5*s.*

LEARN OF JESUS CHRIST TO DIE: Addresses on the Words of our Lord from the Cross, taken as Teaching the way of Preparation for Death. *16mo.* 2*s.*

Mozley.—Works by J. B. MOZLEY, D.D., late Canon of Christ Church, and Regius Professor of Divinity at Oxford.

ESSAYS, HISTORICAL AND THEOLOGICAL. *Two Vols.* *8vo.* 24*s.*

EIGHT LECTURES ON MIRACLES. Being the Bampton Lectures for 1865. *Crown 8vo.* 3*s.* 6d.

RULING IDEAS IN EARLY AGES AND THEIR RELATION TO OLD TESTAMENT FAITH. *8vo.* 6*s.*

SERMONS PREACHED BEFORE THE UNIVERSITY OF OXFORD, and on Various Occasions. *Crown 8vo.* 3*s.* 6*d.*

SERMONS, PAROCHIAL AND OCCASIONAL. *Crown 8vo.* 3*s.* 6*d.*

A REVIEW OF THE BAPTISMAL CONTROVERSY. *Crown 8vo.* 3*s* 6*d.*

Newbolt.—Works by the Rev. W. C. E. NEWBOLT, M.A., Canon and Chancellor of St. Paul's Cathedral.

PRIESTLY IDEALS; being a Course of Practical Lectures delivered in St. Paul's Cathedral to 'Our Society' and other Clergy, in Lent, 1893. *Crown 8vo.* 3*s.* 6*d.*

THE GOSPEL OF EXPERIENCE; or, the Witness of Human Life to the truth of Revelation. Being the Boyle Lectures for 1895. *Crown 8vo.* 5*s.*

COUNSELS OF FAITH AND PRACTICE: being Sermons preached on various occasions. *New and Enlarged Edition.* *Crown 8vo.* 5*s.*

SPECULUM SACERDOTUM; or, the Divine Model of the Priestly Life. *Crown 8vo.* 7*s.* 6*d.*

THE FRUIT OF THE SPIRIT. Being Ten Addresses bearing on the Spiritual Life. *Crown 8vo.* 2*s.* 6*d.*

THE MAN OF GOD. *Small 8vo.* 1*s.* 6*d.*

THE PRAYER BOOK: Its Voice and Teaching. *Crown 8vo.* 2*s.* 6*d.*

Newman.—Works by JOHN HENRY NEWMAN, B.D., sometime Vicar of St. Mary's, Oxford.

LETTERS AND CORRESPONDENCE OF JOHN HENRY NEWMAN DURING HIS LIFE IN THE ENGLISH CHURCH. With a brief Autobiography. Edited, at Cardinal Newman's request, by ANNE MOZLEY. 2 *vols.* *Crown 8vo.* 7*s.*

PAROCHIAL AND PLAIN SERMONS. *Eight Vols.* *Cabinet Edition.* *Crown 8vo.* 5*s.* *each.* *Cheaper Edition.* 3*s.* 6*d.* *each.*

SELECTION, ADAPTED TO THE SEASONS OF THE ECCLESIASTICAL YEAR, from the 'Parochial and Plain Sermons.' *Cabinet Edition.* *Crown 8vo.* 5*s.* *Cheaper Edition.* 3*s.* 6*d.*

FIFTEEN SERMONS PREACHED BEFORE THE UNIVERSITY OF OXFORD *Cabinet Edition.* *Crown 8vo.* 5*s.* *Cheaper Edition.* 3*s.* 6*d.*

SERMONS BEARING UPON SUBJECTS OF THE DAY. *Cabinet Edition.* *Crown 8vo.* 5*s.* *Cheaper Edition.* *Crown 8vo.* 3*s.* 6*d.*

LECTURES ON THE DOCTRINE OF JUSTIFICATION. *Cabinet Edition.* *Crown 8vo.* 5*s.* *Cheaper Edition.* 3*s.* 6*d.*

**** A Complete List of Cardinal Newman's Works can be had on Application.*

Osborne.—Works by EDWARD OSBORNE, Mission Priest of the Society of St. John the Evangelist, Cowley, Oxford.

THE CHILDREN'S SAVIOUR. Instructions to Children on the Life of Our Lord and Saviour Jesus Christ. *Illustrated.* *16mo.* 2*s.* 6*d.*

THE SAVIOUR KING. Instructions to Children on Old Testament Types and Illustrations of the Life of Christ. *Illustrated.* *16mo.* 2*s.* 6*d.*

THE CHILDREN'S FAITH. Instructions to Children on the Apostles' Creed. *Illustrated.* *16mo.* 2*s.* 6*d.*

Ottley.—ASPECTS OF THE OLD TESTAMENT: being the Bampton Lectures for 1897. By ROBERT LAWRENCE OTTLEY, M.A., Vicar of Winterbourne Bassett, Wilts; sometime Principal of the Pusey House. *8vo.* *New and Cheaper Edition.* 7*s.* 6*d.*

OUTLINES OF CHURCH TEACHING: a Series of Instructions for the Sundays and chief Holy Days of the Christian Year. For the Use of Teachers. By C. C. G. With Preface by the Very Rev. FRANCIS PAGET, D.D., Dean of Christ Church, Oxford. *Crown 8vo.* 3*s.* 6*d.*

Oxenden.—Works by the Right Rev. ASHTON OXENDEN, sometime Bishop of Montreal.

PLAIN SERMONS, to which is prefixed a Memorial Portrait. *Crown 8vo.* 5*s.*

PEACE AND ITS HINDRANCES. *Crown 8vo.* 1*s. sewed*; 2*s. cloth.*

THE PATHWAY OF SAFETY; or, Counsel to the Awakened. *Fcap. 8vo, large type.* 2*s.* 6*d.* *Cheap Edition.* *Small type, limp,* 1*s.*

THE EARNEST COMMUNICANT. *New Red Rubric Edition.* *32mo, cloth.* 2*s.* *Common Edition.* *32mo.* 1*s.*

OUR CHURCH AND HER SERVICES. *Fcap. 8vo.* 2*s.* 6*d.*

FAMILY PRAYERS FOR FOUR WEEKS. First Series. *Fcap. 8vo.* 2*s.* 6*d.* Second Series. *Fcap. 8vo.* 2*s.* 6*d.*

LARGE TYPE EDITION. Two Series in one Volume. *Crown 8vo.* 6*s.*

COTTAGE SERMONS; or, Plain Words to the Poor. *Fcap. 8vo.* 2*s.* 6*d.*

THOUGHTS FOR HOLY WEEK. *16mo, cloth.* 1*s.* 6*d.*

DECISION. *18mo.* 1*s.* 6*d.*

THE HOME BEYOND; or, A Happy Old Age. *Fcap. 8vo.* 1*s.* 6*d.*

THE LABOURING MAN'S BOOK. *18mo, large type, cloth.* 1*s.* 6*d.*

Oxenham.—THE VALIDITY OF PAPAL CLAIMS: Lectures delivered in Rome. By F. NUTCOMBE OXENHAM, D.D., English Chaplain at Rome. With a Letter by His Grace the ARCHBISHOP OF YORK. *Crown 8vo.* 2*s.* 6*d.*

Paget.—Works by FRANCIS PAGET, D.D., Dean of Christ Church.

STUDIES IN THE CHRISTIAN CHARACTER: Sermons. With an Introductory Essay. *Crown 8vo.* 6s. 6d.

THE SPIRIT OF DISCIPLINE: Sermons. *Crown 8vo.* 6s. 6d.

FACULTIES AND DIFFICULTIES FOR BELIEF AND DISBELIEF. *Crown 8vo.* 6s. 6d.

THE HALLOWING OF WORK. Addresses given at Eton, January 16-18, 1888. *Small 8vo.* 2s.

Percival.—SOME HELPS FOR SCHOOL LIFE. Sermons preached at Clifton College, 1862-1879. By J. PERCIVAL, D.D., LL.D., Lord Bishop of Hereford. New Edition, with New Preface. *Crown 8vo.* 3s. 6d.

Percival.—THE INVOCATION OF SAINTS. Treated Theologically and Historically. By HENRY R. PERCIVAL, M.A., D.D., Author of 'A Digest of Theology,' 'The Doctrine of the Episcopal Church,' etc. *Crown 8vo.* 5s.

POCKET MANUAL OF PRAYERS FOR THE HOURS, ETC. With the Collects from the Prayer Book. *Royal 32mo.* 1s.

Powell.—THE PRINCIPLE OF THE INCARNATION. With especial Reference to the Relation between our Lord's Divine Omniscience and His Human Consciousness. By the Rev. H. C. POWELL, M.A. of Oriel College, Oxford; Rector of Wylye and Prebendary of Salisbury Cathedral. *8vo.* 16s.

PRACTICAL REFLECTIONS. By a CLERGYMAN. With Prefaces by H. P. LIDDON, D.D., D.C.L., and the LORD BISHOP OF LINCOLN. *Crown 8vo.*

THE BOOK OF GENESIS. 4s. 6d.
THE PSALMS. 5s.
ISAIAH. 4s. 6d.
THE MINOR PROPHETS. 4s. 6d.
THE HOLY GOSPELS. 4s. 6d.
ACTS TO REVELATIONS. 6s.

PRIEST'S PRAYER BOOK (THE). Containing Private Prayers and Intercessions; Occasional, School, and Parochial Offices; Offices for the Visitation of the Sick, with Notes, Readings, Collects, Hymns, Litanies, etc. With a brief Pontifical. By the late Rev. R. F. LITTLEDALE, LL.D., D.C.L., and Rev. J. EDWARD VAUX, M.A., F.S.A. *New Edition, Revised. 20th Thousand. Post 8vo.* 6s. 6d.

Pullan.—LECTURES ON RELIGION. By the Rev. LEIGHTON PULLAN, M.A., Fellow of St. John's College, Lecturer in Theology at Oriel and Queen's Colleges, Oxford. *Crown 8vo.* 6s.

Pusey.—LIFE OF EDWARD BOUVERIE PUSEY, D.D. By HENRY PARRY LIDDON, D.D., D.C.L., LL.D. Edited and prepared for publication by the Rev. J. O. JOHNSTON, M.A., Principal of the Theological College, and Vicar of Cuddesdon, Oxford; the Rev. R. J. WILSON, D.D., late Warden of Keble College; and the Rev. W. C. E. NEWBOLT, M.A., Canon and Chancellor of St. Paul's. *With Portraits and Illustrations. Four Vols. 8vo. Vols. I. and II.*, 36s. *Vol. III.*, 18s. *Vol. IV.* 18s.

SPIRITUAL LETTERS OF EDWARD BOUVERIE PUSEY, D.D. Edited and prepared for publication by the Rev. J. O. JOHNSTON, M.A., Principal of the Theological College, Cuddesdon; and the Rev. W. C. E. NEWBOLT, M.A., Canon and Chancellor of St. Paul's. *8vo.* 12s. 6d.

Randolph.—Works by B. W. RANDOLPH, M.A., Principal of the Theological College and Hon. Canon of Ely.

THE THRESHOLD OF THE SANCTUARY: being Short Chapters on the Inner Preparation for the Priesthood. *Crown 8vo.* 3s. 6d.

THE LAW OF SINAI: being Devotional Addresses on the Ten Commandments delivered to Ordinands. *Crown 8vo.* 3s. 6d.

Rede.—Works by WYLLYS REDE, D.D., Rector of the Church of the Incarnation, and Canon of the Cathedral, Atalanta, Georgia.

STRIVING FOR THE MASTERY: Daily Lessons for Lent. *Cr. 8vo.* 5s.

THE COMMUNION OF SAINTS: a Lost Link in the Chain of the Church's Creed. With a Preface by LORD HALIFAX. *Crown 8vo.* 3s. 6d.

Reynolds.—THE SUPERNATURAL IN NATURE: A Verification by Free Use of Science. By JOSEPH WILLIAM REYNOLDS, M.A., Past President of Sion College, Prebendary of St. Paul's Cathedral. *New and Cheaper Edition, Revised. Crown 8vo.* 3s. 6d.

Sanday.—INSPIRATION: Eight Lectures on the Early History and Origin of the Doctrine of Biblical Inspiration. Being the Bampton Lectures for 1893. By W. SANDAY, D.D., Margaret Professor of Divinity and Canon of Christ Church, Oxford. *New and Cheaper Edition, with New Preface. 8vo.* 7s. 6d.

Scudamore.—STEPS TO THE ALTAR: a Manual of Devotion for the Blessed Eucharist. By the Rev. W. E. SCUDAMORE, M.A. *Royal 32mo.* 1s.

On toned paper, with red rubrics, 2s: The same, with Collects, Epistles, and Gospels, 2s. 6d; Demy 18mo. cloth, 1s; Demy 18mo. cloth, large type, 1s. 3d; Imperial 32mo. limp cloth, 6d.

Simpson.—THE CHURCH AND THE BIBLE. By the Rev. W. J. SPARROW SIMPSON, M.A., Vicar of St. Mark's, Regent's Park. *Crown 8vo.* 3s. 6d.

Strong.—CHRISTIAN ETHICS : being the Bampton Lectures for 1895. By THOMAS B. STRONG, M.A., Student of Christ Church, Oxford, and Examining Chaplain to the Lord Bishop of Durham. *New and Cheaper Edition. 8vo.* 7s. 6d.

Tee.—THE SANCTUARY OF SUFFERING. By ELEANOR TEE, Author of 'This Everyday Life,' etc. With a Preface by the Rev. J. P. F. DAVIDSON, M.A., Vicar of St. Matthias', Earl's Court; President of the 'Guild of All Souls.' *Crown 8vo.* 7s. 6d.

Williams.—Works by the Rev. ISAAC WILLIAMS, B.D.

A DEVOTIONAL COMMENTARY ON THE GOSPEL NARRATIVE. *Eight Vols. Crown 8vo.* 5s. *each.*

THOUGHTS ON THE STUDY OF THE HOLY GOSPELS.
A HARMONY OF THE FOUR GOSPELS.
OUR LORD'S NATIVITY.
OUR LORD'S MINISTRY (Second Year).
OUR LORD'S MINISTRY (Third Year).
THE HOLY WEEK.
OUR LORD'S PASSION.
OUR LORD'S RESURRECTION.

FEMALE CHARACTERS OF HOLY SCRIPTURE. A Series of Sermons. *Crown 8vo.* 5s.

THE CHARACTERS OF THE OLD TESTAMENT. *Crown 8vo.* 5s.

THE APOCALYPSE. With Notes and Reflections. *Crown 8vo.* 5s.

SERMONS ON THE EPISTLES AND GOSPELS FOR THE SUNDAYS AND HOLY DAYS. *Two Vols. Crown 8vo.* 5s. *each.*

PLAIN SERMONS ON CATECHISM. *Two Vols. Cr. 8vo.* 5s. *each.*

Wilson.—THOUGHTS ON CONFIRMATION. By Rev. R. J. WILSON, D.D., late Warden of Keble College. *16mo.* 1s. 6d.

Wirgman.—THE DOCTRINE OF CONFIRMATION CONSIDERED IN RELATION TO HOLY BAPTISM AS A SACRAMENTAL ORDINANCE OF THE CATHOLIC CHURCH: with a Preliminary Historical Survey of the Doctrine of the Holy Spirit. By A. THEODORE WIRGMAN, B.D., D.C.L., Vice-Provost of St. Mary's Collegiate Church, Port Elizabeth, South Africa. *Cr. 8vo.* 7s. 6d.

Wordsworth.—Works by CHRISTOPHER WORDSWORTH, D.D., sometime Bishop of Lincoln.

THE HOLY BIBLE (the Old Testament). With Notes, Introductions, and Index. *Imperial 8vo.*

Vol. I. THE PENTATEUCH. 25s. Vol. II. JOSHUA TO SAMUEL. 15s. Vol. III. KINGS to ESTHER. 15s. Vol. IV. JOB TO SONG OF SOLOMON. 25s. Vol. V. ISAIAH TO EZEKIEL. 25s. Vol. VI. DANIEL, MINOR PROPHETS, and Index. 15s.

Also supplied in 12 Parts. Sold separately.

[*continued.*

Printed in the United States
136094LV00008B/73/A

9 780548 778616